MILITARY SERVICE
IN THE UNITED STATES

The American Assembly, *Columbia University*

MILITARY SERVICE
IN THE UNITED STATES

Prentice-Hall, Inc., *Englewood Cliffs, New Jersey*
A SPECTRUM BOOK

Library of Congress Cataloging in Publication Data
Main entry under title:

MILITARY SERVICE IN THE UNITED STATES
  "A Spectrum Book"
  At head of title: The American Assembly, Columbia
University.
  Includes index.
  1. Military service, Voluntary—United States—Addresses, essays, lectures. 2. Military service, Compulsory—United States—Addresses, essays, lectures.
3. United States—Armed Forces—Recruiting, enlistment, etc.—Addresses, essays, lectures. I. Scowcroft, Brent.
II. American Assembly.
UB323.M54   355.2′2362′0973   81-22744
                                        AACR2

ISBN 0-13-583062-1

ISBN 0-13-583054-0 {PBK.}

Editorial/production supervision by Betty Neville
Manufacturing buyer: Barbara A. Frick
Cover design by Jeannette Jacobs

10 9 8 7 6 5 4 3 2 1

This Spectrum Book can be made available to businesses and organizations at a special discount when ordered in large quantities. For more information, contact:
              Prentice-Hall, Inc.
              General Publishing Division
              Special Sales
              Englewood Cliffs, New Jersey 07632

PRENTICE-HALL INTERNATIONAL, INC. *(London)*
PRENTICE-HALL OF AUSTRALIA PTY. LIMITED *(Sydney)*
PRENTICE-HALL OF CANADA, LTD. *(Toronto)*
PRENTICE-HALL OF INDIA PRIVATE LIMITED *(New Delhi)*
PRENTICE-HALL OF JAPAN, INC. *(Tokyo)*
PRENTICE-HALL OF SOUTHEAST ASIA PTE. LTD. *(Singapore)*
WHITEHALL BOOKS LIMITED *(Wellington, New Zealand)*

Table of Contents

Preface

In the aftermath of the war in Vietnam, the United States replaced the selective service system which had furnished personnel for military service with a program that produced an all-volunteer force. Since that force has been in existence, there has been widespread criticism directed at the program.

It has been criticized because the mental quality of recruits has been considered low, because the forces do not reflect the ethnic, social, and educational composition of the nation accurately, and because the number of readily mobilizable reserves is inadequate. Many of the critics have felt that the situation can be corrected only by return to some system of compulsion or some form of conscription.

In 1980 and 1981, as unemployment increased, the armed forces were better able to fill their quantitative needs and to improve the quality of those electing military service. However, the problem of the reserves remained unresolved.

In these circumstances, The American Assembly believed that it could help achieve a national policy on military service by bringing together a number of citizens who would examine the issue in depth and help clarify the anticipated national debate.

Accordingly, the Assembly retained Lt. Gen. Brent Scowcroft, USAF (ret.), former National Security Advisor, to be director and editor of a project on Military Service in the United States. Under his editorial supervision, background papers on the various points at issue were prepared. From September 17 to 20, 1981, a group of distinguished Americans and two representatives of our NATO allies, met at Seven Springs Center in Mt. Kisco, New York, to discuss the papers and to issue a report which has received wide circulation.

Those background papers have been compiled in this volume, which is published as a stimulus to further thinking and discussion among informed and concerned citizens. We hope the book will serve to evoke a broad consensus about the nature of our problem and the action we should take to meet it.

Funding for this project was provided by the Ford Foundation, for whose timely assistance we are most grateful. The opinions expressed in this book are those of the individual authors and not necessarily those of the Foundation nor of The American Assembly, which do not take stands on the issues they present for public discussion.

William H. Sullivan
President
The American Assembly

Lt. Gen. Brent Scowcroft

Introduction

There is a growing feeling in the United States that one of the fundamental national security issues facing us is that of military manpower. We may in fact be on the threshold of a great national debate to determine whether we should continue to man our military forces through purely volunteer measures or whether we should return to some form of compulsory military service. It is in recognition of the importance of this issue and in the hope of illuminating the many factors involved that these various chapters have been commissioned by The American Assembly.

The issue of a volunteer military force versus compulsory service is not a new one. Indeed, it is virtually as old as the Republic itself. In philosophical terms, it may be an irreconcilable debate, involving, as it does on both sides, fundamental principles of our political life. The idea of the nation in arms and the obligation of every citizen to do his part to defend freedom runs as deep as does the belief in the freedom of the individual and the abhorrence of any involuntary servitude.

Before World War II the question was largely moot, because the nation in most cases had ample time to shift from its libertarian posture to its patriotic obligation mood after a direct

BRENT SCOWCROFT *was formerly assistant to the President for National Security Affairs. A graduate of the National War College, Lt. Gen. Scowcroft taught in the Social Science and Political Science Departments of the U.S. Military Academy and the U.S. Air Force Academy. He has served as special assistant to the director of the Joint Chiefs of Staff and was recently a member of the Townes Panel on Strategic Weapons.*

military challenge to the United States had clearly emerged. That general pattern began to change when an anticipatory draft was inaugurated prior to World War II. But even then the draft was renewed in 1940 by a margin of just one vote, despite the conflict in Europe and darkening war clouds in the Far East.

Following World War II, however, a broadened concept of U.S. national security, the shrinking of our ocean barriers through technology, and the disappearance of other powers able to hold the enemy at bay while we set about building a military force led to a fundamental change—the imposition of a peacetime military draft. An important element of the debate at that time and into the 1960s was not so much the principle of the draft itself but whether it should be selective, in the manner of the World War II draft, or take a more sweeping form through the adoption of some variety of universal service.

That period came to an end with the Vietnam conflict. The selective service draft came under increasing attack, resulting first in a shift to a lottery system of draft selection and ultimately, in 1973, to its abandonment in favor of an all-volunteer military force (AVF). Many of the arguments used to end the draft have found their counterparts in the current debate over the future of the all-volunteer force. In light of some of the arguments now being heard, it is not irrelevant to wonder about the extent to which the revolt against the draft in 1973 was in reality a reaction to the Vietnam conflict rather than to the draft itself.

In any event, murmurings of discontent against the AVF began shortly after its initiation and swelled to a chorus by 1978 with stories, among others, that enlistment quotas were not being met, quality was deteriorating, and the make-up of the armed forces was becoming increasingly unrepresentative. In addition to these doubts about the actual operating effectiveness of the AVF, there was growing concern about Soviet expansionist ambitions, epitomized by the invasion of Afghanistan. Finally, there emerged a national resolve to correct deficiencies in the U.S. military posture which had developed over a number of years, including development of an enhanced ability to project U.S. ground forces in strength to distant parts of the globe. All of these elements have combined to bring the future of the AVF to the forefront of national attention at the present time.

As indicated above, the issues are complex, with heavy philosophic overtones. Proponents of each side tend to argue in support of some more or less idealized version of whichever position they are advocating and to become very specific in criticizing the faults of the system to which they are opposed. It is in an attempt to bring dispassionate analysis to this important subject and to provide factual background for informed discussion that this volume has been prepared.

Critical to any analysis of AVF versus compulsory military service is the size of the armed forces considered to be required and the mix between active-duty and reserve/national guard forces. Clearly a military force the size of that during the 1930s (less than 200,000) could be manned in outstanding fashion with volunteers. Equally clearly, a force the size of that at the peak of World War II (over 12 million) would require the most sweeping kind of compulsory service. Therefore, the first question which must be asked is the size of the armed forces which the United States will require over the coming years. William Kaufmann, in the first chapter, explores this question in terms of the current force posture as reflected in the last Carter administration budget, together with its strategic rationale and possible or probable amendments by the Reagan administration. Kaufmann concludes that the current posture which was designed, even if not actually able, to cope simultaneously with one and one half major military contingencies may not be adequate to the threat of the 1980s. This judgment appears parallel to indications revealed thus far of the thinking of the Reagan administration. Such a conclusion would, of course, place an additional burden on the AVF. Kaufmann would avoid this burden by relying on reserve and national guard forces to meet any additional force requirements. As indicated in chapter 6, by James Lacy, our historical experience with call-up of reserve and guard forces has not been uniformly reassuring, and it brings with it as well its own problems of equity and economic and social costs.

The second chapter, by John White and James Hosek, presents an overview of military manpower issues and provides insights into the best way to think about them. It is designed to be read in conjunction with chapter 3, by Richard Hunter and Gary Nelson, which sets forth the actual experience of the armed forces over the eight years of the AVF. These two chapters should serve to dispel some of the myths which have grown up about the AVF, as well as about the draft years which preceded it. They illustrate the interrelated nature of many of the criteria and the subjective or relative nature of some of the indices of measure. They also indicate the dangers of statistical analysis, which can mistake symptom for cause. The ease with which poor military performance was equated with AVF rather than reduction in readiness and training and the assumption that AVF was satisfactory because it met manpower needs at a time of decreasing force size and increasing manpower pool size are cases in point.

The chapter by Charles Moskos deals with the societal implications of military manpower acquisition. Moskos sets forth some of the ways in which American society as a whole and the military services themselves have changed social character over the years and the implications of those changes for force manning. He describes the inherent tension between concepts of the military as an institution or as an occupation and the impact of force acquisition decisions on the character of the military in this respect.

The final two chapters are advocate presentations, with Richard Cooper persuasively arguing the case for the AVF and James Lacy, with equal persuasiveness, describing the need for a return to compulsory service. It should be noted, of course, that there are many options not falling neatly into either of these categories, such as the proposal outlined by Charles Moskos and that of Representative Paul N. McCloskey as mentioned in the Cooper chapter.

No attempt has been made to force these chapters into a particular mold, other than to attempt to insure comprehensive coverage of the topic. The authors have presented their facts and conclusions in their own way, and some overlap or even contradiction can be expected. If the chapters set forth the data on which judgments can be based and the philosophical and practical premises on which the positions of the two schools of thought rest, they have fulfilled their purpose.

William W. Kaufmann

1

U.S. Defense Needs in the 1980s

For those who follow fashions in defense, the four years of the Carter administration wrought a remarkable change in attitudes toward the armed forces of the United States. President Carter, when he came to office in 1977, insisted that $5 billion could be cut from the fiscal 1978 defense budget; he also proposed a more modest five-year defense plan than had been submitted by President Ford. Before he left office, the same President Carter recommended that during the next five years (fiscal 1982 through fiscal 1986) the United States increase its appropriations for defense each year by 5 percent, after the effects of inflation had been removed, and spend a cumulative total of $1,085.2 billion in constant dollars to maintain and improve the armed forces. President Reagan quickly went him one better with the recommendation that the pace of growth proceed at a rate of 7 percent a year in real terms and that the cumulative total rise to $1,280.6 billion by the end of fiscal 1986. Congress, which had agreed to the earlier reductions, may well acquiesce in the proposed increases.

WILLIAM W. KAUFMANN *is professor of political science at Massachusetts Institute of Technology. Previously he taught at Yale University and Princeton University before joining the Rand Corporation, where he served as head of the Social Science Department. Dr. Kaufmann has edited and written several books. He was recently a contributor to* Setting National Priorities in the 1980s.

In the aggregate, these budgetary totals are impressive. But are they of the appropriate magnitude? Will they buy the defense posture needed by the United States in the decade ahead? To put the question another way, what is the right defense posture for the United States, and what will it cost in dollars and manpower?

The easy answer is that no single, identifiable, optimum posture exists. U.S. defense needs depend on a great many considerations, not the least of which are estimates about the future capabilities of prospective enemies and the degree of conservatism with which these estimates are treated. Inevitably, different planners arrive at differing estimates and judgments. A range of defense postures is bound to result.

The Baseline Program

One way around this problem in current circumstances is to treat the most recent Carter proposals as a baseline program, to understand its logic, and to ask by how much it might be desirable and feasible to augment or decrease the baseline.

COST

The outlines of the financial plan for the baseline program are shown in Table 1. The program would start by consuming about 5.6 percent of estimated GNP in fiscal 1982 and gradually increase that rate to 5.9 percent by fiscal 1986. Since the rate of

TABLE 1. THE BASELINE FIVE-YEAR DEFENSE PROGRAM,
         FISCAL YEARS 1982–1986

Item	1982	1983	1984	1985	1986
Total obligational authority					
Current dollars	196.4*	224.0	253.1	284.3	318.3
Fiscal 1982 dollars	196.4	206.2	216.5	227.4	238.7
Percent real increase	5.3	5.0	5.0	5.0	5.0
Outlays					
Current dollars	180.0	205.3	232.3	261.8	293.3
Fiscal 1982 dollars	180.0	188.2	197.1	207.0	217.5
Percent increase	4.4	4.6	4.7	5.0	5.1

* In billions of dollars.

growth would be somewhat faster than the anticipated rate of growth in the economy, the plan would presumably require a reduced rate of growth in other federal programs or an unlikely increase in taxes.

FORCES

Despite its financial growth, the baseline plan does not call for any marked increase in the current U.S. combat force structure, which is summarized in Table 2. The number of strategic nuclear delivery vehicles, with or without SALT, will probably remain close to existing levels, although their payloads could increase by several thousand warheads, depending on the pace of

TABLE 2.   THE PROGRAMED U.S. COMBAT FORCE STRUCTURE, FISCAL YEARS 1981–1982

	1981	*1982*
Strategic nuclear forces		
Land-based ICBMs	1,052	1,052
Bombers	412	412
Fleet ballistic missile launchers	496	544
Fighter-interceptors		
Active	139	120
Reserve	178	178
General purpose forces		
Army divisions		
Active	16	16
Reserve	8	8
Marine Corps divisions		
Active	3	3
Reserve	1	1
Air Force wings		
Active	26	26
Reserve	11	12
Marine Corps wings		
Active	3	3
Reserve	1	1
Navy carrier wings		
Active	12	12
Reserve	2	2
Naval combatant, amphibious, and auxiliary vessels		
Active	409	429
Reserve	45	45

the Trident submarine and cruise missile programs. Ground combat and tactical air forces will presumably change very little in size, but the Navy's general purpose fleet may well expand by twenty or more ships and submarines. Additional fast sealift and maritime prepositioning ships (floating warehouses for combat equipment and supplies) will gradually enter the force structure as well.

PERSONNEL

Because force increases are likely, at best, to be quite modest under the baseline plan, it does not contemplate any major additions of military or civilian personnel. As far as can now be judged, the number of men and women on the payroll of the Department of Defense is programed to remain at about the level shown in Table 3. Interestingly enough, total military per-

TABLE 3. DEFENSE EMPLOYMENT OUTLOOK: THE BASELINE FORCE

	1964	1968	1975	1980	1981	1982
Active military						
Army	972*	1,570	784	777	775	786
Navy	667	765	535	527	540	555
Marine Corps	190	307	196	188	191	192
Air Force	856	905	613	558	569	587
	2,685	3,547	2,128	2,050	2,075	2,120
Selected reserve						
Reserve personnel						
Army	269	244	225	207	217	237
Navy	123	124	98	87	87	88
Marine Corps	46	47	32	35	37	39
Air Force	61	43	51	59	61	64
National guard						
Army	382	389	395	367	386	398
Air Force	73	75	95	96	98	98
	953	922	897	851	885	923
Civilians						
Army	453	542	401	361	371	382
Navy/Marine Corps	346	433	326	309	317	313
Air Force	338	357	278	244	243	247
Defense Agencies	37	74	73	77	82	83
	1,174	1,405	1,078	990	1,014	1,025

* Strengths in thousands at end of fiscal years.

sonnel (active-duty and reserve) and civilian employees funded by the department—amounting to nearly four million people—are not significantly smaller in number than the total estimated to be employed by the Soviet Ministry of Defense. In the latter case, however, most of the 4.4 million people are in uniform, whereas the United States for some years has been substituting civilian for military personnel in a number of positions formerly classified as military. This practice, along with others, makes it all the more difficult to compare the totals of the two sides in any meaningful way.

RATIONALE

The fact that combat force structure and personnel will not grow with the growth in the defense budget does not mean that the baseline plan is necessarily either ill-conceived or wasteful. Even though the size of a military force may not vary with resources, the effectiveness, mobility, and sustainability of the posture can change substantially, depending on the extent to which funds are allocated to such programs as the operation and maintenance of the forces, the capabilities to move them from the continental United States (CONUS) to potential combat theaters, and the war reserve stocks required to keep them functioning in combat. At one end of the spectrum, the force may be a facade, with only the outward appearances of effectiveness. At the other end, because it has the equipment, maintenance, training, supplies, and mobility necessary for maximum performance, its potential may be fully realized.

The baseline program seeks to move precisely in this latter direction. It does so by what might be called full funding of all those appropriation accounts related to effectiveness, mobility, and sustainability. However, full funding is not reached until fiscal 1984. The premise behind the program presumably is that it is a more efficient use of resources to round out and improve existing capabilities than to create still more expensive force structure that has only limited effectiveness and lacks the airlift or sealift to deploy it to a theater in any useful period of time.

Students of bureaucratic politics will insist that the resulting posture, or any other posture for that matter, is simply the product of various more or less parochial and conflicting interests.

Whatever the merits of that claim—and there are bound to be some—a great deal more lies behind the baseline program and the evolving posture than the interplay of rival bureaucratic forces. Despite the battles that erupt periodically between the military and the civilians, among the services, and between executive and legislative branches, a considerable and systematic, if somewhat glacial, planning effort plays a major role in shaping the defense program and posture. Logic and analysis may not be the only determinants of decisions in the Department of Defense, but they do help to explain why U.S. forces have their present size and composition. It is even possible to reconstruct both the nature of the problem confronted by successive defense planners and the reasoning behind their attempts to deal with it.

The problem itself has three major components. The first, quite simply, is that the outside world has become critically important to the United States for reasons that are as much political and strategic as they are economic and historical. Not only do Americans depend increasingly on international trade and the import of energy and raw materials for their well being, but with the advent of nuclear weapons, long-range bombers, and ballistic missiles, they can also be threatened in their own territory as well as overseas. Clearly they have a major stake in seeing that the outside world remains reasonably stable, that pluralism and a measure of order in international relations continue to exist, that issues among states be peacefully resolved, and that threats to order and stability be deterred if possible and contained where necessary.

The second component of the problem is that order and stability have been undermined by a number of forces, not the least of which have been the policies and power of the Soviet Union. For the United States, indeed, much of the difficulty in protecting its interest has come from having to deal simultaneously with the local causes of instability and the support given by the Soviet Union and its clients to the more extreme proponents of change. A balanced and synchronized deployment of diplomatic, psychological, economic, and military incentives to peaceful change within a framework of international pluralism has proved a complicated, burdensome, and often frustrating task.

The task has been made all the more difficult by the third component of the problem: the relatively modest role played by

America's allies within the postwar system of collective security. Unlike the period between World Wars I and II, which allowed the United States to watch events overseas as an interested by-stander and limited participant, the postwar era has thrust on American statesmen the position of both leadership and bulwark of the non-Soviet world. That position, in turn, has taxed the United States with a far weightier military establishment than any it had previously maintained in peacetime.

The United States has taken a number of steps to deal with this problem. It has accepted unprecedented formal treaty commitments—in Latin America, Europe, Southeast Asia, and Northeast Asia—and has undertaken several less formal but almost equally binding pledges to nations in the Middle East and Southwest Asia. After an initial postwar period of almost complete disarmament and atomic euphoria, American planners decided that the country could not rely solely on a nuclear defense posture and, with varying degrees of enthusiasm, began to restore its conventional capabilities. By the early 1960s, not only were the nonnuclear forces coming to absorb the bulk of the defense budget, but plans were also afoot to obtain the capability, in conjunction with allies, simultaneously to fight two major nonnuclear conflicts and a lesser one. Although the Nixon administration subsequently decreed that the Sino-Soviet split would permit the plan to be modified—and one of the major (hypothetical) conflicts was dropped from the planning books—the nonnuclear emphasis continued, at least as far as the defense budget was concerned. However, while the long-range strategic nuclear forces were kept at a relatively high state of readiness and alertness, the conventional forces would have required additional resources and considerable time to reach a comparable condition. In effect, a bet was made through most of the 1970s that any crisis of the future would have a sufficiently slow fuse to permit what would amount to a mobilization of the conventional forces, or more accurately, the acquisition of all the assets needed to make the existing force structure militarily effective.

A number of events have now caused a change in the assessment both of the urgency of the security problem and of the U.S. responses appropriate to it. There are no readily available and reliable data to indicate that war, revolution, terror, and sabotage are more prevalent than they were a decade ago. But the general impression exists that international turbulence is increasing and that Central America, so close to home, and the areas of the Middle East and the Persian Gulf, so important to the United States, are becoming especially vulnerable to it: witness the insurgencies in Nicaragua and El Salvador, the revolution in Iran, the periodic disruption of oil supplies, and the sporadic crises in both regions. Not only is this instability considered bad in and of itself, but it is seen as a standing invitation to Soviet meddling and even direct intervention. The evidence suggests, moreover, that the Soviets will respond to the invitation, if they do not actually create for themselves the opportunity to be invited. Cuban forces in Angola supported by the USSR, Cuban units and Soviet advisers in Ethiopia, Soviet advice and assistance to South Yemen and Syria, the Soviet invasion of Afghanistan, and the Soviet threat to Poland are not easy to characterize as restraint or contributions to peace and orderly change.

Exactly why the Soviets have been behaving in this particular way remains a matter of controversy. It is possible to believe that the ideology which led Khrushchev twenty years ago to support "wars of national liberation" continues to motivate Russian leaders. Imperial ambitions, which caused them to bargain with Hitler forty years ago for control of the Persian Gulf, cannot be excluded as a factor. Despite the relative restraint these leaders have shown in their quarrel with China, dreams of Soviet world hegemony may still inspire them. Sheer paranoia and the belief that if they do not divert and disrupt the capitalist countries, capitalism will destroy them, could be the driving force behind their activities. What cannot be in doubt, however, is a Soviet military build-up which has continued with undiminished vigor for nearly twenty years, with detente and without it, with SALT and without it.

From the standpoint of the baseline planners, there no longer is much danger that the character and magnitude of the Soviet build-up will be underestimated. The main risk now is that both will be exaggerated.

That there could be some exaggeration is understandable. The Soviet military establishment, after all, has expanded a great deal since 1964 and the advent of Brezhnev. It should be recognized, however, that most of the expansion has occurred in two areas. The strategic nuclear forces, and particularly the number of Soviet intercontinental ballistic missiles (ICBMs) and submarine-launched ballistic missiles (SLBMs), have increased markedly, from several hundred to several thousand. The ground forces have also expanded, largely because the number of Soviet divisions in the Far East has approximately tripled since 1964. Substantial modernization of the Soviet capability has taken place as well. But nothing has occurred that could not have been anticipated, given a Soviet government with the will and the authority, the resources, the technological skills, and, above all, the time to upgrade its military weapons and equipment. As a consequence, the capabilities are unquestionably larger and more effective than they were twenty years ago. Even so, the development has been evolutionary rather than revolutionary. In the circumstances, the baseline planners see the future Soviet challenge as more serious than the threat of the past—and one that no longer permits the United States to live off the defense it inherited from the 1960s—but still manageable without the declaration of a national emergency or institution of crash programs.

STRATEGIC NUCLEAR PROGRAMS

To the baseline planners, deliberation seems particularly in order where the strategic nuclear forces are concerned. For some years now, U.S. objectives for these forces have been relatively modest: deterrence of nuclear attacks, stability in both crises and over the long run so that neither side would consider its second-strike forces seriously threatened, and the achievement of these objectives through unilateral programs undertaken preferably within the constraints of increasingly comprehensive measures of arms control.

The military conditions under which these objectives could be achieved have been seen as four in number:

1. the maintenance of offensive capabilities so designed that, through a combination of warning and various protective measures, a large percentage of the inventory could survive an enemy first strike;
2. the diversification of these capabilities over a triad of offensive systems—ICBMs, SLBMs, and bombers—so that an enemy would face an intract-

able problem in trying to knock out all three, and a virtually unsolvable problem in attempting to defend against the differing angles and trajectories of attack produced by such different forces;

3. the coverage with these forces of a comprehensive list of targets—military, logistic, economic, and industrial—but with the ability to withhold parts of the force so as to give the President a range of choice, including the option of responding to a selective attack with an appropriately tailored destruction of enemy targets; and

4. restraint in programs (together with care in their design) so as to minimize first-strike threats to Soviet forces and jeopardy to the conclusion of future arms control agreements.

To maintain these four conditions, baseline planners have developed a countervailing strategy. This strategy postulates that the United States, in designing forces for a nuclear war and deterrence, will not seek to achieve a meaningful strategic superiority, especially given the difficulties and costs associated with trying to do so. But all necessary measures in U.S. programs and war plans will be taken to ensure that the Soviet leadership can have no rational expectation of achieving meaningful superiority either.

The Soviet build-up of strategic nuclear forces is seen as having undermined several of the conditions of deterrence and stability, but not as having eliminated the ability of the United States to respond effectively to a first strike. The most serious development has been the evolution of the Soviet ICBM force in size, reliability, and accuracy to the point where it will soon have to be treated (at least for planning purposes) as capable of destroying up to 95 percent of the U.S. Minuteman/Titan force. Further improvements in Soviet air defenses could also make the penetration of manned bombers to their targets increasingly hazardous by the mid-1980s. In addition, continued Soviet development of antiballistic missile defense systems and construction of civil defense shelters for elite groups and some portion of the urban population could be interpreted to mean that Soviet leaders continue to strive for the overall capability to conduct, and survive virtually intact, a thermonuclear war.

Despite this range of aggressive and costly measures, baseline planners remain reasonably confident that the U.S. strategic nuclear forces on a second strike will be able to cause unacceptable damage to a large number of targets in the Soviet Union.

There are, to be sure, uncertainties about the precise effectiveness of such a retaliation. But Table 4 illustrates what a second strike might be expected to accomplish against a hypothetical Soviet target list, even after the loss of most of the ICBMs, all the nonalert bombers on the ground, and all ballistic missile submarines that might be in port. In such an all-out retaliation, the force could probably deliver on the order of 3,600 warheads from a normal (day-to-day) alert, and cover approximately 38 percent of a comprehensive target list, including large numbers of soft (vulnerable) targets. However, hard targets would not be covered at all. As many as 5,800 warheads could probably be delivered under conditions of a crisis when a great deal more of the force would be put on a high (generated) alert, and as much as 81 percent of the target list could be covered. However, few hard targets would be covered and would have to be attacked by late-arriving bombers.

TABLE 4. CURRENT SECOND-STRIKE U.S. STRATEGIC FORCES VERSUS A HYPOTHETICAL SOVIET TARGET LIST. POTENTIAL TARGET COVERAGE AFTER A SOVIET SURPRISE ATTACK

Targets in the USSR		Targets Covered	
Type	Number	Day-to-Day Alert	Generated Alert
Nuclear			
Hard	1,400	—	436
Soft	600	600	600
Tactical			
Army	200	200	200
Frontal aviation	200	200	200
Navy	30	30	30
Nonurban			
Energy	500	500	500
Transportation	1,000	208	1,000
Economic	1,000	—	1,000
Urban-Industrial	200	200	200
Total	5,130	1,938	4,166
Percent of list	100	38	81

Aside from the vulnerability of the ICBMs to surprise attack and of penetrating bombers to improved air defenses, the main weakness of the U.S. strategic nuclear posture is the lack of a survivable capability to destroy very hard targets in the Soviet Union within an hour or less of an attack. This weakness means that the Soviets could enjoy a sanctuary for their ICBMs during the initial phases of an exchange and, more important, that they would have no peacetime incentive to move the missiles from silos to a more costly basing mode. Without such an incentive, they would be in a position to transfer substantial resources from their ICBM accounts to such troublesome activities as upgraded air defenses and antisubmarine warfare, steps which would increase the vulnerability of the other two legs of the triad.

Quite apart from these vulnerabilities, all three legs of the U.S. triad have been aging and require systematic modernization. Thus, the MX ICBM with its ten warheads and high accuracy will not only have the ability to threaten Soviet ICBM silos and other hard targets; presumably it will also be made more survivable than the Minuteman. Long-range air-launched cruise missiles deployed on as many as 120 B-52G heavy bombers, combined with improved penetration aids for the B-52H, will counteract improved Soviet air defenses in the 1980s, and a follow-on bomber based on the Stealth technology will further degrade those defenses in the 1990s. The Trident submarine combined with the C-4 missile (Trident I) for both the new submarine and twelve of the thirty-one Poseidon boats will reduce any potential weaknesses in the sea-based component of the strategic forces. In addition, as hedges against further Soviet offensive and defensive measures, research and development in antiballistic missile systems will be increased, and more exotic weapons based on high-energy lasers and particle beams will be pursued.

In short, all three legs of the triad will be strengthened as well as modernized. Table 5 suggests what might be the expected effectiveness of the upgraded U.S. forces on a second strike against a comprehensive target set in the Soviet Union. As can be seen, the improved forces should be able to cover 72 percent of the targets from a day-to-day alert status. In the more probable event of a generated alert, the forces might cover all the targets on the list, including hard targets. Furthermore, the upgraded capability would presumably provide still further options to the National Command Authorities, since it would increase their ability to withhold forces from, or commit them to, selected portions of the target list.

Admittedly, the strategic competition will be accelerated somewhat, with or without SALT, because of the Soviet threat to the ICBMs, and the planned U.S. response to it. But another more stable and less dynamic equilibrium could be within reach once both sides have moved away from ICBMs in silos and bombers with large radar and infrared cross sections.

TABLE 5.   PROGRAMED SECOND-STRIKE U.S. STRATEGIC FORCES VERSUS
            A HYPOTHETICAL SOVIET TARGET LIST. POTENTIAL TARGET
            COVERAGE AFTER A SOVIET SURPRISE ATTACK

Targets in the USSR		*Targets Covered*	
Type	*Number*	*Day-to-Day Alert*	*Generated Alert*
Nuclear			
Hard	1,400	—	1,400
Soft	600	600	600
Tactical			
Army	200	200	200
Frontal aviation	200	200	200
Navy	30	30	30
Nonurban			
Energy	500	500	500
Transportation	1,000	1,000	1,000
Economic	1,000	972	1,000
Urban-Industrial	200	200	200
Total	5,130	3,702	5,130
Percent of list	100	72	100

THEATER NUCLEAR PROGRAMS

The baseline planners have been a great deal less confident about programs related to what are mistakenly called the theater nuclear forces. This is hardly surprising. What exists here is not an independent capability but a number of warheads (thousands of them), a few vehicles specialized for their delivery, and various systems which can shoot or drop nuclear as well as nonnuclear ordnance, but are basically part of the conventional forces.

U.S. policy as to the functions of this rather miscellaneous collection of delivery systems and weapons has been and remains ambivalent. When the concept of tactical nuclear warfare was first advanced, it was expected that the United States would retain a monopoly of weapons for this purpose for some time, and that a powerful advantage would thereby be conferred on the defense, despite the assumption of overwhelming Soviet superiority in ground forces, especially in Europe. While much of this thinking hung on long after the Russians had broken the tactical monopoly, most˘ defense planners have now reached rather different conclusions about the utility of these capabilities. One of those conclusions is that because of allied sensitivities and presumed Soviet advantages in conventional forces, the United States must continue to be able to threaten a first use of nuclear weapons in the theater so as to help deter a nonnuclear attack. A second and probably more realistic conclusion is that the capabilities are needed to serve, at a minimum, as deterrents to a first use of nuclear weapons by the Soviet Union.

This latter function would presumably result in a considerable emphasis on second-strike capabilities. Such capabilities would have three primary tasks:

1. the destruction of enemy units in and near the battlefield;
2. the degradation to the extent possible of opposing nuclear capabilities; and
3. the interdiction of follow-on forces through attacks on the units themselves and on their lines of communication.

Since Soviet peripheral attack units—intermediate and medium-range ballistic missiles and medium bombers—could also be brought to bear on the theater, they too might have to be targeted. In the past, that task has been assigned to the U.S. strategic nuclear forces, including a portion of the Poseidons. Whether that solution will be acceptable in the future remains to be seen.

Ground force units, such as companies, can be considered targets in the same way as airfields, bridges, tunnels, and missile installations. Accordingly, it becomes possible to relate the need for warheads and delivery systems to the number of potential targets and arrive at what might be considered an appropriate force size and composition. And in the past, the weapons and delivery systems deployed to Europe and elsewhere for tactical use have been considered more than sufficient according to this rough test. Deemed more urgent than additional weapons have been improvements in the command-control communications for existing capabilities, increases in their survivability, and replacement of older warheads with newer and more efficient devices better tailored to their targets.

Since about 1976, however, the Soviets have been gradually replacing their old peripheral attack and theater nuclear delivery systems with more modern capabilities. The most publicized of these newer systems have been the Backfire bomber and the mobile SS-20 intermediate-range ballistic missile, which carries three independent warheads. Other than with alleged improvements in accuracy, none of these developments increases the vulnerability of the U.S. deployed nuclear capabilities or reduces the target coverage they provide. About the only difference is that under certain conditions, the U.S. strategic forces might find the SS-20s more difficult to target than the SS-4s and SS-5s they replace. Whether now, any more than during the last twenty years, the United States would attack these targets on a first strike must remain a moot question. What good it would do to attack them on a second strike must be left to the imagination.

It has been argued, nonetheless, that the loss by the United States of nominal strategic superiority (however meaningless it has proved) now gives the Soviets an advantage in the theater with their peripheral attack capabilities that must be countered. Whatever the merits of this argument, and of the claim that the Soviets can exercise something called "escalation dominance" in a theater—that is, deter NATO from escalating a conflict beyond the level preferred by the USSR—baseline planners have felt obliged to concoct a program for the deployment to Europe, under U.S. control, of 572 Pershing II ballistic missiles and ground-launched cruise missiles capable of reaching targets in the Soviet Union. They also propose to modernize shorter-range NATO capabilities with the deployment of new Lance missile warheads which could be converted to enhance radiation weapons (more popularly known as neutron bombs) and a new eight-inch nuclear round for the M110A1 howitzer.

NONNUCLEAR PROGRAMS

Despite the public and academic fascination with the nuclear competition and its theologies, the baseline planners consider the greatest defense needs to center on the U.S. conventional forces. Why they feel this way is easy enough to understand. Despite the advent of the nuclear age, all the wars of the past thirty-six years have been nonnuclear. The United States, with only one brief exception, has made its conventional capabilities the cutting edge and mainstay of its defense posture for twenty years. It could even be argued that in contrast to the 1940s and 1950s, the United States has reversed the rhetoric of the Truman and Eisenhower years and come to place main, but not sole, reliance on its nonnuclear forces for deterrence and defense.

To determine what the magnitude of these forces should be, planners have made a number of assumptions about potential enemy threats, allied contributions, and U.S. objectives. It was postulated originally that the USSR would be capable of undertaking one major attack, most probably in Europe, and that its Chinese ally would have the means and ambition to launch another attack more or less simultaneously, either in Korea or in Southeast Asia. It was assumed, in addition, that a small but hostile country, such as Cuba, might engage in activities sufficiently dangerous to require military countermeasures at the same time but on a lesser scale. Later, as the extent of the Sino-Soviet estrangement became evident, these assumptions were modified, and the potential dangers were reduced to the occurrence of one major and one minor contingency for the purposes of conventional force planning. After more than a decade, these assumptions have not been revised.

It has also been postulated that in most contingencies the allies under attack would bear the main burden of the defense, and that the United States would have the responsibility of making up any deficiencies in that defense. Furthermore, for reasons of military efficiency as well as political expediency, it has been accepted that containment of the threat would have to be based on a forward defense. Space would not be traded for time.

To meet these commitments, and at the same time minimize the size of the forces to be maintained, it was decided in the early 1960s that the United States would limit its overseas deployments of ground forces to Europe, keep the bulk of its nonnuclear capability in the CONUS, and depend primarily on intercontinental mobility to protect its power into a threatened theater in a timely fashion. While any resulting conflict might be quite short, as had been the case in successive Arab-Israeli wars, hedges against longer campaigns would be needed. Naval forces would be required primarily to guard essential lines of communication to allies in Europe and Asia, to blockade and interdict any Soviet forces that might sally forth from the Barents Sea and Sea of Japan, and to project power with amphibious forces and attack carriers in places where land bases might not be available. For nearly twenty years, this is the approach that has dominated the planning of the conventional forces.

Once it was decided to prepare for one major and one lesser contingency, capabilities were adjusted so that, at least in principle, they could deploy more or less simultaneously to several theaters, as shown in Table 6. However, because of resource constraints and the U.S. tradition of relying on time and mobilization to strengthen the active-duty forces prior to moving them overseas, important components of the posture have been missing. Several regular Army divisions depend on reserve components for some of their maneuver battalions; war reserve stocks are below minimum objectives; heavy airlift capable of moving the largest Army equipment (which continues to grow in volume and weight) is in short supply; ground forces are out of balance with the lift to move them promptly to places where they might be needed. The fighting potential of the force, in sum, has not been fully realized.

The Soviet conventional build-up was bound eventually to challenge the wisdom of this relatively relaxed U.S. posture. Admittedly the bulk of that build-up has taken place in the Far East. But Soviet units facing Western Europe have been enlarged, given more support forces, and modernized with new fighter-attack aircraft, new tanks, infantry fighting vehicles, self-propelled artillery, and new air defenses organic to the ground forces. Military airlift has also been expanded. And the Soviet navy continues to grow in sophistication if not in size. Long-range Backfire aircraft with air-to-surface missiles are being added to Soviet Naval Aviation. A small force of relatively light carriers armed with jump-jets and helicopters has made its appearance. New classes of surface combatants, led by the battle cruiser *Kirov,* are being deployed. Nuclear attack submarines with cruise missiles and torpedoes are replacing diesel boats, though on less than a one-for-one basis.

Perhaps as important as the build-up itself is the ability the

TABLE 6. HYPOTHETICAL ALLOCATION OF U.S. CONVENTIONAL CAPABILITY FOR CONTINGENCIES

Theater	Army Divisions	USMC Divisions	USMC Wings	Air Force Wings	Carrier Battle Groups	Convoy Escorts	Attack Submarines	Amphibious Ships
North Atlantic	–	–	–	–	2	60	32	–
Central Europe	14	–	–	23	–	–	–	–
Norway	–	1	1	–	1	–	–	10
Mediterranean	–	–	–	–	2	–	7	–
Persian Gulf	–	1	1	–	2	–	–	50
Indian Ocean	–	–	–	–	–	–	7	–
Western Pacific	–	–	–	–	2	30	32	–
Korea	2	1	1	3	–	–	–	–
CONUS/ Caribbean*	–	–	–	–	3	16	20	–
	16	3	3	26	12	106	98	60

* Includes ships and submarines in overhaul and training.

Soviets have demonstrated to mount an unopposed invasion of Afghanistan (major fighting began following the introduction of Soviet troops) with perhaps five or six relatively small division forces, hold their deployments steady in the Far East, develop a substantial military threat to Poland, continue to look strong in East Germany, and provide support and encouragement to foreign revolutionary groups and governments. This perhaps inadvertent demonstration of a potential for multiple operations, set against the background of U.S. dependence on overseas oil and the revolution in Iran, has understandably set off a review of the U.S. nonnuclear posture and a number of recommendations on how to improve and operate the posture.

Even before Iran and Afghanistan, substantial efforts were underway to strengthen the U.S. forces already in Europe, elicit more capability from the NATO allies, and augment the U.S. ability to provide large air and ground reinforcements within two weeks of a Soviet mobilization against Western Europe. With the sudden turbulence and apparent menace in Southwest Asia, the attention of the baseline planners shifted to the problem of how to provide more substance to the U.S. forces supposedly acquired for a lesser contingency. The upshot has been that increased resources are going to existing forces so as to realize more fully their combat potential. Emphasis is being given to improving their maintenance, training, and sustainability. Efforts are being made to retain key enlisted personnel. And plans are afoot for the rapid movement of CONUS-based capabilities through a combination of stabilized overseas deployments (including naval forces on station more or less permanently in the Indian Ocean), prepositioned equipment for the ground forces on land and at sea in special logistic ships, some fast sealift, and a great deal of additional airlift to supplement the existing fleet of C-141 and C-5A aircraft.

What this amounts to, briefly, is that the baseline planners do not see the need for any change in the basic strategic concept of being prepared for one major and one minor nonnuclear contingency. Nor do they anticipate having to acquire a larger force structure. Rather, they see their task as one of making the existing forces respond to contingencies in a timely fashion, with primary attention being given to the rapid deployment of forces to Europe and the Persian Gulf.

What the U.S. nonnuclear posture should be able to accomplish, if and when the baseline programs are carried to completion, can be readily summarized. Although there is disagreement on this score, conventional wisdom has it that 15 U.S. divisions and 23 fighter-attack wings, in conjunction with roughly 30 allied divisions and 3,000 combat aircraft, would suffice (on the average) to withstand a nonnuclear attack against Germany by as many as 85 to 90 Warsaw Pact divisions and 100 regiments of tactical aircraft. Another 3 U.S. divisions and 5 air wings (which would include Marine Corps aviation), similarly, are considered adequate either to help South Korea defend successfully at the demilitarized zone or to keep the Soviets from reaching the oil fields of southwestern Iran. That would still leave a Marine Corps division and air wing for Norway.

To sum up, the baseline planners see international stability as having become somewhat precarious, and the threats to U.S. vital interests as having increased, as a result of both local grievances and the behavior of the Soviet Union which is less cooperative than in the past and supported by a greater nuclear and nonnuclear capability. To respond to these dangers, the baseline planners seek to move more or less simultaneously to accelerate the modernization of all major combat capabilities, reduce the vulnerability of the strategic nuclear forces, deploy a long-range theater nuclear delivery capability as a counterweight to the Soviet SS-20 missile and the Backfire bomber, provide greater readiness and sustainability for existing nonnuclear forces, and increase the overseas prepositioning of material and the airlift deemed necessary to the rapid deployment of these forces. Presumably all five programs could be completed without exerting additional pressure on the existing war production base or making any further demands on the pool of manpower eligible for military service.

The Reagan Program

How much of a departure from this baseline does the Reagan program represent? In the commitment of resources the difference is fairly striking, as can be seen in Table 7. However, it is probably too early to say how firm the commitment is to the budgets projected for the last four years of the five-year defense plan. As of 1981, the budgets for these out-years are more symbols of what the administration thinks it wants to do than they are reflections of a carefully prepared departure from the baseline program. How much of a departure actually takes place will only become visible when the President submits his successive defense budgets.

To be sure, there is a great deal of talk that something new will emerge. The chairman of the Joint Chiefs of Staff hinted in early 1981 that "our strategy should be to apply our strengths against the weaknesses of the adversary, not just necessarily at the point of attack (which may be the enemy's strength) but across a wide array of painful vulnerabilities." The secretary of the navy, in resurrecting the goal of a 600-ship fleet, also threatened to unleash carrier battle groups in waters close to the Soviet Union. The secretary of defense once more extolled the virtues of neutron bombs. However, if these statements have more than rhetorical significance, they will probably have greater impact on future military operations than on current force planning.

TABLE 7. THE REAGAN AND BASELINE FIVE-YEAR PROGRAMS, FISCAL YEARS 1982–1986

Item	1982	1983	1984	1985	1986
Total obligational authority					
Reagan program	222.2*	238.4	255.1	272.9	292.0
Baseline program	196.4	206.2	216.5	227.4	238.7
Outlays					
Reagan program	184.8	205.6	218.1	245.3	263.3
Baseline program	180.0	188.2	197.1	207.0	217.5
Percent real increase (TOA)					
Reagan program	14.6	7.3	7.0	7.0	7.0
Baseline program	5.3	5.0	5.0	5.0	5.0

* Amounts in billions of fiscal 1982 dollars.

It is the case, nonetheless, that as of mid-1981 the Reagan amendments to the defense budgets for fiscal 1981 and fiscal 1982 were serious and detailed. Between them, they added more than $32 billion in future spending to the baseline program. Some of these resources go to new initiatives. Research and development are proposed for what is called a long-range combat aircraft, pre-

sumably an interim penetration bomber to serve as a replacement
for the B-52H until such time as a Stealth aircraft becomes available. The long-lead items for a new nuclear-powered attack carrier and amphibious ship are to be ordered. And three older
ships—one carrier and two battleships—are to be taken out of
mothballs. However, most of the proposed appropriations go, for
all practical purposes, to an acceleration of the baseline program.
Levels of modernization, readiness, sustainability, and deploy-
ability scheduled to be funded under the baseline program in
fiscal 1984 would now be funded in fiscal 1981 and fiscal 1982.

Whether the Reagan planners will continue that thrust cannot
yet be stated with confidence. As is inevitable with any new
administration under the pressure of congressional budgetary
deadlines, its initial proposals are almost bound to be variations
on the themes propounded by its predecessors. That should not
be taken to mean, however, that the future will simply hold
more of the same. Indeed, given the resources at least tentatively
reserved for defense in the five-year economic and financial plan,
there is room for a considerable change in the baseline program.
A rough estimate suggests that full funding of the baseline defense posture over the period 1981–86 would require on the
order of $1,090 billion calculated in 1982 dollars. Since the
Reagan administration budgets $1,280.6 billion (also in 1982
dollars) over the same period, more than $190 billion will pre-
sumably be available for new programs. In default of a clear-cut
administration plan for their use, it may not be excessively
presumptuous to consider where and to what effect these additional resources, or some subset of them, might be invested.

Increments to the Baseline

It should be noted that, in principle, there is never any
difficulty in finding serious defense uses for budgetary increments.
Capabilities to perform particular tasks can be given greater
confidence of achieving their objectives. Thus, if two nuclear
warheads would give an 84 percent probability of destroying a
given target, three would raise the probability to about 94 percent. Additional tasks can also be assigned to the armed forces.
Thus, if nineteen divisions may be adequate as the U.S. contribution to a simultaneous defense of Western Europe and

South Korea, as many as twenty-three divisions might be required to deal with more or less simultaneous contingencies in Western Europe, South Korea, and the Persian Gulf. How far to go in buying these additional capabilities will obviously depend a great deal on what are seen as possible dangers and their imminence. But it will also depend on the risk preferences of the policy makers and on what will have to be given up in order to acquire the incremental capabilities.

In these respects, defense has often been considered analogous to insurance. The nation can always buy more and better coverage of its assets. As with rich individuals, it has a great deal to lose from the international equivalents of accident, fire, and theft. Large insurance policies make sense. There is, however, a point at which this analogy breaks down. Unlike most insurance, defense may generate countermeasures. Even though the United States may keep adding to its military arsenal for purposes of insurance, the USSR may decide to do the same, and vice versa. Except when war is actually underway, or is seen as inevitable, all-out build-ups or even more modest attempts to gain some margin of superiority over a well-to-do, alert, and resourceful opponent may prove counterproductive, as the Soviets themselves are likely to discover in the years ahead, despite the lag in the U.S. response to their build-up.

More is not always better. Accordingly, the issue in considering additions to the baseline posture is not so much whether additional capabilities could be used. It is rather more this: how many additional capabilities the United States can use before running into diminishing returns to scale, finding itself preparing for unlikely or inconsequential contingencies, and producing compensating or excessive countermeasures from abroad. The issue is not easy to resolve.

STRATEGIC NUCLEAR NEEDS

In principle, the opportunities for further investment in strategic nuclear capabilities are considerable. It may prove difficult to justify a target list much larger than the one that already exists for the U.S. offensive forces. But more than the currently programed number of warheads could certainly be used to improve coverage of the targets on a second strike and to increase the probability of destruction against particular targets such as silos, nuclear weapons storage sites, and various command bunkers. For these kinds of purposes, a doubling of the planned MX ICBM force could readily be argued. As a backup or complement to the MX, the Trident II missile could be given greater funding, thereby providing the submarine leg of the strategic triad with a better hard target kill capability. If there are uncertainties about extending the life of the B-52s through the 1980s, and if delays are possible in the useful application of Stealth technology to heavy bombers, a case can also be made for going ahead with production of the interim bomber being proposed for development by the Reagan administration. More resources could readily be allocated to such active and passive defense measures as antiballistic missile defenses, manned interceptors, advanced surface-to-air missiles, and population shelters designed to withstand fallout and even blast effect.

All told, these kinds of improvements to the strategic nuclear offense and defense could absorb on the order of $70 billion (in fiscal 1982 dollars) over the 1981–86 period. Whether they would be worth their cost is at best uncertain. On the surface, many of the measures sound attractive. But it is probably safe to say that no one at present can spell out with authority how, short of being able to execute a disarming first strike, either the United States or the Soviet Union could prosecute a strategic nuclear campaign to anything like a favorable conclusion. As a corollary, it also remains difficult to demonstrate that the strategic forces have any political utility except against nonaligned, nonnuclear, or weak nuclear powers.

In default of any such demonstration, which would surely have to be more serious than a comparison of opposing warhead inventories after one or more hypothetical (and hygienic) nuclear exchanges, the case remains strong for proceeding with the baseline program of modernizing the triad and maintaining a second-strike, countervailing capability. The case for going much beyond that program and posture remains to be proved.

THEATER NUCLEAR NEEDS

Something of the same problem exists at the tactical nuclear level. Here, as with the strategic nuclear forces, arguments can be made for adding more warheads and delivery systems so as to cover existing targets more confidently and to cover a wider range of targets. But the truth of the matter is that the power of nuclear weapons, so far, has outstripped the ability of both the United States and the Soviet Union to adapt to it.

A commonplace of the 1950s was that just as armies had come to terms with gunpowder, so they would learn to live and die with, if not love, the Bomb. So far, however, the learning process has been very slow indeed. Nuclear campaigns can be described in the abstract, and ground forces supposedly can operate in a nuclear environment, at least on paper. But it requires the suppression of much information and enormous effort of the imagination to believe that, in such an environment, units could hold together and fight with anything like the cohesion and coordination they achieve with such difficulty in the face of nonnuclear fires.

Admittedly, the Soviet Union could simply leapfrog the nuclear battlefield with its peripheral attack forces, as it has been in a position to do for twenty years, and destroy all or parts of Western Europe from a distance. But the United States could wreak similar vengeance, however pointless it might be, on all or parts of Eastern Europe. What either side would gain from such massive barbarism, or how the threat of it could be turned to political profit, escapes comprehension.

Threats, to be more than bluffs, must have the potential for something greater than self-defeating action in back of them. This being the case, most nuclear threats are bound to be empty under present and foreseeable conditions. Even so, it has been argued that regardless of the military realities, perceptions of the military balance are what count in the behavior of nations. This supposedly indicates that at least the European allies of the United States must have the reassurance of intermediate-range U.S. nuclear capabilities on European soil as counterweights to Soviet peripheral attack capabilities. The rationale is that somehow it will be easier for the President to commit these capabilities than the more distant ICBMs, bombers, and submarine-launched ballistic missiles.

For better or worse, the baseline program caters to these alleged perceptions with $6 billion worth of Pershing ballistic and ground-launched cruise missiles. To proceed beyond the baseline program, without enhancing the survivability of this force, hardly promises to provide a worthwhile return on what could amount to a substantial investment.

NONNUCLEAR NEEDS

The utility of adding to the conventional forces is quite another matter. The Soviets probably have a number of obstacles to overcome before they can attain truly global power on a conventional scale. It still seems to take them several months rather than days to mobilize a fully ready attack force of any magnitude. Their logistic system is weak and susceptible to breakdown. It remains questionable whether they have accumulated the war reserve stocks necessary for more than a few weeks of large-scale and intensive fighting. They lack the maintenance capability to support moderately sophisticated equipment in the field. Their geography and climate force them to divide their navy into four fleets, and leave them vulnerable to long-range blockades. Their air and ground forces in the Far East and Southwest Asia must operate at the end of weak lines of communication. They face ethnic as well as economic problems.

That is the good news. The bad news is that the Soviets have been working hard to minimize or remove these obstacles. It may not be excessively pessimistic in the circumstances to believe that with time a considerable degree of success will attend their labors. Exactly what Soviet success will portend for the United States and its allies cannot be foretold with confidence. Before too long, however, and perhaps before the end of the decade, it would not be surprising to discover that the Soviets could commit more forces to an attack on Western Europe than is currently assumed for planning purposes, and that they—along with other states hostile to the United States—could mobilize and threaten action in at least three separate theaters. Nor will it be out of the question for them to acquire well-protected and well-equipped overseas bases that would permit some Soviet naval forces to escape their current geographical constraints.

Even if only a few of these possibilities came to pass, they could strain to the breaking point both allied capabilities and the forces in the U.S. baseline program. Under such conditions fewer than the optimum number of ground and tactical air forces could be committed to each of the theaters under attack; alternatively, one theater might have to be sacrificed (for later recovery) in order to save the other two.

A military crisis in Western Europe, quickly followed by similar confrontations in Korea and Southwest Asia could prove especially testing. Such a sequence of events would probably result in a large-scale commitment of U.S. reinforcements to Germany and South Korea. As a consequence, little in the way of active-duty ground and tactical air forces would be left over for the Persian Gulf, and reserve units would not be deployable for several months.

Suppose that the navy had two carrier battle groups in the Arabian Sea when this world-wide crisis erupted. It would still be able to deploy antisubmarine and antiair warfare forces along the barriers formed by Japan and Greenland, Iceland, and the United Kingdom. In conjunction with allies, it could also begin protecting convoys in the North Atlantic and Western Mediterranean. But it would be hard pressed to launch early amphibious operations in Norway and Southwest Asia. Sea lines of communication in the Western Pacific and Indian Ocean might become vulnerable.

Exactly how big a deficit in U.S. conventional forces such a sequential and world-wide crisis would cause is not easily calculated. Under some conditions, it could run to 4 divisions, 6 fighter-attack wings, and perhaps as many as 60 frigates and destroyers. If the Soviets were able to mobilize what might be considered the high instead of the median threat to the Central European front—as many as 120 Warsaw Pact divisions—and if there were trouble in the Caribbean as well, the deficit (assuming no further allied contributions) could run as high as 13 divisions and 15 fighter-attack wings. Amphibious ships and their escorts would also be in short supply.

To illustrate more explicitly the implications of these depressing possibilities, Table 8 shows existing and needed forces deployed to deal with sequential contingencies in Europe, Korea, and Southwest Asia. Table 9 assumes the same sequence of events, but postulates the high Warsaw Pact threat to Central Europe and instabilities in the Caribbean.

How plausible is such a world-wide conflagration? How realistic is it to believe that the Soviets and their clients could undertake such a demanding enterprise, especially if the anti-Russian ferment continues in Eastern Europe? And why would the United States and its allies necessarily respond to the challenge in this

TABLE 8. POTENTIAL DEPLOYMENTS, DEFICITS, AND NEEDS IN U.S. CONVENTIONAL FORCES: MEDIAN THREAT

Deficits are shown in parentheses

Theater	Army Divisions	USMC Divisions	USMC Wings	Air Force Wings	Carrier Battle Groups	Convoy Escorts	Attack Sub-marines	Amphibious Ships
North Atlantic	—	—	—	(1)**	2	60	32	—
Central Europe	15	—	—	20(3)	—	—	—	—
Norway	—	1	1	—	1	—	—	10
Mediterranean	—	—	—	—	2	—	7	—
Persian Gulf	(2)	1(1)	1(1)	3	2	(30)	—	50(50)
Indian Ocean	—	—	—	—	—	(30)	7	—
Western Pacific	—	—	—	(1)**	2	30	32	—
Korea	1(1)	1	1	3	—	—	—	—
CONUS/ Caribbean*	—	—	—	—	3	16	20	—
Total	16	3	3	26	12	106	98	60
Deficit	(3)	(1)	(1)	(5)	—	(60)	—	(50)
Needs	19	4	4	31	12	166	98	110

* Includes ships and submarines in overhaul and training.
** Land-based substitutes for carrier-based aircraft in Iceland and Japan.

TABLE 9. POTENTIAL DEPLOYMENTS, DEFICITS, AND NEEDS IN U.S. CONVENTIONAL FORCES: HIGH THREAT

Deficits are shown in parentheses

Theater	Army Divisions	USMC Divisions	USMC Wings	Air Force Wings	Carrier Battle Groups	Convoy Escorts	Attack Sub-marines	Amphibious Ships
North Atlantic	–	–	–	(1)**	2	60	32	–
Central Europe	15(8)	–	–	20(9)	–	–	–	–
Norway	–	1	1	–	1	–	–	10
Mediterranean	–	–	–	–	2	–	7	–
Persian Gulf	(2)	1(1)	1(1)	3(1)	2	(30)	–	50(50)
Indian Ocean	–	–	–	–	–	(30)	7	–
Western Pacific	–	–	–	(1)**	2	30	32	–
Korea	1(1)	1	1	3(1)	–	–	–	–
CONUS/Caribbean*	(1)	–	–	(1)	3	16	20	–
Total	16	3	3	26	12	106	98	60
Deficit	(12)	(1)	(1)	(14)	–	(60)	–	(50)
Needs	28	4	4	40	12	166	98	110

* Includes ships and submarines in overhaul and training.
** Land-based substitutes for carrier-based aircraft in Iceland and Japan.

particular way or at the nonnuclear level? As usual, there are no certain answers to these questions. It is no underestimate of the Soviets to say that they have responded cautiously and deliberately to the many opportunities and difficulties that have come their way since 1945. It is also the case, however, that they have been less than finicky about exploiting the opportunities or disposing of the difficulties (real and imagined) with the direct or indirect application of military power.

There is good reason to expect that a number of comparable difficulties and opportunities will arise in the future for the Soviet Union. There is equally good reason to believe that even more than in the past the Soviet leadership will make use of the instrumentality on which it has lavished so many resources, and the only one in which it can have much confidence. The bear of the 1980s may prove gentle and benign; it could be confident and aggressive. As likely as not it will be wounded, desperate, dangerous, and still very strong.

Of course, the Soviets may still be laboring mightily but ineffectually to surmount the obstacles that have prevented them from realizing their full military potential. The Russian record on this score, however, suggests great tenacity of purpose and considerable, if gradual, achievement. The strategic nuclear forces of the Soviet Union have grown steadily in size and sophistication. Its navy has evolved from a coastal to a blue-water fleet. Where ground and tactical air forces were once heavily concentrated west of the Urals, a two-front capability of impressive proportions is now poised in the East as well as in the West. It is, on the whole, a record that discourages much betting against increased Soviet strength and the development of still more Soviet military options.

Conclusion

How the United States and its allies might choose to deal with these potential threats is as uncertain as everything else. U.S. forces could indeed be directed to attack Soviet vulnerabilities rather than counter alleged Soviet strengths. However, skepticism must be in order about the operational significance of such abstractions. Political leaders are rarely willing, without specific and powerful cause, either to abandon critical theaters or to expand a conflict in order to follow the principle of exploiting some Soviet weakness. Indeed, that the descendants of *Overlord* (the Normandy invasion) should now be looking for soft underbellies is a remarkable reversal of history and roles.

As for the notion that a large conflict would escalate to some kind of nuclear exchange, there is not much to say except that nuclear weapons do not go off spontaneously. Someone has to fire them. Both the United States and the Soviet Union have understandably refrained from taking this particular step. And there is no persuasive reason to believe that they will become more enthusiastic about such a step in the future. If conventional resources fall short of needs, political concessions may prove more acceptable than a leap into the nuclear unknown. As usual, it proves easier to talk about using nuclear weapons than to authorize their release. Defense planners who are serious about maintaining the national security rather than arguing some doctrinal point are unlikely to be taken in by such talk.

What should be evident, in the final analysis, is that there is no cheap and easy way to deal with so much uncertainty. A gamble can be taken, and the baseline program takes it, that the future will conform to U.S. expectations of it. Conversely, hedges can be taken out against the possibility that the future will be less generous, and that we should be better armed to deal with contingencies that may be low in probability but high in prospective danger.

If the latter course should be taken, a hierarchy of nonnuclear hedges becomes imaginable. For illustrative purposes, however, the needs postulated in Tables 8 and 9 can be regarded as two major levels of protection that might be warranted in the face of future uncertainties. These hedges would add the equivalent of 4 to 13 divisions, 7 to 16 tactical air wings, and at least 110 surface combatant and amphibious ships to the current force structure. Fully manned, they would result in substantial increases in defense military and civilian personnel. A rough estimate suggests that, depending on the magnitude of the hedge chosen, these increases could amount to as many as:

Thousands of Personnel

	Median Hedge	Conservative Hedge
Army	200	810
Navy	70	70
Marine Corps	50	50
Air Force	41	115
Total	361	1,045

Basically, personnel increments of this order could be acquired by one or a combination of several means: recruitment of further volunteers, institution of some form of compulsory service, greater use of the selected reserve, and (at least where the service support structure is concerned) employment of more civilians.

As will be recalled from Table 3, current plans already call for a paid selective reserve force of 923,000 people by 1982. The United States will have to pay on the order of $11 billion in fiscal 1982 for these reservists. Yet large portions of them are excluded for all practical purposes from plans for an initial U.S. response to military contingencies. In the event of an emergency, a number of companies and battalions might be called up immediately to round out, augment, and support the active-duty ground forces. But most of the organized units would be deployed, if at all, only after months of refitting and retraining, assuming that the equipment and facilities were already available.

These capabilities could obviously be tapped and, at a price, tapped more rapidly than current plans anticipate. If recruitment for the National Guard and Reserve continues to increase, and if the combat units could be brought to full readiness in a matter of days instead of months, the need to expand to active-duty forces and rely on conscription would decline dramatically. To speed the call-up process, reserve component units could be given more, and more modern, equipment at the expense of the ambitious baseline programs for prepositioning stocks of material overseas, especially in Europe. In addition, whatever the source of additional ground, naval, and air personnel, an expansion in the war production base for aircraft, tanks, and other weapons would almost certainly have to be anticipated. Several years would be required to obtain that expansion.

This is not the place to decide which among the basic choices is least painful. Each has its advantages and drawbacks. Improvement of, and greater reliance on, the National Guard and Reserve might prove more feasible than a return to conscription. But whatever the choices, an equally fundamental issue remains to be resolved. It is whether the United States, in the face of uncertainties about the USSR, its allies, and a host of other factors—as well as the large opportunity costs that go with defense spending—needs to hedge more than the baseline program does against the possibility of an increasingly turbulent and dangerous environment.

Even if the Reagan program is not adopted in full, or is scaled down by as much as $100 billion in real terms over the five-year period, the resources for considerable hedging will still be at the disposal of the armed forces. There is little doubt, moreover, that the resources could be profitably used, since the case for buying more insurance than is contained in the baseline program has considerable force.

This does not automatically mean that additional resources will be allocated in ways most likely to earn the greatest possible return on the investment. The military services, like most consumers, can never have all their wants satisfied. Even with the Reagan increases, or some variant of them, hard choices will have to be made—choices, in all probability, that the Joint Chiefs of Staff cannot and should not be asked to make for themselves.

The temptation to compromise and give each service its "fair" share will be enormous. It is to be hoped that the civilian leadership of the Pentagon will not succumb to that temptation and will choose instead to lead. If it does, it will find that the signposts to the future are not all that difficult to read. In general terms, they can be seen as directions of the following order.

1. With or without SALT, the United States must surely keep up its end of the strategic nuclear competition, even as it tries to slow down the dynamics of its military interactions with the Soviet Union. What this means, in effect, is that:
   a. the USSR must not be allowed to get away unpenalized with threats such as it has developed to the U.S. Minuteman force;
   b. the Soviets must not be allowed to believe they can obtain military or political leverage with these forces;
   c. the United States, for its part, should forget about wasting resources on trying to achieve some form of numerical superiority, high con-

fidence, extended deterrence, or the chimera of "surgical" exchanges with minimal effect on population; and

d. the highest U.S. interest in designing these capabilities is in maintaining a credible deterrence to their use by others.

The baseline program already strengthens substantially each leg of the strategic nuclear triad. It also forces the Soviets to review the future of their own ICBM force and provides hedges against further Soviet efforts to destabilize the strategic balance. In the circumstances, the case for going beyond the baseline program for the U.S. strategic forces is not at this juncture persuasive.

2. The theater nuclear capabilities, such as they are, should not be treated as the salvation of the West, a source of walking-around money for diplomats anxious to please or bribe U.S. allies, or a new field of experimentation for the arms control community. These are marginal military instrumentalities. They are useful, at best, as second-strike deterrents to the tactical employment of nuclear weapons by others. The commitment to the deployment of long-range theater nuclear forces in the form of Pershings and ground-launched cruise missiles has been made. To add hedges by means of further, vulnerable, long-range or short-range delivery systems does not appear to be a profitable enterprise. Trying to protect existing inventories makes more sense.

3. The conventional capabilities become the critical component of the U.S. arsenal once the nuclear backdrop is firmly in place. As such, they need and deserve the bulk of the resources allocated to defense. To the extent that additional hedges are to be acquired against the uncertainties of the future, they should be taken out primarily with the conventional forces. In designing hedges, it will be desirable for defense planners to:

a. abandon the force planning concept which allows for only one major and one minor contingency;

b. substitute a planning approach which concentrates on contingencies in such specific theaters as Europe, Southwest Asia, Korea, and Central America;

c. dedicate, equip, train, and supply capabilities for these particular theaters and for the protection of the sea lines of communication to them;

d. rely in the short term primarily on a combination of deployed forces and sealift for reinforcements rather than on the costly long-term baseline program of prepositioned equipment, overseas bases, and airlift—a system which may never be fully tested in peacetime and therefore would probably fail in an emergency; and

e. consider the National Guard and Reserve as an option for the principal force augmentations, unless it can be demonstrated that some form of conscription is politically and economically more feasible.

If these general directions are followed, what kind of a defense posture might the United States have in hand by the end of the decade? Table 10 illustrates three of the main possibilities. Neither Posture A nor Posture B would ensure the cessation of local and regional rivalries, terror, or revolution. But Posture A would have a good chance, and Posture B a still better one, of forestalling even a desperate Soviet leadership with an improved military capability from engaging in unprovoked aggression or from overtly exploiting international turbulence. It is doubtful that either of these postures, or still larger ones, would be able to accomplish much more.

TABLE 10. POSSIBLE FUTURE U.S. DEFENSE POSTURES

	Baseline Posture	Posture A	Posture B
Strategic nuclear forces			
Land-based ICBMs	1,000	1,000	1,000
Bombers	410	410	410
Fleet ballistic missile launchers	600	600	600
Fighter-interceptors	300	300	300
General purpose forces			
Army divisions	16	19	28
Marine Corps divisions	3	4	4
Marine Corps wings	3	4	4
Air Force fighter-attack wings	26	31	40
Attack carrier battle groups	12	12	12
Convoy escorts	106	166	166
Nuclear-attack submarines	98	98	98
Amphibious ships	60	110	110

John P. White and James R. Hosek

2

The Analysis
of Military Manpower Issues

Introduction

As in the past, we can be assured that the future will bring continuing debate about the adequacy of U.S. defenses and, indeed, their purposes. A major component of the debate concerns the provision, training, and capability of our military forces. Manpower issues were prominent during the presidential election campaign of 1972 when the continuation of conscription was weighed against the introduction of a voluntary accessions system.

JOHN P. WHITE *is chairman of Interactive Systems Corporation. Before entering government service as assistant secretary of defense for Manpower, Reserve Affairs, and Logistics at the Department of Defense and later as deputy director of the Office of Management and Budget, Dr. White was senior vice president of The Rand Corporation and a member of the board of trustees of that organization.*

JAMES R. HOSEK *heads the Manpower, Mobilization, and Readiness Program at The Rand Corporation. His research has been in the area of labor economics and most recently has focused on enlistment decision-making and retention behavior. Prior to joining Rand in 1973, Dr. Hosek was at the National Bureau of Economic Research and Yale's Institution for Social and Policy Studies.*

Of course, that debate continues. And the manpower debate has other dimensions which receive less public prominence, but are equally important. They pertain to such issues as the structure and adequacy of military compensation, the quality of training, the size and capability of the reserves, the appropriate retention rate for skilled manpower, and the effectiveness and efficiency of the retirement program. As with the larger national security debate, the manpower debate occurs against the backdrop of a large ongoing system. It is a system where change is incremental and slow, although there are notable exceptions, such as the introduction of the all-volunteer force (AVF). Here, as with the larger debate, there is a tendency to forget the institutional setting and, more importantly, to ignore the interrelatedness of the system while discussing any particular issue.

This chapter is intended to provide an introductory description to the military manpower system and to provide a context for the discussion of changes to that system. While the chapter relies on some current and recent manpower policy issues for the sake of illustration, we do not intend to prescribe or advocate particular policy alternatives. The presentation emphasizes the importance of assessing the long-term, systemic implications of policy change. In our view, the opportunities for improvement depend significantly upon the actions of the institutional blocs of the military manpower system. We take these blocs to be Congress, the White House, the civilian leadership in the Department of Defense, the uniformed services, and the service personnel themselves. As we argue below, the service personnel are often not directly active participants in policy deliberations, but their prospective responses to policy changes tend to define the range of reasonable and effective policy actions. Beyond these blocs, there stands the larger reality that how our military forces are obtained, equipped, and managed tends to reflect the values of society at large. Consequently, when debating manpower issues, one must try to understand the implications of proposed changes upon society, i.e., whether society will support the alternatives under consideration.

The consequences of change depend upon the larger, long-term consequences of specific policy changes. Our orientation is toward the systemic evaluation of the costs and consequences of policies on the defense system as an institution as well as society at large. This emphasis may take some of the excitement out of what are often emotional issues, but it is essential to effective debate and realization of improvements over the current system.

The next section, on content, provides some information on the size and composition of the armed forces, as well as demographic data on such factors as the sex, age, education, and race make-up of the forces. Manpower requirements are discussed, and selected aspects of the cost of military manpower are described in the following two sections. The section on the institutional setting discusses the institutional blocs and uses various manpower issues to illuminate their positions and preferences. Finally, the last section, relying upon the previous ones, discusses some manpower policy alternatives bearing on three areas: compensation choices, skill mix and training, and alternative institutional arrangements for accessions.

Context

As William Kaufmann's discussion reminds us, deterrence and combat capability are the ultimate purposes for having a large standing armed force. Relative to the period between the World Wars, the U.S. has maintained a large force since World War II. Table 1 shows that the force of 4.3 million active-duty personnel at the World War I peak had shrunk to only 343,000 by 1920. That force level more or less persisted until the onset of World War II. By the peak in mid–1945, over 12 million individuals served on active duty. By 1947 the force had been reduced to about 1.6 million. As national defense strategy has evolved in the postwar period, the global basing of forces has remained important, and, of course, the threat from the USSR and, intermittently, from the People's Republic of China has remained cause for concern about a significantly large deterrence capability. Since the Korean War, the U.S. armed forces have ranged from 2 to 3 million personnel, although a transitory peak of about 3.5 million occurred in 1969 during the Vietnam War. Since the advent of the AVF in 1973 the force has declined in size from 2.25 million to about 2 million in 1981. The Reagan

TABLE 1. ACTIVE-DUTY MILITARY PERSONNEL, SELECTED YEARS, 1918–1979

	Year	Total (000s)
World War I Peak	1918	4,315
	1920	343
World War II Peak	1945	12,124
	1947	1,583
Korea Peak	1952	3,685
	1955*	2,935
Vietnam Peak	1969	3,460
	1972	2,323
AVF Era	1973	2,252
	1974	2,162
	1975	2,128
	1976	2,083
	1977	2,074
	1978	2,062
	1979	2,027

* Command strength.
Compiled from *Selected Manpower Statistics FY79.*

administration contemplates enlarging the force by 200,000 by 1986.

Table 2 reveals that the proportion of young men required by the services has dropped dramatically since 1960, as measured by the number of young men on active duty, ages seventeen to twenty, divided by the number of eighteen-year-old males. The latter provides a measure of the pool that feeds the flow into the military. In 1960 the proportion stood at over 50 percent, but it had fallen to 41 percent by 1970 and below 30 percent by 1972. This decline was largely driven by the increase in the pool of eighteen-year-olds, which rose from 1.262 million in 1960 to 1.913 million in 1970. That increase continued during the 1970s but at a much slower pace; the peak size of the pool came in 1970 (2.171 million). These demographics made the AVF feasible.

However, the male population will decline steadily until 1986, reaching a projected low of 1.783 million—an 18 percent drop

TABLE 2. MALE YOUTH AND ACTIVE-DUTY MEN AGES SEVENTEEN TO TWENTY,
1969–1979

Year	Male Population 18 Years Old (000s)	Young Men on Active Duty Ages 17–20 (000s)	Percent
1960	1,323	644	49
1961	1,507	685	45
1962	1,424	732	51
1963	1,409	703	50
1964	1,398	638	46
1965	1,929	603	31
1966	1,729	930	54
1967	1,794	1,038	58
1968	1,791	983	55
1969	1,858	942	51
1970	1,913	780	41
1971	1,958	705	36
1972	2,005	565	28
1973	2,045	594	29
1974	2,069	553	27
1975	2,146	539	25
1976	2,150	523	24
1977	2,142	501	23
1978	2,136	468	22
1979	2,171	454	21

Source: *CPS Series 25, Population Characteristics, Selected Manpower Statistics FY79.*

from 1979. By 1989 it will grow to 1.895 million, which is on the order of 150,000 below the average prevailing in the 1970s.

It is possible that the demographic decline in male youth can be offset by greater utilization of women on active duty or by an expansion of the Department of Defense civilian work force. Over the 1970s the proportion of the armed forces made up of women increased markedly (Table 3). This change reflected a conscious policy on the part of the Department of Defense to increase the number of qualified women in the face of increasing difficulty in recruiting high-quality men. But the change also reflected changes in societal values and the shifting career objectives of young women. Whereas women constituted one in

TABLE 3.   ACTIVE-DUTY FEMALE PERSONNEL AND PERCENT OF ACTIVE-DUTY PERSONNEL, 1973–1979

Year	Total (000s)	Percent
1973	55	2.4
1974	75	3.5
1975	97	4.6
1976	109	5.2
1977	119	5.7
1978	134	6.5
1979	151	7.4

Source: *Selected Manpower Statistics FY79.*

every forty active-duty personnel in 1973 (or 2.4 percent), they were one in every thirteen personnel by 1979 (or 7.4 percent). Whether or not the role of women in the armed forces will be expanded in the 1980s remains to be decided. The same holds for the Department of Defense civilian work force and contract personnel, whose services tend to substitute for certain activities of the active-duty force (e.g., some administrative and maintenance activities). In 1979 there were 1 million Department of Defense civilian employees, a decrease of 130,000 from the level prevailing in 1973 (Table 4).

Some other trend lines with respect to the character of the force over time will assist in gaining perspective. For example, Table 5 displays the constancy of the relative size of the services since 1973.

TABLE 4.   DEPARTMENT OF DEFENSE CIVILIAN PERSONNEL

Year	Total Civilians (000s)
1973	1,133
1974	1,164
1975	1,131
1976	1,091
1977	1,065
1978	1,061
1979	1,036

Source: *Selected Manpower Statistics FY79.*

TABLE 5. DISTRIBUTION OF ACTIVE-DUTY PERSONNEL BY SERVICE

Year	Army	Navy	Marine	Air Force	Total
1973	801*	564	196	691	2,252
1974	783	546	189	644	2,162
1975	784	535	196	613	2,128
1976	779	525	192	585	2,081
1977	782	530	192	571	2,075
1978	772	530	191	570	2,063
1979	759	524	185	559	2,027
		Percent Distribution			
1973	35	25	9	31	100
1974	36	25	9	30	100
1975	37	25	9	29	100
1976	38	25	9	28	100
1977	38	26	9	27	100
1978	37	26	9	28	100
1979	37	26	9	28	100

Source: Selected Manpower Statistics FY79.
* In thousands.

In contrast, the reserve forces have shrunk dramatically (during the Vietnam War over 90 percent of nonprior service reservists had joined to avoid the draft) and only recently have shown a modest increase (Table 6). While there may be continued hope for improvements in the strength of the reserves, in the future it is not realistic to assume dramatic changes in force size, given current accession and incentive policies. This represents a serious issue for mobilization planners.

These problems are magnified by related concerns about the readiness of the reserves. Will the reserves be ready to fight? This question is critical under the current Total Force Concept, which requires the reserve forces to play an integral role with the active forces in any major conflict. This is most important for the Army. Of the Army's twenty-four divisions, eight are in the Army reserve forces. In addition, the Army National Guard has twenty-two combat brigades and the Army Reserve has another three combat brigades. The reserve forces constitute over half of the Army's combat strength, particularly in regard to support service capability.

Currently, just under 14 percent (one in seven) of active-duty personnel are officers, a value that has held steadily throughout the 1970s (Table 7). As Hunter and Nelson discuss in more detail, the median age of the enlisted force has risen from 23.9 to 24.5 from 1973 to 1979 (Table 8). At the same time, the percent of the enlisted force with over four years of experience inched upward from 40 to 41 percent (Table 9). The gradual climb in age and experience may reflect the departure of young personnel who entered during the draft years, either by being

TABLE 6. RESERVE STRENGTH, OFFICER AND ENLISTED, NOT ON ACTIVE DUTY, 1970–1978

Year	Officers	Enlisted	Total
1970	686*	2,953	3,639
1971	718	3,186	3,904
1972	752	2,959	3,711
1973	728	2,684	3,412
1974	715	2,349	3,065
1975	702	1,954	2,656
1976	697	1,686	2,383
1977	694	1,554	2,249
1978	664	1,445	2,109

Compiled from *Selected Manpower Statistics FY79.*
* In thousands.

TABLE 7. ACTIVE-DUTY OFFICER PERSONNEL AS A PERCENT OF TOTAL ACTIVE-DUTY PERSONNEL, 1970–1979, BY SERVICE

Year	Army	Navy	Marine Corps	Air Force	Department of Defense
1970	12.6	11.7	9.6	16.4	13.1
1971	13.3	12.0	10.2	16.1	13.7
1972	15.0	12.4	10.0	16.8	14.5
1973	14.5	12.5	9.8	16.6	14.3
1974	13.5	12.3	9.9	17.2	14.0
1975	13.1	12.3	9.5	17.2	13.8
1976	12.6	12.0	9.8	17.0	13.4
1977	12.5	12.0	9.8	17.0	13.3
1978	12.7	11.8	9.6	16.8	13.3
1979	12.8	11.9	9.8	17.2	13.5

Compiled from *Selected Manpower Statistics FY79.*

TABLE 8. MEDIAN AGE AND AGE DISTRIBUTION OF MALE MILITARY PERSONNEL, 1973–1979

Year	Median Age	Age Distribution				
		17–20	21–24	25–29	30+	Total
1973	23.9	27.0	28.9	18.4	25.7	100
1974	24.0	26.7	28.4	19.0	25.9	100
1975	24.1	26.8	27.7	20.0	25.5	100
1976	24.2	26.8	27.1	21.0	25.1	100
1977	24.4	26.0	27.2	21.8	25.0	100
1978	24.3	24.6	28.0	21.6	25.8	100
1979	24.5	24.4	27.9	21.5	26.2	100

Compiled from *Selected Manpower Statistics FY79.*

TABLE 9. PERCENT OF ENLISTED PERSONNEL WITH OVER FOUR YEARS OF SERVICE, BY SERVICE, 1973–1977

Year	Army	Navy	Marine Corps	Air Force	Department of Defense
1973	34	40	27	50	40
1974	32	41	25	51	39
1975	34	44	25	52	40
1976	35	42	25	53	41
1977	37	42	26	54	41

Source: *Selected Manpower Statistics FY79.*

drafted or draft-induced, and who accordingly may have not had as strong a taste for military life as did those entering voluntarily.

In any case, Tables 8 and 9 remind us that a large portion of the active-duty force is young and relatively inexperienced. About 25 percent of the force is between seventeen and twenty years old, and upwards of 60 percent (three out of five) has no more than four years of experience. In the civilian sector the frequency of job changing is greatest among youth, so the appearance of substantial turnover among junior military personnel is not wholly unexpected. Data show (Table 10) that of the 355,000 persons entering active-duty service in 1976, more than 33 percent had left the force within three years. And of the roughly 66 percent continuing to the point of first-term reenlistment, only about 33 percent decided to reenlist. By the time subsequent

TABLE 10. SELECTED PERSONNEL FLOW VARIABLES FOR ACTIVE-DUTY MALE
ENLISTED PERSONNEL, 1973–1979

Year	Total Accession (000s)	First-Term Attrition Rate*	First-Term Reenlistment Rate	Career Reenlistment Rate
1973			26.1	82.2
1974	356	36.8	28.0	80.5
1975	369	35.1	36.3	82.3
1976	355	33.5	34.3	77.6
1977	333	—	35.9	75.3
1978	—	—	36.0	71.2
1979	—	—	33.9	67.2

* Percent of accessions leaving active duty within thirty-six months of accession date.

Source: Columns 1 & 2, Defense Manpower Data Center tabulations; Columns 3 & 4, *Selected Manpower Statistics FY79.*

reenlistment points occur, the turnover rate has fallen dramatically. The final column in Table 10 indicates that 77.6 percent of those eligible to reenlist at the end of the second term, or high point, did so. However, the late 1970s witnessed a decline in the career reenlistment rate; the rate had dropped to 67.2 percent by 1979. Needless to say, the trends alone tell nothing about whether they are desirable or disadvantageous, or about how to change them.

In every year since the beginning of the AVF the services have been able to maintain the active-duty force close to authorized size. However, over the past several years concerns have arisen about force quality, first from field personnel who complained about increased difficulty in training new recruits, and subsequently from the discovery that the aptitude test taken by all recruits had been misnormed. When the norming error had been corrected, it was found that more recruits fell into lower test score groups than originally measured. This can be seen in the large proportion of nonprior service personnel whose Armed Forces Qualification Test (AFQT) score placed them in "Category IV," which lies near the lower end of the range and forms the lowest test score category acceptable to the services. Table 11 reveals that 30 or more percent of the accessions from 1977 to 1980 were Category IVs. The problem was most acute in the Army, which took in from 44 to 52 percent Category IVs, figures well in

TABLE 11. PERCENT OF NONPRIOR SERVICE ENLISTED ACCESSIONS WHOSE TEST
SCORES PLACED THEM IN AFQT CATEGORY IV, SELECTED YEARS
1952–1980

Year	Department of Defense	Army	Navy	Marine Corps	Air Force
1952	39	44	33	43	33
1956	27	27	32	35	18
1960	14	17	7	16	12
1964	15	20	11	9	4
1968	25	28	17	22	17
1972	16	18	18	20	8
1974	10	18	3	8	1
1977*	30	44	21	27	6
1979*	30	46	18	26	9
1980*	33	52	17	27	10

* These percentages were computed so as to correct for the norming error.
Source: Statement of Acting Assistant Secretary of Defense on Manpower, Reserve Affairs, and Logistics (Robert A. Stone), February 24, 1981, p. 12.

excess of the anticipated numbers at the time of recruiting. Since the discovery of the AFQT norming error, the quality mix of recruits has improved. Enlistment contracts being written at present by the Army consist of under 25 percent Category IVs.

It is perplexing that such a major measurement error could go undetected for several years. For instance, one might have expected a concurrent decline in the educational attainment of the force, but there was little evidence of that. To the contrary, the education statistics that are routinely tracked by the Department of Defense revealed a slight increase in the percent of enlisted personnel (first-term as well as career) who were high school graduates (Table 12). The figure rose from 87.8 percent in 1976 to 89.4 percent in 1978. In any case, the aftermath of the norming error yielded a rider to the fiscal year 1980–81 pay increase bill, which compelled the Department of Defense to recruit no more than 25 percent Category IVs during fiscal year 1981 and for the Army to recruit at least 65 percent high school graduates. For fiscal year 1982, the 25 percent Category IV constraint was imposed on each service and increased to 20 percent in fiscal year 1983. Although these constraints would not have presented serious problems to the services in the past, they are more important

TABLE 12. ESTIMATED PERCENT OF OFFICERS AND ENLISTED PERSONNEL BY EDUCATION LEVEL, 1973–1978

	Officers		Enlisted	
Year	Some College	College Graduate	High School Graduate	Some College
1973	93.6	82.0	86.2	15.8
1974	94.2	83.8	86.7	15.7
1975	95.0	86.2	87.4	16.6
1976	94.6	86.6	87.8	17.9
1977	96.1	88.3	87.8	18.5
1978	95.9	88.5	89.4	17.3

Compiled from *Selected Manpower Statistics FY79*.

today. That concern is driven by the declining size of the youth cohort, the worry that military compensation may not keep pace with the civilian sector, and the continuing military demand for "high-quality" recruits.

Manpower Requirements

Each year the Department of Defense issues a statement of manpower requirements. The requirements emerge from an assessment of the roles and missions of the services under various wartime scenarios, at one extreme, as well as an assessment of the workload associated with specific tasks (e.g., repairing a jeep) at the other. The planning process mixes the top-down and bottom-up approaches. As a result, the manpower requirements that emerge represent a blend of considerations, some based on subjective evaluations of how to cope with uncertain situations and others based on detailed, quantitative "manpower engineering" techniques.

Given the uncertainty about when and where the next war will occur, whether it will be nuclear or nonnuclear, long or short, and so forth, the Department of Defense statement of manpower requirements is problematical.

The services employ different but related techniques for determining manpower requirements. Broadly speaking, the process begins with a review of what the service is supposed to do under various wartime scenarios (its "missions") and how well different configurations of resources would accomplish the missions (its "capability"). The review provides guidance regarding the number and kinds of wartime combat and combat-support structures. For example, the services use scenarios to help judge the mix of units that would be effective in accomplishing specific objectives in the context of a scenario, and the judgment depends on assumed rates of attrition of men and material as the battle progresses. In some cases, simulation models are used to depict the course of utilization of military resources during an engagement; in other cases there is more reliance on individual opinion and historical analogue. Working backward from a determination of the wartime requirement, the review gives peacetime support requirements, which depend on the desired surge capacity during mobilization and on peacetime workloads. Also, budget considerations enter the planning process, as the services must decide where to cut or where to add to their resources and capability in the face of defense spending changes. Indeed, much of the planning is incremental, with the current requirements carried over from previous years, implicitly indicating a continuity in both the nature of perceived threats and how to respond to them. Consequently the changes that occur are largely evolutionary, e.g., the gradual development of a rapid deployment force and the multiyear phase-in of new weapons systems. The determination of requirements includes not only what the services think they need in order to meet the mission requirements, but also the reality of what they think they can get and how much it costs.

The services also conduct detailed bottom-up planning. Here the focus falls on the best way to man and equip a tank unit, an infantry battalion, a ship, or an air squadron. As an example of how the bottom-up process works, the Army relies on its Table of Organization and Equipment (TOE) to obtain the manpower and equipment levels for a tank unit to accomplish its wartime mission. The number of combat-type positions in the unit depends on tactical doctrine, desired firepower, and the number of weapons. Each weapon has a prescribed set of operators. Following this, the TOE supplies guidance on TOE service and support (e.g., mess, maintenance, supply). Depending on the specific environment in which the unit will be deployed, the number of combat and support personnel authorized for the unit may be modified, and so on. The actual authorized levels (which may be different from the stated requirement) are not always achieved; in a sense, they represent an upper boundary on the unit's resources, yet they have been constructed to provide assurance that the unit can accomplish its wartime mission.

For purposes of personnel management, the peacetime manpower requirements in combat, service, and support activities are entered as data into an "objective force" planning model, which aggregates the data in various ways. The models can generate profiles of the objective force (i.e., the desired force as built up from the peacetime requirements) by years of service and pay grade. These profiles can then be compared with profiles as predicted from the current, actual distribution of personnel. This comparison serves to reveal probable shortfalls or surpluses of manpower relative to requirements. The comparisons can be done force-wide or by selected occupational area. Also, the objective force models can be arithmetically manipulated to yield insights regarding the number of accessions required to meet future manpower requirements by years of service, pay grade, and skill. Also, they can produce simulations of the effects of alternative retention behavior and promotion opportunities. An example of such a model is the Air Force's Total Objective Plan for Career Airmen Personnel (TOPCAP).

If nothing else, such models lay out the preferences of the services with respect to the key characteristics of the force. They highlight the differences in the structure of the services as determined by differences in mission, doctrine, and manning philosophy. The objective force structures are useful in developing criteria for examining the value of proposed changes in incentives, recruiting, etc. For example, to the extent that the services indicate a preference for a more experienced force, it is useful to examine what incentives provide for increased retention and at what cost.

Perhaps the most difficult "demand" problem is determining the mobilization or surge requirement. Planning for mobilization depends heavily on the character of the conflict, e.g., to what extent it calls for various types of personnel, whether prepositioned supplies are adequate, whether the conflict will be brief or protracted. For many scenarios, the essence of surge planning pivots on the legal constraint that the nation cannot add trained manpower to the force sooner than *ninety* days from the onset of conflict. Afterwards, freshly trained recruits can augment the deployed forces. Consequently, mobilization planning pays heed to standing reserve forces, which can be called up during the mobilization and which provide crucial buffer support. Moreover, rapid mobilization is a major reason for having male youth register with the Selective Service System in order to avoid delay during a national emergency. In light of the uncertainty, complexity, and political difficulty of these issues, they receive inadequate attention.

During peacetime, the manpower and equipment levels often fall short of authorized levels, which are sometimes less than the formally stated requirements. Such shortfalls arise at the cost of reduced military preparedness but at a savings of freeing resources for other purposes during peacetime. Given the various techniques for determining requirements and the constraints on resources, it is not surprising that judgments vary regarding the appropriate levels of authorizations and requirements. There is no right answer to meet all of the various contingencies, particularly since the probability is very high that a future war will be considerably different from any of the contingencies.

Finally, we should mention that the requirements determination process has occasionally been challenged on several technical, but nonetheless important, aspects. First, standard manning guidelines typically specify a single configuration of the number and skill levels of personnel for a given task. But in many cases a variety of alternative configurations (e.g., fewer but more highly skilled personnel) may be able to accomplish the same task. By specifying alternative configurations, planners would have more latitude in selecting the least costly one or in finding the one best suited to the existing (short-run) supply of personnel. Second, trade-offs between equipment and men are possible; spare parts, for instance, can substitute for some highly skilled maintenance personnel. Some logistics/manpower models recognize such trade-offs, but until recently the models were incapable of simulating the trade-offs under wartime scenarios that involve variables reflecting the attrition of material, equipment failure rates, and repair times. And they remain relatively weak inputs in the decision process.

The Costs of Military Manpower

This section reviews selected aspects of the costs of military manpower. We begin by examining manpower outlays as a proportion of the defense budget followed by a review of the amounts spent on specific components of the manpower budget and a comparison of military versus civilian earnings.

Although much of the discussion will be descriptive, the principal point is that compensation can be an effective policy tool for shaping the size of the force as well as its skill and experience mix. Changes in compensation change the attractiveness of military service, and that in turn affects recruitment, retention, individual performance, and the overall force profile. In many cases the responsiveness of recruitment or retention to a change in compensation can be estimated with considerable accuracy; occasionally, the Office of the Secretary of Defense (OSD) utilizes controlled experiments for this purpose. These estimates can then be applied to evaluate the manpower consequences of alternative compensation policies. This procedure of quantitative estimation and prediction has been used successfully in predicting the results of different recruiting and retention incentives, ranging from across-the-board pay increases and bonuses to educational and retirement benefits. Thus we should keep in mind the different perspectives with which to view the costs of military manpower. By one perspective, the costs indicate the budgetary outlays associated with a force of existing size, skill, and experience. By another perspective, the costs can be thought of as an outcome of the process by which policy makers attempt to choose cost-effective modifications of the compensation package and, in so doing, hope to improve the recruitment, retention, or performance of the force.

MANPOWER COSTS IN THE DEPARTMENT OF DEFENSE BUDGET

The cost of military manpower has increased in absolute terms but declined in relative terms over the recent past (Table 13). One reason for the decline in the share of the budget allocated to manpower is the increase in outlays for operations and maintenance. Those outlays rose from 28.8 percent of the defense budget in 1978 to 32.1 percent in 1980. A second reason is the increase in the cost of military retirement; the budget share grew from 6 percent to 9.3 percent over the same period. Of course, changes of even a couple of percentage points result in large dollar changes, e.g., one percent of the fiscal year 1979–80 budget represented over $1.25 billion.

TABLE 13. FEDERAL BUDGET OUTLAYS FOR ACTIVE AND RESERVE MILITARY PERSONNEL, 1973–1980

Year	$ Billion	Percent of Department of Defense Military Budget
1973	23.2	31.7
1974	23.7	30.5
1975	25.0	29.4
1976	25.1	28.6
1977	25.7	26.9
1978	27.1	26.3
1979	28.4	24.7
1980	30.6	24.0

Source: Statistical Abstract of the United States, 1980, Table No. 595, p. 368.

Table 14 presents the components of military pay and defines the primary components as regular military compensation (RMC), special pay, supplemental benefits, and other allowances. RMC consists of base pay, expenditures on food and housing, and a tax adjustment to account for the fact that the food and housing components of compensation are not taxed. Reaching nearly $26 billion of the $41 billion total, RMC dominates the other components of pay. Supplemental benefits are next in line at $13 billion; however $9 billion takes the form of retirement benefits which are deferred rather than current compensation. The $35 billion; however $9 billion takes the form of retirement benefits remaining categories, and close to $4 billion of that derives from medical care and the government contribution to social security. In addition, special pay accounts for about $1 billion, and the commissary and exchange and other allowances make up the remaining $1 billion.

These various components have been relatively stable from year to year. The stability derives from the gradual nature of changes in military policy since the advent of the AVF in 1973.

TABLE 14. ESTIMATED MILITARY COMPENSATION COSTS (IN MILLIONS OF FISCAL YEAR 1978 DOLLARS)

Category	Fiscal Year 1979
Regular military compensation	$24,438
Base pay	17,311
Quarters allowance [1]	5,202
Subsistence allowance [1]	1,925
Supplemental benefits	14,529
Retirement benefits	10,149
Medical care	2,918
Government contribution to Social Security	1,027
Commissary and exchange	435
Special Pays	864
Bonuses	283
Hazardous duty [2]	265
Sea duty	27
Medical personnel [3]	139
Other [4]	150
Other allowances [5]	565
Separation payments [6]	322
Total Department of Defense	$40,718

[1] Excludes tax advantage.

[2] For flying duty, submarine duty, parachuting duty, and demolition duty.

[3] Includes pay for physicians, dentists, veterinarians, and optometrists; medical officers' variable pay; and physicians' and dentists' continuation pay.

[4] Proficiency pay, foreign duty pay, diving duty pay, and personal money for flag and general officers.

[5] Includes uniform or clothing, overseas station, family separation, and dislocation allowances pay. Also death gratuities, mortgage insurance, burial costs, and missing in action pay.

[6] Includes terminal leave, lump-sum readjustment, severance pay, and early-release pay.

Source: Report of the President's Commission on Military Compensation, 1978.

In particular, the size of the active-duty force has decreased only slightly since 1975, when the post-Vietnam manpower reductions were completed. Also, the military pay scale has been stable.

The pay scale is revised annually in order to maintain comparability with pay changes in the private sector. The authority for pay comparability between civilian employees and military personnel derives from the Rivers Amendment, sponsored by Mendel Rivers, chairman of the House Armed Services Committee, in 1967. Under the Rivers Amendment, a pay index based on white-collar civilian employees serves as the basis for adjustments to the military pay scale. At first the pay adjustment was confined to base pay, but a subsequent revision permits base pay as well as cash allowances for quarters and subsistence to rise by the same percentage as the index. However, the secretary of defense can channel as much as 25 percent of the base pay increase to quarters and subsistence allowances. Some recent military pay bills have taken an additional step by proposing that pay increases, which have typically been applied across-the-board, be targeted on selected pay grade or years-of-service groups. For instance, the fiscal 1979–80 pay bill (authorizing an 11.7 percent pay increase for fiscal year 1980–81) permitted the Department of Defense to reallocate up to 25 percent of the increase by grade and years of service. The pay of a careerist could thereby have been increased relative to the pay of a first termer, which would help alleviate the suspected pay compression under the current pay scale and promotion structure. Still, the administration chose to apply the increase across-the-board; it was thought that military pay had not kept pace with the private sector, so a "catch-up" was in order at all pay levels.

Expenditures on food and housing amounted to $6.9 billion in fiscal year 1977–78, the payments being made both in cash and in kind. Military personnel living off base or in rental housing on base receive cash payments, and personnel living in nonrental housing on base, such as barracks or bachelor officers quarters, receive in-kind payments; most junior and many unmarried personnel live in nonrental housing on base. The gradual aging of base housing facilities, many of which date from World War II, has led the services to devote increased attention to their upgrading and replacement. Further, because of inflation and the widespread real estate boom in the U.S., off-base housing became increasingly expensive to military personnel during the 1970s. These developments helped spur passage of a more generous housing allowance in fiscal year 1979–80, the so-called variable housing allowance (VHA). Under the VHA, military personnel can receive the difference between the average cost of nongovernment housing for individuals of a specific pay grade in a high-cost area of the U.S. and 115 percent of the cash allowance for quarters.

This benefit may turn out to be exceedingly expensive and reflects the standard problem with changes hurriedly passed because of "emergency" need. There is a strong tendency to underestimate their cost, both in the short and long runs. In addition, the VHA is the kind of compensation innovation that should have been subject to experimental implementation, or at least more gradual phasing, in order to understand better how it would actually work, iron out the administrative problems, and gain a better estimate of its cost.

Retirement benefits are the second largest component of military manpower costs. Of the $10.2 billion paid to military retirees in fiscal year 1978–79, over 80 percent went to nondisability retirees, who form the largest single group of beneficiaries (Table 15). Outlays to military retirees have grown at a remarkable pace since the 1950s, and in part because of this rapid rate of growth, questions have arisen about the amount of future outlays and, more fundamentally, about whether the retirement system should continue in its present form. Currently, the system provides for nondisability retirement after twenty years of service. Fewer than 10 percent of entering enlisted personnel and perhaps 15 percent of entering officers can expect to reach the twenty-year point. The benefit amount depends on base pay (not RMC) at the time of retirement and rises from 50 percent of

TABLE 15. MILITARY RETIREMENT BENEFITS BY CATEGORY OF RETIREE FOR FISCAL YEAR 1978–79

Category	Number	Total Benefits ($ million)
Nondisability	976,500	$ 8,313
Temporary disability	11,300	59
Permanent disability	141,000	1,029
Fleet reserve	97,800	673
Survivor benefit plan	57,600	190
Total	1,284,200	$10,264

Source: *FY1979 Department of Defense Statistical Report on the Military Retirement System*, p. 13.

that amount, if retirement occurs at twenty years of service, to a maximum of 75 percent of base pay at thirty years of service. Prior to FY82, twice annual cost-of-living adjustments were made in order to compensate for the effects of inflation; however, adjustments will occur once a year beginning in FY82. Contrary to most retirement systems, no vesting occurs until completion of twenty years of service. On the other hand, active-duty personnel who complete twenty years may begin receiving their benefits upon "retirement."

Outlays to military retirees grew steadily during the 1970s: from 3.6 percent of the defense budget in fiscal year 1969–70 to 9.3 percent in fiscal year 1979–80. The trend in the budget share going to retirees derives from still longer trends in the growth of the population of military retirees (Table 16). The number of retired officers grew by a factor of four from 1955 to 1979, and the number of retired enlisted personnel rose twice again as fast. From roughly 100,000 each of retired officers and enlisteds in 1955, the beneficiary pool increased to about 400,000 officers and 800,000 enlisteds in 1979. Although we do not show data for all years, steady growth occurred.

The volatility of end strength during 1935 to 1959, driven by manpower build-ups during World War II and the Korean War, bears little relationship to the smooth pattern of increase in retirees over 1955–1979, the period of retirement fed by the earlier years. Thus large fluctuations in the size of the active-duty force have not been associated with fluctuations in the num-

TABLE 16. RETIRED OFFICERS AND ENLISTEDS, 1955–1979

Year	Officers	Enlisteds
1955	87.3*	93.5
1960	122.4	132.7
1965	193.6	287.0
1970	263.4	501.5
1975	330.0	713.9
1979	289.8	838.7

* In thousands.
Source: FY1979 Department of Defense Statistical Report on the Military Retired System.

ber of retirees, because the management of force size occurs predominately among the first few years of service.

All active-duty military personnel and their dependents are eligible for free medical care on base. Off-base medical care is covered by the military health insurance system, CHAMPUS, which has an annual deductible of fifty dollars per individual (or one hundred dollars per family) for outpatient care, a coinsurance rate of 20 percent, and has a small daily fee for inpatient care. As Table 14 shows, the cost of these medical benefits stood at $2.9 billion in fiscal year 1978–79. Viewed from the perspective of the individual, annual health expenditures in the civilian sector were then on the order of $250 per person for insurance, as well as direct outlays on medicine, physician visits, etc. To a rough approximation, the military probably provided the same value of care to its personnel, although a finer comparison would also consider such aspects as accessibility, range of services, and quality of care.

The military employs a variety of special pays to encourage recruitment or retention in selected skills, to compensate for hazardous duty, to adjust for high costs of living abroad, and for other purposes. For example, reenlistment bonuses were paid to nearly 25 percent of all active-duty enlisted personnel in 1979. Hazardous duty pay, such as jump pay, sea pay, flight pay, and sub pay, plus other special pays (including foreign duty pay, cost-of-living allowance, overseas housing allowance, and more) were received by about 40 percent of enlisted personnel in 1979. Thus bonuses and special pays are used widely by the military to supplement RMC. In fiscal year 1979 special pays amounted to $864 million in 1978 dollars (see Table 14), and since then the use of bonuses has expanded.

With this information about RMC, retirement benefits, medical care, special pays, and bonuses in mind, we next present tabulations that compare the earnings of enlisted personnel with civilian sector employees. The comparisons provide a general idea of whether military pay is comparable to private sector pay, but, unlike the index used in implementing the Rivers Amendment, we do not limit the civilians to only those in white-collar jobs.

CIVILIAN VERSUS MILITARY EARNINGS

Our earnings comparisons, developed with the assistance of Christine Peterson at Rand, utilize data from two surveys of individuals, the May 1979 Current Population Survey and the 1979 Department of Defense Survey of Officers and Enlisted Personnel, which was administered in the spring of 1979. Each of these data sets permits us to construct monthly earnings variables. The civilian earnings variable represents gross (pretax) monthly earnings of workers who are not self-employed. The definition of the military variable is more complex because of the many components of pay that must be considered. Still, we think our military pay variable offers a reasonable indication of pay in the armed services, although with some limitations.

Our military pay variable consists of three basic components: regular military compensation, special pays, and reenlistment bonuses. RMC is constructed in two steps. First, using an individual's reported year of service and pay grade, we look up his base pay in the fiscal year 1978–79 military pay table. Second, even though some personnel (especially those in the first term) receive quarters and subsistence in kind, we add to base pay the average reported cash allowances for quarters and subsistence as computed for personnel receiving these in cash This procedure assumes that the value of the in-kind benefits equals the average cash allowance. Special pays are averaged in as reported. Bonuses, which are reported in a lump sum amount, are prorated to a monthly basis by assuming a thirty-six-month term of reenlistment. Because that is the minimum term, the prorating procedure yields monthly bonus amounts that are biased upward. However, most reenlistments are for the thirty-six-month term. Our military pay could include some allowance for medical care, commissary and exchange privileges, the government contribution to social security, and other more minor factors. Also, the data unfortunately exclude data on enlistment bonuses, which if included, would increase military pay in the eighteen to twenty age range and to a lesser extent among higher age groups.

Tables 17 and 18 present average monthly pay by age group for males with a high school education. Table 17 refers to whites and Table 18 to blacks. The comparisons are limited to persons with a high school education in order to control for differences in the educational composition by sector. About 70 percent of all enlisted personnel have a high school education (and no higher education), and the vast majority of these are graduates rather than equivalency diplomates (GEDs). In viewing the tables, keep in mind that military personnel are disproportionately young, so the first two or three age groups have the heaviest concentration of personnel. (About 50 percent of enlisted males are age eighteen to twenty-three versus about 30 percent in the civilian sector, relative to the overall age range of eighteen to forty-five years.)

TABLE 17. CIVILIAN AND MILITARY MONTHLY EARNINGS, WHITE MALE HIGH SCHOOL GRADUATES, 1979

Age	Civilian	RMC + Special Pays + Bonuses	Ratio Mil./Civ.
18–20	795	823	103
21–23	1,046	934	89
24–26	1,203	1,108	92
27–29	1,265	1,188	95
30–32	1,365	1,248	92
33–35	1,404	1,330	95
36–38	1,464	1,397	95
39–41	1,482	1,447	98
42–45	1,535	1,573	102
Average	1,261	1,081	86

For whites the ratio of military to civilian pay begins near unity and then declines to 89 percent for ages twenty-one to twenty-three. Then it gradually builds back to unity by the late thirties. For blacks the pattern of relative earnings is about the same, but it begins with military blacks averaging 32 percent more than their private sector counterparts. The ratio then dips down to unity in the midtwenties and rises to about 130 percent by the late thirties. In other words, relative earnings of blacks distinctly exceed those of whites. These racial differences reflect black/white earnings differences in the private sector, for our data show (Table 19) that black/white earnings equality exists within the military using earnings as defined above.

TABLE 18. CIVILIAN AND MILITARY MONTHLY EARNINGS, BLACK MALE HIGH SCHOOL GRADUATES, 1979

Age	Civilian	RMC + Special Pays + Bonuses	Ratio Mil./Civ.
18–20	$ 632*	$ 837	132
21–23	842	969	115
24–26	1,039	1,053	101
27–29	987	1,186	120
30–32	1,091*	1,275	117
33–35	1,195	1,382	116
36–38	1,321*	1,416	107
39–41	1,121*	1,488	133
42–45	1,144*	1,481	129
Average	1,020	1,077	106

* Cell has less than thirty people.

TABLE 19. MILITARY EARNINGS FOR WHITES AND BLACKS, HIGH SCHOOL GRADUATES, 1979

Age	White	Black	Ratio Black/White
18–20	$ 823	$ 837	102
21–23	934	969	104
24–26	1,108	1,053	95
27–29	1,188	1,186	100
30–32	1,248	1,275	102
33–35	1,330	1,382	104
36–38	1,397	1,416	101
39–41	1,447	1,488	103
42–45	1,573	1,481	94
Average	1,081	1,077	100

These comparisons do not control for many differences in the civilian/military terms of employment that might give rise to relative wage differences. In the military one wears a uniform, works within a formal hierarchy of command, rotates to different geographical locations (often without choice), bears the risk of going to war, and apparently works more hours per week. We tabulate that the average civilian high school graduate works 42.5 hours per week, which contrasts to 52.6 hours per week for military personnel (as reported in the Department of Defense survey). Earnings comparisons could also be extended to whether the wife accompanies the husband in the military, the wife's employment opportunities, and her earnings.

We conclude the earnings comparisons by simply noting two points. First, allowing for a fairly brief lag attributable to the survey process, the above exercise indicates that it is possible to make timely yet detailed comparisons between military and civilian compensation. Second, while such comparisons are a necessary input for policy evaluation, by themselves they are inadequate to tell whether the armed services offer correct and sufficient incentives for performance and retention.

The Institutional Setting

We have discussed the overall context, requirements, and composition of military manpower. But it is also important to understand the institutional setting in which any change must take place. Like all public policy issues, military policy changes tend to highlight particular problems at any given time and to introduce solutions to those problems without an adequate understanding of the attendant effects of the solutions. The preference functions of the various actors are important when considering possible changes. First, their preferences give insights into what the overall outcomes will be. The institutions, particularly the services, tend to view the changes in terms of their benefits and deficiencies in their own larger institutional setting. Second, the preferences of the particular parties display their values and therefore reveal decision criteria, some of which are not explicit. Finally, the role of the various parties in any given issue will provide a strong indication of whether or not proposed changes will be successful.

The principal players in this discussion are four: the individual service member, the services, the administration, and Congress. We will discuss each of these, principally by illustration. We can illustrate the preferences of the parties with reference to a number of general policy issues: overall readiness and combat performance, emphasis on cost-effectiveness, compensation, attrition and retention, and flexibility of choice and the quality of life.

THE INDIVIDUAL

The individual plays a central, but often muted, role in the debate. Obviously, it is important that the system attract a range of qualified individuals to perform complicated tasks, in peacetime as well as wartime. These individuals represent an array of talents and preferences. Their performance will change under different conditions (policies), but it is highly problematic how particular changes affect performance. It is not obvious that more is better, be it compensation or quality of life, or, conversely, that hardship alone hardens individuals to face the rigors of the tasks of the professional military.

The other three policy actors are continually concerned about the effect of changes on military manpower performance to solve particular problems, but with none of them being able to judge those effects adequately. As a result, the role of the individual tends to be that of a modifier on the policy proposals of the other three parties. Because individuals respond to manpower policy adjustments, their prospective reactions control the limits within which changes can be made. One reason why many key issues, particularly compensation and related personnel issues such as rotation and quality of life, lend themselves to policy analysis is that the individuals affected change behavior in ways that can be predicted as well as tracked. This can be seen in measures of accessions, reenlistments, indiscipline, etc. Consequently their subsequent behavior, predicted or real, directly affects policy choices. For example, the length of tour for a soldier in Germany is not only driven by the best military judgments about combat training and unit effectiveness, but also by indiscipline rates and morale factors that have had the Army move toward shorter tours in recent times. The arguments for shorter tours were made by the senior unit commanders, not by the personnel specialists. And their arguments were basically in terms of the morale and discipline problems that ensue toward the end of a lengthy tour.

A similar illustration involves the number of military personnel who are married. Over time the number of married active-duty military has risen steadily, particularly among first termers. This argues for an increasing concern with amenities which are not necessary for single people. It can be seen directly in the congressional proposals to reduce the number of dependents in Europe. Objectively, most policy makers would agree that dependents in Europe are a burden. However, the services and each succeeding administration have reluctantly opposed any changes in the current provision for accompanied tours, because they perceive a major reduction in career attractiveness from such a change.

The increasing concern with the reduction in continuation rates beyond the first reenlistment is another illustration. The services, particularly the Navy, have experienced a significant loss of trained manpower in the middle years of service. The services have argued that these losses are due to inadequate compensation and can be cured by increases in pay and allowances. But the problem runs much deeper. Surveys indicate serious disenchantment with many aspects of service life, beginning with the leadership of their superiors, living conditions, rotation policies, etc. At the same time, the services may be right in the sense that increases in compensation may obviate some of these other perceived inadequacies. The point is that a change in behavior, which is regularly measured, caused a compensation policy shift.

In summary, while the individual is at the heart of both policy and policy changes, he is a relatively silent or at least an inarticulate participant in the debate, other than for the important fact that behavioral responses of the individual can shape policy. Indeed, the individual often defines the limits of policy change.

THE SERVICES

The services shoulder the obligation of meeting the overall mission requirements. The other institutions are basically concerned with these objectives also. But the military has embodied these concerns as the very essence of their professional obligation. As a consequence they tend to be conservative in the estimate of the requirements to meet any particular situation. Coupled with this overall conservatism is a strong desire to have the ability to manage the force under as few constraints as possible. Consequently, the services have a strong preference for increasing compensation and monetary benefits because doing so will make service life more attractive. At the same time it will increase service flexibility in terms of the other personnel policies, e.g., rotation, promotion rates, tour lengths. On the other hand, the services show less sensitivity to cost-effectiveness than do the Congress and, certainly, executive branch civilian leaders. By definition cost-effectiveness means only providing expenditures that are necessary to meet a defined requirement whereas the services would far rather err on the side of increased expenditures, again, not because they are profligate, but because they derive added institutional benefits from these expenditures.

A priori, one would expect the uniformed military to have a strong preference for low attrition rates in the first term, whereas, in fact, this has turned out not to be the case. As was discussed in the section on manpower requirements, attrition rates rose markedly during the seventies and have remained relatively high. The institution of the all-volunteer force carried with it a very strong signal from Congress that discipline problems were to be reduced. Throughout the Vietnam War not only had the draft become a major political issue, but so had the resultant disciplinary measures taken by the military on those who had entered the service. The large numbers of complaints from the individuals involved and their parents were politically unattractive to Congress. The services responded to these signals and to their own preferences by allowing commanders to discharge people who were perceived to be unfit for service or unhappy with service, and as a result attrition rates among first termers rose markedly. This provided the attendant benefits of fewer leadership problems, a marked reduction in the infrastructure needed to deal with disciplinary cases, and practically the elimination of complaints from Congress regarding military discipline. Attempts on the part of civilian leadership and certain elements in Congress to reduce these attrition rates on cost-effectiveness grounds have been resisted by the services.

The service resistance to major retirement reforms is also instructive. Retirement reforms proposed by the Carter administration were designed to increase the attractiveness of the service for individuals in the eight- to twelve-year range, among other things. The proposals guaranteed grandfathering of all active-duty people who entered up to the day of their enactment and, in fact, provided the choice between the old system and the new for those in their first term. Coupled with an increase in attractiveness for those in their eighth to twelfth year of service were lower monetary penalties for leaving for those in the twelfth to twentieth year of service. The services argued that the pay proposal that accompanied the retirement changes was inadequate. But their fundamental concern had to do with losing the flexibility that they now enjoy because of the lock-in effect of twenty years of service. The retirement reforms would have forced a full range of attendant changes in other personnel policies in order to maintain the attractiveness of service to those between twelve and twenty years of service. This was not the public reason for resistance, but it was the principal reason.

The services have been reluctant to switch from straight pay to bonuses. They place high value on the attendant benefits that go with increased across-the-board compensation even though it is demonstrably more expensive and less efficient. This can be illustrated by the recent introduction of a variable housing allowance (VHA). The services insisted that the VHA be provided outside the calculation of regular military compensation. They wanted the new benefits to be a true add-on that could not be traded off easily against other kinds of compensation in the annual budget proposals.

THE CIVILIAN EXECUTIVE LEADERSHIP

For our purposes the Office of the Secretary of Defense and the Executive Office of the President can be treated as one actor, although one would never think so while involved in the process. At the executive level there is considerable emphasis upon cost-effectiveness and cost trade-offs. In addition, there is a heavy reliance on numerical indicators of personnel system performance. This reflects the orientation of the actors at this level and also less commitment to the broader and less well-defined institutional concerns of the services. The annual cycle of program and budget development forces them to focus on resource constraints and trade-offs. Consequently, there is a heavy emphasis on attempting to create cost-effective personnel and compensation policies that will provide adequate performance measures at minimum costs. This emphasis on trade-offs is reflected in the defense budget itself, as well as in the broader process of establishing the President's total budget each year. It is not just that the executive leadership views the relative size of the various elements of the defense budget as choices within a fixed constraint, but also that it has a requirement to mesh personnel policies with related policies concerning the civilian work force. This is particularly true with respect to military-related agencies such as the Public Health Service and the Veterans Administration, but also for the rest of the executive branch. This orientation is manifested in a strong preference for bonuses and other flexible pay devices, retirement reform, reduced attrition, and reduced rotation. On the other hand, the civilian leadership in the Pentagon often sees its interest as the same as the services and engages in intense debates with the Executive Office of the President. For example, Secretary of Defense Caspar Weinberger's initial proposal to exempt a large portion of military pay from income taxes was quickly withdrawn by the administration because of its broader implications.

One added illustration should suffice. In the President's budgets for FY78 and FY79 there was great pressure to hold down the compensation of government employees, both military and civilian, as a part of the government's overall commitment to anti-inflation policies. The administration judged that this policy would not result in serious changes in personnel performance, and that turned out to be true for civilians. But it was not true for the military. The administration found it difficult to develop a rationale in the context of its broader policies to decouple military and civilian pay and allow military pay to rise. At the same time there was a strong reluctance to abandon the legal mechanism that provided for military pay to rise each year on the average provided to civilians. This difficulty stemmed in part from a reluctance to abandon this mechanism and once again make military pay an annual political issue. While this reluctance was finally overcome, in large measure through pressures and actions of Congress, military pay increases came quite late and only after a deterioration in accessions and retention.

THE CONGRESS

The most difficult institution to discuss in summary is Congress. It does not speak with one voice, but some generalizations can be made. Historically, Congress has been reluctant to provide increased power to the secretary of defense in personnel matters, for example, enhanced power to manipulate the bonus system.

At the same time, there is a continuing desire on the part of Congress to "do what's right for the troops," while, conversely, there is a reluctance to be perceived as wasting money on military expenditures. We are all familiar with the swings in national and congressional mood that change these generalizations. Also, the armed services committees tend to view the uniform services as their constituents in the conventional model of constituency politics in Congress. In addition, in the last decade, the debate over the effectiveness of the AVF has colored basically every military compensation issue brought to the Hill. In each and every case there is an undercurrent as to whether the measures proposed will enhance military capability and military personnel effectiveness, or whether they will continue merely to shore up a system which many consider inappropriate and unworkable.

Finally there are numerous actors in the executive branch and Congress (e.g., domestic cabinet officials and social service committees) who are not attuned strongly to the needs of the military personnel system, but are involved in implementing public policy choices that directly affect the military personnel system. Some are closely related, such as policies to improve benefits for veterans (which may in fact reduce retention). Others are more general, such as the introduction of the Comprehensive Employment and Training Act, other kinds of youth employment programs, and the broadly based provision of grants and loans for higher education. And at the more general level of government, fiscal and monetary policy are concerned with controlling civilian wages and inflation while increasing civilian employment opportunities. Consequently, we need to remember that the military manpower debate is not played out in isolation, but in the context of broader social issues.

Alternative Approaches for Improved Efficiency and/or Lower Cost

This section discusses several areas of interest in defense manpower policy, including compensation choices, skill mix and training, and alternative institutional arrangements for accessions. These issues are important in themselves and, in addition, offer salient illustration of policy evaluation and modification. The discussion expands on the argument that policy decisions involve multiple criteria and that the consequences of one policy often

bear on the workings of others. The interrelated nature of manpower policies provides good reason for obtaining a thorough
understanding of the expected effects of policy changes before
they are implemented. To gain such an understanding, policy
analysts and decision makers require access to information. In
cases where adequate information is not readily available, surveys
and controlled experiments are valuable. Analyses of such data
have the advantage of producing estimates of the direction and
magnitude of policy effects. When a range of options can be
analyzed, the information can be enormously valuable not only
in shaping the most cost-effective policy, but also in gaining a
sense of whether certain side effects are inevitable or avoidable.

Our three topical areas, compensation choices, skill mix and
training, and alternative institutional arrangements or accessions,
are themselves interrelated. Thus, the discussion will flow from
one to the next, revealing some of the interconnections along
the way.

In textbook economics, workers receive a wage rate set by
market forces through the interaction of supply and demand.
Neither firm nor worker can affect the equilibrium market wage,
as they are assumed to be only two agents among the many that
comprise the market. This notion contrasts sharply with compensation practices utilized by firms, especially firms employing
more than a few workers. Compensation is used as a management
tool; the terms of the compensation package are shaped according
to the specific objectives desired, e.g., lower turnover of labor,
greater assembly line production, less absenteeism, higher motiva-
tion for achievement, and so forth. Thus, the simple market wage
in the textbook model has been replaced by a multifaceted compensation package, and workers, rather than simply comparing
the wage at one firm versus that at another, are viewed as evaluating the utility (personal satisfaction) of the firm's compensation
package versus other firms' packages. This paradigm applies also
to the armed forces. The reason is simple: the armed forces must
compete with the private sector for labor. This fact imposes a
discipline on setting the terms of military compensation, for the
less competitive the military package, the greater the loss of
workers to the private sector.

As discussed in the section on military manpower costs, the
pay of military personnel is adjusted annually to keep pace with

a pay index based on earnings of civilian white-collar workers. It is doubtful that the index adequately captures changes in fringe benefits as opposed to direct monetary compensation (wages and salaries). The importance of fringe benefits in the overall civilian compensation package has grown rapidly in the past decade, perhaps because of a growing demand for such "earmarked" compensation, and perhaps because it offers some tax shelter. In the past few years, a number of larger firms have introduced so-called "cafeteria benefit plans" in which the worker can select among different options for health insurance, dental coverage, pension plans, tax deferred annuities, and so on. The military system, in the meantime, except for the VHA, has not substantially altered the nature or level of its fringes. As a result, the military pay package may be less competitive than perceived from the pay comparability adjustments, and, of course, the discrepancy may be sizable in certain occupational areas where private sector fringes have advanced rapidly. Further, the retention consequences of fringe benefit discrepancies may depend on the specific nature of the difference, e.g., dental care or educational benefits. To some extent, the military is making amends, for example, the proposed extension of dental care benefits to the dependents of active-duty personnel. But the military benefit package is not evaluated against a comprehensive and quantitative understanding of what the private sector offers. (Only in the past few years has the federal government begun a systematic assessment of private sector benefit packages by means of surveys undertaken by the Office of Personnel Management.)

Another, long-recognized rigidity in the military manpower system is the preference for port-of-entry hiring. Almost all accessions to the enlisted force are nonprior service youth with little labor force experience or skill. If experienced nonprior service workers in the private sector want to join the services, the workers face the same skill ladder as inexperienced workers and must begin at pay grades that may be well below their skill levels. In comparison, private firms typically hire at all skill levels and pay commensurately. This raises the question of whether the military pays a premium for its hiring policy. Some experiments permitting the lateral entry of civilians could shed light on whether they were equally productive, motivated, and willing to follow orders; whether their retention was equally high; and whether they could be obtained at any significant saving of costs in the manpower system (e.g., determine whether enlisting a skilled mechanic is cheaper than recruiting and training an inexperienced one, and then paying him enough to keep him).

The success of a lateral-entry accession program would hinge on another unique feature of military compensation relative to private sector compensation. Because the latter varies by occupation but military pay scale does not (apart from special pays and bonuses), one would expect the response to a lateral entry program to differ by occupational area. Indeed, the lack of pay variation across occupational areas in the military probably underlies some of the retention problems now occurring among midcareer personnel. As an antidote, some suggest modifying the pay scale to allow occupational pay differentials. But before accepting the wisdom of such recommendations, it is useful to know whether these retention problems (and personnel shortages) typically persist over time. If so, permanently increasing military pay in those specialties could relieve the shortages. Such is the case with medical officers, who do, in effect, have augmented pay. But in many other cases it is less clear how long the shortage will exist and what caused it. For instance, the commercial aviation industry has produced volatile swings in the demand for pilots and navigators, yet the severest movements tend to be of short duration. The development of models to help predict these swings can aid the Air Force and Navy in managing their pilots. And how should the management be done—through more pilots, tighter commitment contracts, or more pay? If pay for pilots were permanently increased, then in slack periods in the commercial aviation industry, military pilots would be overpaid. Ironically, sharp increases in the demand for additional pilots in the private sector might still occasionally create a harmful shortage in the military, even at the higher pay rate.

These problems of overpayment and underpayment would vanish under a system allowing an occupation's pay to vary freely with pay in corresponding occupations in the private sector. But such a system needs to define the "corresponding" occupations and to make pay adjustments in fairly short order. Moreover, it is by no means clear that workers would be content not knowing how much they would make from one period to the next. Introducing year-to-year flexibility in pay scales creates a new risk for military personnel, who presumably would demand higher pay in each period in order to remain as content as before. Besides, the character of the military career is so much different from that of the conventional civilian environment that it is not simple to tailor a system that is a close analog of civilian systems, even for peacetime, hence, the continued resistance to the frequent calls for adoption of a salary system.

These kinds of considerations lie behind the growing usage of bonuses as a flexible means of meeting transitory shortages, while the substructure of RMC continues steadily from period to period. But still far too little is known about the existence and size of *persistent* wage differentials between military personnel and private sector employees in given occupations to reach any convincing judgment about the cost-effectiveness of occupational premiums within the military.

With respect to retirement pay, the military retirement system's provision for vesting at twenty years of service creates an incentive for active-duty career personnel to remain in the service until then. The draw of retirement pay increases as retirement nears, and it provides a strong incentive for personnel with fifteen or more years of service to stay, even under unsatisfactory conditions: "it all counts on twenty."

This incentive applies to less productive and more productive soldiers alike, and it is argued that the existing system unfortunately does little to remove the deadwood from the force. Among others, the President's Commission on Military Compensation (PCMC) proposed the vesting of retirement benefits in conjunction with a later start date of benefits (age sixty-five instead of end of service). These provisions would encourage personnel to leave rather than stay until their twentieth year of service. At the same time, more midcareer personnel (eight to twelve years) could eventually qualify for retirement benefits than under the current system, thereby increasing retention among this important group. As a consequence of the increased retention behavior, the PCMC projected a decline in front-end accession requirements during the transitional phase from the existing system to the steady state of the new system. Had the PCMC recommendation been adopted when proposed in 1978 (it was not), the decline in the accession requirements would have fortunately coincided with the decline in the size of youth cohorts in the mid–1980s—an opportunity that has now largely passed.

A key aspect absent from analyses of the retirement system is its effect on quality, i.e. does it tend to retain higher or lower quality personnel, or is it neutral. Advocates of earlier vesting suggest that such a policy would encourage the less productive personnel to leave earlier. The reason is that retirement benefits depend on pay grade; so for two soldiers starting at equal pay grades after, say, ten years of service, the less productive one has a lower expected pay grade were he to stay twenty years, hence more incentive to leave early. Whether that would in fact be the case may only be learned from further empirical analysis or experimentation. In particular, it needs to be determined whether the lower quality personnel would expect sufficiently lower wages in the private sector so that the military service continued to be their best alternative. In addition, the services may be less reluctant to release marginal performers who have made a career commitment.

Concern with the productivity of personnel carries over into the issue of skill mix and training. Pressure to review the appropriateness of the existing experience and grade profiles comes from various sources (the services, the Office of Management and Budget, the Office of the Secretary of Defense, outside defense analysts) and at times may seem contradictory. For instance, on the basis of empirical work indicating that on-the-job performance rises with experience (years of service), the *Defense Resource Management Study* recommended further investigation of the possibility of moving toward a more senior force. Having a higher content of the force in the five-plus years of service range would, it is argued, reduce recruiting demands, lower training costs, and yield greater returns on the training that is given. Movement toward a more senior force would entail some redefinition of the job content associated with higher pay grades. Presumably the higher enlisted grades (say E-5 through E-7) would become less oriented toward administration and supervision and more toward production-line activities. The implications of such changes on morale and retention remain unknown.

Pointing in the other direction, toward a less senior force, is the growing concern of retirement costs. As mentioned earlier, the retired population currently stands at roughly 800,000 enlisteds and 400,000 officers, and since the mid–1950s the enlisted portion has grown approximately twice as fast as the officer portion. Furthermore, the experience profile of the force indicates that once an enlisted person attains ten to twelve years of service, the odds of making it to twenty (and thereby qualifying for retirement benefits) are very high. Thus a fear of ever-increasing outlays for retirees motivates the notion of trimming the senior force or changing the retirement system.

Clearly, the essence of the issue is who should be kept and for how long. It is complex for reasons deriving from the difficulty of measuring an individual's productivity or the productivity of the unit to which he is assigned. Success so far with written and hands-on performance tests has been limited. The Army has made the most extensive use of such tests, although the other services have programs to develop performance measures. To date most testing has been confined to performance during the first term of service, so it is not an accepted conclusion that the same methods can be effectively applied to later terms (and higher skill levels), where supervisory and managerial activities gain prominence. Moreover, test development has dwelt on individual, not unit, performance. Little is known about how the composition of a unit (age, race, education, skill mix) affects the productivity of an individual much less that of the group as a whole. Thus, the extension of testing beyond the first term and to units should be done in order to establish a foundation for analyzing the skill mix of the force.

Assuming that accurate measures of productivity were found, the productivity gains of a more experienced force could be weighed against the costs of higher active-duty compensation and greater likelihood of qualifying for and drawing retirement benefits. At the same time, the implications of changing the force's skill mix on the objective force would have to be examined—would wartime capability be enhanced or impaired? And the compensation package would have to be reviewed to see whether additional incentives for retention were required and, if so, how much they would cost. All of this would be necessary because the objective is not merely to increase the average experience level of the force, but to do so in a cost-effective way and without degrading force strength, flexibility, and readiness with respect to surge and wartime requirements.

Turning to alternative institutional arrangements for meeting accessions requirements, there are several, including the AVF, a partial draft to meet shortfalls under a voluntary system, a full draft, a draft for reserves, a national service obligation, and others. By and large, these systems differ most obviously in their ability to meet first-term accession goals and, concomitantly, in their Department of Defense budget cost. Under the AVF, compensation must be sufficiently high to attract the required recruits; bonuses aid in directing recruits to areas of potential shortfall. Under a partial or full draft, individual compensation can be less; eligible individuals, if drafted, have a legal obligation to serve. Under a national service obligation, military service would be one of presumably several alternatives for discharging, say, a two-year "debt" of service to the country. Like the partial draft, a system of national service could run in conjunction with the AVF (or for that matter, in conjunction with a partial draft).

Any system that does not pay individuals a wage commensurate with their opportunity wage will tend to have attrition and retention problems. These problems will be exacerbated if military service is compelled rather than voluntary, but will be mitigated to some extent if the involuntary system has shorter obligatory terms of service and offers compensation above the opportunity wage. Hence detailed comparisons of the relative advantages and costs of alternative procurement systems can be meaningfully done for specific system alternatives.

It is true that a draft should bring in personnel more socially and educationally representative of youth as a whole. Whether those drafted would be better soldiers and equally well motivated to serve remains debatable. However, restructuring the AVF recruiting goals and compensation package has the potential to accomplish the same objective. On the other hand, uncertainties about the costs of maintaining a viable AVF remain, as well as uncertainties about its effectiveness. To the extent that costs arise from pressures to recruit more and higher quality recruits, there may be options to mitigate those pressures. These options include increased usage of prior-service personnel, of Department of Defense civilian employees, manpower substitutes (such as additional spare parts in lieu of additional repairmen), weapons systems with lower manning and/or skill requirements for operation and maintenance, and compensation policies that improve the retention of midcareer personnel, especially those in critical specialties.

Conventional wisdom about the AVF versus other procurement

systems suggests that their differences are concentrated in the first term of service. Put differently, regardless of the procurement mechanism, the traditional problems of managing the career force will remain. After all, the career force has always been voluntary, draft or not. But, unfortunately, this observation falls short of recognizing the differences in attrition, retention, and performance that may emerge across alternative systems. Barring major changes in the structure of compensation, non-AVF systems will likely experience higher attrition and lower first-term reenlistment; if so, accession requirements will increase. Under an involuntary system an increase in accession requirements will have scant effect on accession costs but will increase training requirements. Further, higher attrition and lower retention may aggravate possible efforts to move toward an experience profile with more personnel in the five to twelve years of service range. Depending on the weight of arguments, such as that more sophisticated weaponry dictates longer tenure among military personnel or that productivity rises sufficiently fast with years of service to justify a more senior force, a more junior, conscripted force having greater attrition and turbulence could jeopardize force readiness and flexibility as well as worsen cost-effectiveness. Putting the point more positively, the strategy for adapting a non-AVF system should specify the best way to use personnel likely to be around for a short time. The strategy should also attempt to devise mechanisms that can give early indication of an individual's propensity to stay on active duty until the completion of his first term and beyond. One possibility would be stiff penalties for early departure, but that is unlikely to be politically acceptable. As noted above, another option is to restructure the compensation profile so that initial earnings are lowered and subsequent earnings are raised, thus providing greater incentive for personnel to stay to the end of their terms and to reenlist.

In conclusion, these issues highlight the basic themes of our argument: the complexity and systemic nature of the institution, the important first and subsequent order effects of policy changes, the key role that can be played by analysis and evaluation, the opportunities for improvement, and the importance of the key actors to the overall outcome. The challenges of the coming years are significant, but the opportunities for meeting them are well within the limits of our resources and abilities.

Richard W. Hunter and Gary R. Nelson

3

Eight Years with the All-Volunteer Armed Forces

Assessments and Prospects

Introduction

The authors have been asked to assess the experience of the active military forces under the all-volunteer force (AVF) of the 1970s and to project the potential problems of the 1980s. To be most useful, such analysis needs to be set in the context of the

RICHARD W. HUNTER *is assistant director for Compensation Program Development in the U.S. Office of Personnel Management (formerly the Civil Service Commission). Previously he held the positions of staff director, Military Personnel Policy, and director, Manpower Program Analysis, in the Office of the Secretary of Defense. Dr. Hunter is the author of numerous studies and articles on manpower and compensation issues, including* Use of Women in the Military *and* The Educational Incentives Study.

GARY R. NELSON *is associate director for Compensation in the U.S. Office of Personnel Management. Dr. Nelson previously was the deputy assistant secretary of defense for Requirements, Resources, and Analysis in the area of manpower and logistics and was a member of the staff of the 1970 Presidential Commission on the All-Volunteer Armed Forces (the Gates Commission). He and Dr. Hunter are coauthors of the comprehensive Department of Defense study,* America's Volunteers: A Report on the All-Volunteer Armed Forces.

defense environment. This introduction sets such a context and discusses the terms used in military manpower and the criteria for evaluation. The second section analyzes recruitment incentives and the success of the AVF. The third section provides more detailed manpower and personnel data in the context of the manpower equation, and the final section presents the results and conclusions.

THE DEFENSE ANALYSIS ENVIRONMENT

In assessing defense programs, balance is extremely important. The finest weaponry that can be built may prove useless if it cannot be maintained and operated by the people in the armed services or if there are insufficient spare parts or munitions or if the command-and-control systems fail to communicate the orders to use it. On the other hand, the defense establishment is so large and so complex that it is difficult to make simultaneous solutions of all the potential variables to achieve the needed balance. To classify issues into one of the following five major categories helps to provide a framework for analysis:

1. new weapon systems development and procurement;
2. munitions, spare parts, and other consumables for war reserve;
3. operations, maintenance, and training;
4. command and control (including intelligence); and
5. manpower and personnel.

There is a propensity for flashy new weapons systems with great promise, such as the MX missile system, the B-1 bomber, multi-purpose cruise missiles, or a new tank or ship to dominate defense spending at the expense of items in the other four categories. This is understandable. Such systems create excitement both in the press and among participants in the defense decision process. The problem is that such systems often promise more capability than they eventually deliver, and payoffs are almost always a long way in the future. Long-range planning, development, and procurement of high capacity weapons are essential to the long-term defense posture, but they can absorb an enormous share of the limited funds allocated for maintaining a defense posture in peacetime and must be balanced against the needs in the other four areas. This calls for a trade-off between long-term capability and current readiness.

When the intensity of the Arab-Israeli conflict of 1973 is compared to peak battles in other wars, the potential drain on war reserves begins to raise serious concerns. It led General Alexander Haig, when he was NATO commander in Europe, to observe that any major NATO–Warsaw Pact war in Europe would be a "come-as-you-are war." With the demonstrated potential of a twenty-four hour a day offensive many times the intensity of the Battle of the Bulge in World War II, current levels of war reserves could be exhausted in a matter of a few days. In the budget allocation process, however, the accumulation of munitions, petroleum, spare parts, and other war reserve consumables is not very dramatic and can easily be deferred for another year or two during a budget squeeze. This has happened in the past and may happen again. It has an adverse effect on short-term capacity to sustain a high-intensity limited war beyond a week or two. The ability to contain and sustain a high-intensity war in Europe is a basic assumption in the manpower mobilization plan that underlies almost all of the reserve programs and much of the active-force program. If the United States does not expect to contain and sustain any massive attack in Europe with conventional weapons, then much of the current force structure, unit composition, weapon procurement, manpower programs, and mobilization contingency plans are misdirected.

Linked with the war reserve issue are operations, maintenance, and training. In a "come-as-you-are war," the state of the "you-are" (i.e., readiness) is a direct function of the level of training and maintenance. The literature is replete with concerns about low levels of readiness, training of personnel, and maintenance of equipment. Horror stories are told of tanks that will not operate and gunners that cannot shoot their cannons, let alone hit the target. There has been a tendency to cite poor quality recruits and low retention of trained personnel and thus to blame the problem on the AVF. In many instances the problems were created by reduced training time, simulation to save expensive fuel and munitions, and the curtailment of field maneuvers that sustain skills learned in training and weld units together into combat ready teams or crews. Over the years the increasing cost of munitions, fuel, and consumables and restrictions on places to train have led to persistent reductions in field training with live ammunition. Recurring budget squeezes have intensified the pressure. On top of this, periodic shortages of petroleum have led to other severe cutbacks in the military use of fuels for training and operation. The net result has been reduced readiness for conventional forces, equipment that is not in working order, personnel who do not know how to fix or operate it, makeshift efforts to make do, and a charge that the problem is poor quality people in the military. Often the recommended solution is a return to the draft.

When any of the other elements falls short, the people are expected to compensate and adjust. The question that then becomes relevant is can the services recruit and retain sufficient people with the right skills to meet their needs in the 1980s.

The answer to that question requires more than economic equations or counting high school diplomas. It rests on the commitment of a nation, of a people, to do whatever is necessary to preserve their freedom and way of life. That attribute is not easily measurable and always tends to be a quality attributed to previous generations of Americans and held questionable for the current generation. World War II author Robert Sherrod in *Tarawa* noted that the U.S. generals in 1942 questioned whether the GIs of that war were up to the standards of the doughboys of World War I. In 1918 questions were raised wondering if the doughboys who were going "over there" were as good as the boys who stormed San Juan Hill. Generals in the Civil War lamented the poor commitment of their troops and longed for the good old days when men endured the hardships of Valley Forge. Current problems always seem to be the most trying ever faced, and the past is remembered as better than it was. But it is true that the basic resolve, the strength of America, comes from the homes of America and is only heightened and sharpened by military training. There is no reason to believe that the current generation of teenagers has any more or less of these intangible qualities than any other generation, nor that the next generation will be stronger or weaker than this one.

The nonquantifiable intangibles often make more difference between losing and winning in war than battle plans or econometric analysis. Nevertheless, analysis does have a relevant role in understanding that resources are available, what can be done to correct weaknesses, and what can be expected to happen if certain incentives are changed. This chapter will focus on those aspects that are quantifiable. But in reviewing the literature discussing the manning of the armed forces in the late 1970s and the 1980s, one is struck by how often the arguments turn on the loss of these intangibles that "used to be." The arguments run that somehow, if we just had the draft in operation, everything would be okay. The late Representative William A. Steiger of Wisconsin put this in perspective in testimony before his colleagues while they were debating a report prepared for Representative Robin L. Beard of Tennessee, critical of the volunteer Army.

I would like to share with you the findings of a study I have made regarding the state of the Army. In pursuing this matter, I visited three installations: Fort Meade, Fort Gordon, and Fort Hood. My goal was to talk to the commanders and the troops, in headquarters and in the field, in order to gain insight into their views on Army life and the readiness of our force.

To enhance my ability to get at the facts I arrived unannounced at each post, making a brief courtesy call at the post headquarters, and then spent several intensive days talking with personnel at all levels of the Army. The following material highlights some of the major recurring themes I encountered:

Volunteers repeatedly said that recruiters had misled them as to the job opportunities and assignments.

Dependents stated that medical care was difficult to obtain and, when given, was delivered in a callous and impersonal manner.

Experienced commanders stated that discipline had never been worse; that rates of court-martials, article 15s, and absences were at all-time highs.

Units were often unable to train due to the absence of key personnel.

Senior enlisted men complained that the quality of troops had declined significantly and that the growing number of individuals in mental group IV had made training and discipline nearly impossible.

Personnel at all levels complained that crimes of violence had seriously eroded the quality of life on post; at one installation, I was warned to avoid numerous areas on post after dark because they were dominated by the criminal element.

Medical personnel told me of rampant drug abuse.

Facilities were in a general state of disrepair; barracks were characterized by severe deterioration of the plumbing, as well as the outside structure;

gyms and recreation facilities were not only structurally deficient, but also lacked adequate equipment; soldiers frequently complained about the lack of off-duty activities and an inability to get to a major city for entertainment.

Mr. Chairman, these views simply highlight the more serious problems that I found. My tour was not made [recently] but in 1971, at the height of the draft. I bring these matters to your attention to place into perspective critiques of the Volunteer Army. For such criticisms to be fully appreciated, it must be recognized that problems are generated by the large, bureaucratic organization that is our Army, whether it be volunteer or drafted. The young people from Wisconsin—and Georgia and Tennessee—who join the Army today are no less willing than their predecessors to tolerate unsatisfactory conditions.

I would like to commend my colleague, Mr. Beard of Tennessee, for sponsoring an in-depth study of today's Army. There is much in his report that I can agree with, because it reflects my own study of the Army during the draft. Indeed, any of us who served as Members of Congress during the draft era know of these problems because we have voluminous case-worker files filled with allegations of recruiter malpractice, command abuse, inadequate equipment, poor facilities, and a multitude of other problems. Some were verified, others were not. But the point to remember is that because such difficulties predate the AVF, they cannot be cured by a return to the draft.

The military is a complex enterprise. Any detailed examination will expose major flaws or shortcomings—if not in quality of personnel or training in weapons then in the length of time or the cost to produce complex new weapons or the difficulty of maintaining them or, finally, in the resulting readiness of the forces. Private corporations of similar complexity (and probably similar problems) can be judged on results—the financial accomplishments of the enterprise. We are able to judge our military forces only in wartime. And attempts to gauge our capability in peacetime focus primarily on deficiencies rather than capabilities. This is understandable, particularly given the questionable outcome of military operations in Vietnam and the very sizable military build-up in both conventional and strategic forces by the Soviet Union and the Warsaw Pact in the past fifteen years (see Kaufmann, chapter 1).

So in analyzing our experience under the all-volunteer force and examining its prospects for the future, it is well to remember three major points.

1. Manpower is only one of many inputs to military capability.

2. Manpower problems that exist today may not be occurring for the first time and are not necessarily caused by the all-volunteer force.
3. Alternative manpower systems may produce problems even greater than those existing today.

CRITERIA FOR JUDGING THE AVF

The authority to draft men into military service expired in June 1973. The last draft call was issued the previous November. To date we have had eight years of current experience with the AVF. Dependence on volunteers to staff a small peacetime military has been the rule in American history rather than the exception. The cold war period of the post-Korea 1950s and the pre-Vietnam 1960s was the only period in U.S. history in which a peacetime draft was maintained for more than a few months. It also was the first time the U.S. found it necessary to maintain large standing peacetime armies. In 1973 the nation began its first sustained effort to maintain an active-duty armed force of over 2 million people in uniform without conscription. Thus, the experience since 1973 with the AVF is unique in American history.

To evaluate this experience, we need to define the expectations for the volunteer force and the national defense requirements for military personnel in general. In doing so, we will also define the most common terms used in military personnel management.

The 1970 President's Commission on an All-Volunteer Armed Force (the Gates Commission) set two main objectives for the all-volunteer force: to meet peacetime military manpower requirements without conscription and to attract persons of adequate quality to meet the requirements of military jobs.

The chapters by Kaufmann and by White and Hosek have given a thorough introduction to national defense and to defense manpower policy. We need to supplement this material only with a few specialized definitions. To begin with, *average strength* refers to the average number of people in a service during a year, while *end strength* is the number on the last day of the fiscal year.

The two most common categorizations of military personnel strengths are between officers and enlisted personnel and between first-term and career personnel. *Officers* are the managers of the service and include those military personnel who are commissioned officers of the United States whose appointment requires the advice and consent of the Senate and who serve at the pleasure of the President. Officers do not have terms of service, although there are minimum obligations for newly commissioned officers, and officers serve until they resign, are released from active duty, or are placed on the retired lists of the various armed services. The vast majority of officers (92 percent) hold baccalaureate degrees or have higher education, and although a few are promoted from the enlisted ranks, recent graduates of universities are the primary source of new officers. (*Warrant officers* serve in many technical or semiprofessional jobs and usually are included with officers, although they generally come from the enlisted ranks and do not have as extensive formal educations.) *Enlisted personnel* sign a fixed term of service contract ranging from two to six years and are discharged upon completion of that contract. Enlisted personnel represent technicians and supervisors. *First-term personnel* are on their initial contract or obligated service, while *careerists* are those who have reenlisted or stayed beyond their initial obligated service. To simplify calculations, officer and enlisted personnel with less than four years of service often are considered first-term, and those with four or more years of service often are considered to be careerists.

TABLE 1. OVERALL DEPARTMENT OF DEFENSE STRENGTH

	First-Term	Career	Total	Percent
Officers	64,000	214,000	278,880	14
Enlisted	1,014,000	746,000	1,760,000	86
Total	1,078,000	960,000	2,038,000	100
Percent	53	47	100	—

Recruitment is the process of obtaining volunteers to enter the services from the civilian communities. The draft, when it is in force, is operated by the Selective Service System to require civilians to enter the military involuntarily. Whether recruited or drafted, accessions who have no prior military experience are called *nonprior service* (NPS) accessions. *Reenlistees* are those who have previously enlisted in the services and are enlisting again. A reenlistment could occur on the same day as the discharge so that there would be no "broken service" but rather a continuous period of service, or it could be after several months or even years after discharge. Those who reenlist after substantial broken service are usually rerecruited from the civilian community and are referred to as *prior-service accessions*. Those who reenlist at their units either without broken service or after a short break in service are not recruited by the recruiting commands and for purposes of this chapter will be called reenlistments.

Accessions are those people who are joining the service in a given year, while *losses* or *separations* are those who leave the service. Accessions and separations apply to both officer and enlisted, first-term and career personnel. Officer accessions are those entering the officer corps of the services whether from enlisted status or civilian life, usually as a result of completing a baccalaureate degree or equivalent education. There are very few officer accessions to the career force. Enlisted accessions do involve both first-term and career personnel. For purposes of analysis of service accession programs, a number of categorizations of accession are made, including sex, education, test scores, service, component within service, among others. Another category that is important is the *military occupation* in which the individual has enlisted or been assigned. The various services have different classification systems, but a Department of Defense system divides military personnel into ten categories, as shown in Table 2.

Almost every job found in civilian life must also be performed by someone in at least one of the armed services. When a man

TABLE 2. OCCUPATIONAL DISTRIBUTION OF MILITARY PERSONNEL

Occupation	*Army*	*Navy*	*Marine Corps*	*Air Force*
Infantry, armor, and gun crews	23.3	3.7	23.3	6.4
Electronic equipment repair	4.2	13.0	4.4	13.0
Communication/intelligence specialist	9.4	8.3	6.7	7.0
Medical/dental specialist	5.2	5.1	0.0	4.3
Other technical specialists	2.1	1.1	1.7	3.4
Administrative and clerical	15.8	9.7	13.3	21.2
Mechanical equipment repair	14.4	26.5	15.7	22.7
Craftsmen	2.3	5.6	2.6	5.4
Service and supply workers	10.6	5.4	11.1	9.0
Other (including trainees)	12.8	21.4	20.9	7.5
Total	100.0	100.0	100.0	100.0

or woman enlists in a service he or she usually enlists for a specific job in one of these occupations, is trained in that skill, and serves there for several years. As Table 2 illustrates, there are many jobs needed to operate the armed forces that are not directly related to combat arms and only a relatively few jobs in the combat arms occupations.

Not everyone, however, who signs an enlistment contract completes the conditions of that contract. Some are discharged early to reenlist and are considered reenlistments the same as those who complete the period of contracted service and reenlist. But many are discharged or otherwise leave service before the completion of their contracted obligation. This phenomenon is called *attrition*. *First-term attrition* is the loss of members before they complete their first enlistment. *Retention* is in some sense the opposite of attrition; it is the measure of those members in the service at the beginning of a year who are still in the service at the end of that year.

During the draft years, obtaining more draftees was not a problem, but desertion, AWOL, and apathy often were. So, with the draft, many members of questionable value were retained, often in confinement, because the services did not want to "reward" poor service with "liberation" from military obligation and thus provide a stimulus for misconduct among draftees with no particular desire to serve. In an all-volunteer environment, such constraints were no longer relevant, and those who did not do well in training or appeared unable to adjust to military life were simply discharged.

As a result, as White and Hosek have shown, attrition was higher under the AVF than originally anticipated. However, attrition is expensive and obtaining additional recruits is difficult, so efforts were made to reduce attrition as the recruiting market became more difficult after 1975.

The services' recruiting and retention policies combined with the collective decisions of thousands of individual Americans to enlist and, having enlisted once, to reenlist determines who serves in a volunteer military force. A question often asked is how representative of society are the armed forces. In this view *representativeness* compares the proportion of various groups in the society to their proportion in the military. Analysts often measure representativeness in terms of age, race, sex, economic status, and geographical distributions. Under the AVF, the racial and sexual composition of the armed forces has changed significantly, as will be discussed later.

With these terms defined, the next section will evaluate the AVF in terms of the three criteria which are the most obvious tests for such an evaluation.

1. The first and most obvious test is the ability to meet personnel strength requirements.
2. A second test is the ability to attract quality recruits to military service, where quality means the ability to be trained to accomplish the military jobs.
3. A third test is the ability to retain trained and qualified enlisted personnel and officers in order to provide the leadership and experienced personnel necessary to accomplish the defense mission.

Recruitment Incentives and Experience of the AVF

The performance of the volunteer force in its eight years of existence has been characterized by highly varying results. In some years the military services have appeared to be almost awash in volunteers and, although the results of recruitment have not produced an exact copy of the draft era first-term force, average education levels and test scores compare favorably with anything from the draft era. In other years the services have had enormous difficulty recruiting an adequate number of enlisted personnel. In 1979, the Army failed to meet established strength objectives for the only time in the volunteer era. In 1980 objectives were attained, but only at a sacrifice in the quality of the volunteers.

While no single measure of recruitment is a totally adequate indicator of success, the number of nonprior service male high school (diploma) graduate recruits—or more properly, the enlistment rate of this group—is a useful measure. This is an appropriate statistic because (1) it measures *nonprior service* recruits, or those *new* to military service, and (2) male high school graduates are the primary recruiting market for the military. Recruiters have seldom taken all the women who want to enlist and clearly prefer high school graduates to nongraduates. Table 3 compares the number of such recruits within the eighteen-year-old male population for the volunteer-era fiscal years 1974 through 1981 and calculates an enlistment rate and an index. Figure 1 shows the calculated enlistment rate. Three years stand

TABLE 3. ENLISTMENT TRENDS, 1974–1981

Fiscal Year	H.S.D.G. Male	18-Year-Old Males 3-Year Moving Average**	Enlistment Rate	Index 1975 = 100
1974	213,000	2,039,000	10.44	89.5
1975	243,000	2,083,000	11.66	100.0
1976	245,000	2,135,000	11.47	98.4
1977	241,000	2,159,000	11.16	95.7
1978	206,000	2,156,000	9.55	81.9
1979	191,000	2,163,000	8.83	75.7
1980	201,000	2,159,000	9.31	79.8
1981	223,000*	2,145,000	10.39	89.1

* Estimate based on nine months data.
** Includes the year before and the year after.

out in this comparison: fiscal year 1975, the best recruiting year in the volunteer era; fiscal year 1979, the worst year; and fiscal year 1981, in which recruitment made a strong resurgence.

Between 1975 and 1979 the number of male high school (diploma) graduate recruits declined from 243,000 to 191,000. Because the population of eighteen-year-old males grew slightly during this period, the percentage decline in enlistment rates was a larger value of 24.3 percent. Enlistments from this group resurged in fiscal year 1981, however, so that we estimate the

Fig. 1. *Annual Enlistment Rates: High School (Diploma) Graduates, Male.*

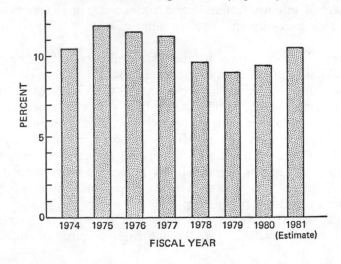

final results to show enlistments of approximately 223,000, or about 18 percent above the enlistment rate of only two years earlier.

The different recruiting results in these three years are closely related to the economic incentives for entering military service as opposed to remaining in the civilian sector. The factors of principal interest are:

1. variation in youth unemployment rates;
2. trends in military pay versus pay in civilian alternatives;
3. enlistment bonuses available in particular military occupations; and
4. changes in educational incentives, particularly the elimination of the G.I. Bill in 1977 as a recruiting incentive.

At the same time, we want to explore other reasons for the recruiting decline between 1975 and 1979 and its subsequent rebound, for example, lower requirements for military personnel produce fewer enlistments, and other factors, such as a bad press on the volunteer force, which also lower public opinion of military service.

Unemployment—In 1975, the United States hit the bottom of the deepest recession since the 1930s. Unemployment for the labor force as a whole exceeded 9 percent for the first time since before World War II. Youth unemployment for males aged sixteen to nineteen averaged 18.5 percent for the fiscal year. While fiscal year 1979 would not appear to qualify as a boom period, the overall unemployment (aged sixteen to nineteen years) averaged 15.9 percent, an improvement of nearly 15 percent since 1975.

Unemployment tends to improve military recruiting in two ways. First, the prospect of some probability of unemployment reduces the individual's valuation of the financial returns of civilian employment and makes military service more attractive. Second, for those directly affected by unemployment, military service may appear to constitute the only economically viable alternative. Econometric studies linking military recruitment and unemployment rates suggest that a 15 percent reduction in youth unemployment produces between a 3 percent and a 7.5 percent decline in military recruiting.

Fiscal year 1981, which did not experience the peak unemployment periods of 1975, actually had higher youth unemployment than the earlier period (19.8 percent versus 18.5 percent). Thus, any reduction in recruiting in 1979 due to a tighter labor market for youth workers would have been completely offset by changes in economic conditions since then.

Military versus Civilian Pay—Trends in military pay in the past decade have, until recently, been generally unfavorable to first-term military pay. There are two reasons for the sluggish growth in military pay. First, military pay was linked for most of this period to the overall average increase for general schedule employees—federal white-collar workers. Their pay is in turn related to the pay of private sector white-collar workers through the Professional, Administrative, Technical, and Clerical (PATC) Survey. In general, pay rates have grown less rapidly for white-collar workers than for blue-collar workers in recent years. Second, between 1974 and 1979, a change in the survey definition and two consecutive pay caps have retarded both military and federal white-collar pay increases by about 6 percent.

In the past two years, military pay has increased relatively more rapidly. The federal government, to counteract perceived recruiting difficulties and problems with the loss of senior enlisted personnel and officers, legislated larger pay increases for fiscal year 1981 and 1982. The military received an increase of 11.7 percent for October 1, 1980, and the increase for October 1982 is expected to be approximately 14 percent.

Empirical researchers have never found fully satisfactory measures of civilian wage rates to use as the market wage for prospective military recruits. Hence, to measure the relative change in military pay relative to civilian wages, we have listed five separate indices: (1) average weekly earnings in the private sector, (2) the annual PATC survey, (3) average weekly earnings in manufacturing, (4) the aggregate of blue-collar surveys used to set rates in the federal wage system, and (5) the minimum wage.

A composite of these five measures shows that military pay declined 10 percent relative to civilian pay between fiscal years 1975 and 1979 (see Table 4). Empirical results based on AVF-era data show that a 10 percent reduction or increase in military pay produces a 10 percent decline or increase in the enlistment rate. The earlier Gates Commission report in 1970 concluded such a pay change would produce a 12.5 percent change in enlistments, which was itself near the conservative range of estimates produced

TABLE 4. MILITARY AND CIVILIAN PAY INDEXES, FISCAL YEAR 1975 THROUGH FISCAL YEAR 1981

	Fiscal Years		
	1975	1979	1981
Military pay	100	126	151
PATC survey	100	136	166
Ratio to military	—	+8%	+10%
Average weekly earnings, total private	100	136	158
Ratio to military	—	+7%	+4%
Federal wage surveys	100	141	170
Ratio to military	—	+12%	+13%
Average weekly earnings, manufacturing	100	145	172
Ratio to military	—	+15%	+14%
Minimum wage	100	138	160
Ratio to military	—	+10%	+6%
Average—five indexes		139	165
Ratio to military		+10%	+9%

by its own studies. Thus, on the basis of pay alone, we would expect a 10 percent decline in enlistments between fiscal years 1975 and 1979.

From 1979 to 1981 military pay tended to keep pace with non-military pay. These data, however, do not include the 14 percent increase for October 1981. This increase was requested in President Reagan's budget in February 1981 and was certainly used by recruiters during this period of time in signing up recruits for the summer of 1981. (The original budget request would have provided a 5 percent increase in July and a 9.1 percent increase in October. Instead, Congress passed a 14 percent increase effective October 1981.) Military pay increases, both awarded and expected, had a positive effect on recruitment in fiscal year 1981.

A pay relationship that deserves special note is between the minimum wage and military enlistment. From 1975, when the minimum wage was $2.10, to 1979, when it reached $2.90, the minimum wage grew 38 percent. Military base pay calculated on a forty-hour week was below the minimum wage, and cash regular military compensation was less than the minimum wage if the longer work week of military personnel was considered. Table 5 shows E-2 enlisted pay compared to the minimum wage since 1970.

TABLE 5. COMPARISON OF E-2 BASIC PAY WITH FEDERAL MINIMUM WAGE

Fiscal Year	Basic Pay	Hourly Military Wage*	Minimum Wage**	Percentage
1970	$127.80	$0.74	$1.60	46
1971	149.10	0.86	1.60	54
1972	320.70	1.85	1.60	116
1973	342.30	1.97	1.60	123
1974	363.30	2.10	2.00	105
1975	383.40	2.21	2.10	105
1976	402.60	2.32	2.30	101
1977	417.30	2.41	2.30	105
1978	443.10	2.56	2.65	96
1979	467.40	2.70	2.90	93
1980	500.10	2.89	3.10	93
1981	558.60	3.22	3.35	96

* Hourly wage is calculated as twelve-months basic pay divided by fifty-two weeks at forty hours per week.
** *Source: History of Federal Minimum Wage under the Fair Labor Standards Act,* Table 11a.

Enlistment Bonuses—The Department of Defense will pay enlistment bonuses to those who choose to enlist in military specialties that are particularly hard to fill. By far the largest share of enlistment bonuses has historically gone to those who entered the combat arms: infantry, armor, artillery, and combat engineering. By helping match people and specialties, the bonuses assist the military services in filling all the jobs that may be open. Although the primary effect of bonuses is on the *distribution* of enlistees, the availability of bonuses can also affect the *number* of enlistees. Persons may be attracted to bonus specialties who would not otherwise enlist. More importantly, diverting enlistments to less attractive specialties may free other jobs which are easier to fill.

Table 6 shows Department of Defense enlistment bonuses for fiscal years 1974 through 1981. The program was very active for fiscal years 1974 through 1976, but was cut back severely for fiscal years 1977 through 1980. Only in 1981 did it grow significantly. This, of course, is consistent with the observed recruiting results for fiscal years 1975, 1979, and 1981. Unlike the other incentives discussed, we do not attempt to estimate the magnitude of this effect, and indeed the effects at any point in time may depend on the precise use of bonuses by the Department of Defense.

TABLE 6. DEPARTMENT OF DEFENSE ENLISTMENT BONUSES, 1974 THROUGH 1981

Fiscal Year	Total Enlistment Bonuses in Millions of Current Dollars	Total Enlistment Bonuses in Millions of 1975 Dollars*	Average Bonus per Enlistee in 1975 Dollars
1974	$43.0	$45.3	$114
1975	58.8	58.8	140
1976	68.5	64.4	162
1977	30.3	27.1	70
1978	34.1	28.5	91
1979	42.7	33.8	107
1980	50.6	37.4	104
1981	76.9	50.9	150

* Deflated by military pay index.

Elimination of the G.I. Bill—at the end of calendar 1976, new enlistees were offered a reduction and contributory educational benefit in place of the G.I. Bill. The G.I. Bill provided tuition payments and cash stipends for up to forty-five months at a total value of $14,000 for single veterans ($16,500 for married).

The G.I. Bill was discontinued because of concern over its lack of efficiency. New recruits discounted the significance of the deferred benefit inherent in the bill and indicated a preference for the more immediate and tangible benefits of a cash payment, even if its net value was less. Many of those for whom the G.I. Bill was not a strong drawing factor at the time of enlistment took advantage of the benefit on leaving the service. This made it a costly benefit. Thus, even though it was an attractive incentive for many recruits, it was not a cost-effective recruiting incentive. Moreover, it often was not cost-effective in the broader societal context. Because it was a benefit only to those who took formal training and education, individuals who derived only a marginal benefit from this training would still make use of this generous benefit. (The best known examples of marginal value courses are pilot-training courses, supposedly for those who would become commercial pilots, and electronics courses resulting at completion with the building of a color television.) Those who favored the G.I. Bill pointed out that it returned several times its cost in increased productivity and argued that it was a social overhead capital investment in the youth of America.

None of the arguments for or against the G.I. Bill are meant to imply that it had no recruiting punch, but rather that the punch was weak relative to the high cost. The annual cost of the G.I. Bill in a steady-state AVF was $1.5 billion per year. While termination of the G.I. Bill was justified as a cost savings measure by the administration at the time, Congress increased financial aid to higher education by an amount about equal to the savings that same year. This was seen by some as being counterproductive. In effect the nation was still paying for the G.I. Bill but was no longer receiving military service—a G.I. Bill without the G.I.

The new Veterans Educational Assistance Program (VEAP), begun for those signing enlistment contracts after January 1, 1977, is a benefit where the government would match the individual's educational savings at a two-for-one rate. The maximum government matching contribution under this formula is $5,400. In addition, the Secretary of Defense is authorized to make additional contributions (VEAP kicker) as may be necessary for accession and retention incentives. This system was meant to focus the educational benefits on those who cared enough to save at least $50 per month toward their education. While the system has a great deal of flexibility and is still being tested, the change in name may be hurting it. Perhaps it needs to be marketed as "the New G.I. Bill."

White and Hosek suggest a range in effects from eliminating the G.I. Bill of between 5 percent and 10 percent of initial enlistments.

Noneconomic Factors: Fewer Military Recruits Needed—Because of higher retention rates and reduced turnover and because of some reductions in the number of military personnel, the number of recruits needed each year since 1977 has been 50,000 to 100,000 fewer than were needed each year between 1974 and 1977. Military service represents a range of jobs and working conditions. Some are more attractive than others, and, although bonus awards and other techniques are used to make less desirable jobs more attractive, they remain harder to fill. Thus, when fewer *total* jobs are available, fewer *good* jobs are available, and it may be harder to attract high school graduate recruits who often are interested in only one or two skills that in years with small recruiting requirements are likely to be over subscribed early in the year.

This hypothesis suggests some relationship between the number of high school graduate recruits and the total number of recruits sought. Figure 2 graphs these two enlistment areas. Total male recruits sought in fiscal years 1974 through 1977 ranged between 356,000 and 382,000; since 1978 total male recruits have declined 25 percent, to between 275,000 and 310,000. Thus, the argument goes, if more positions were available, more high school graduates would be recruited.

While this hypothesis helped explain the poor recruiting experience in the low requirement year of 1978 and the increased success in 1980, it is of little help in explaining 1979 and 1981. When requirements returned to more normal levels in 1979, the number of high-quality recruits remained low. The *net* effect of higher recruiting totals in 1979 made recruiting problems harder, not easier. Moreover, the surge in total recruits for 1981 was accompanied by a *decline* in total male enlistments. Hence, whatever effects exist between total accession requirements and the ability to recruit male high school graduates were rather weak compared to the other factors at play in 1979 and 1981.

Other Reasons—A number of other reasons have been heard for why recruiting may have suffered in the late 1970s:

Fig. 2.   *Total and High School Graduate Male Recruits, 1973–1981.*

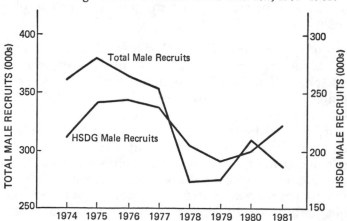

1. a bad press on the problems of the all-volunteer force;
2. a low public opinion of military service, buttressed by continued anti-Vietnam sentiment;
3. trends by youth away from blue-collar jobs and military enlisted service toward college and white-collar jobs;
4. large-scale CETA programs offering jobs to many youths who would otherwise enlist in the military; and
5. growing federally-sponsored scholarship programs which make it possible for low and moderate income youth to attend college without a military service commitment (a G.I. Bill without the G.I.).

Such reasons are not entirely without merit and indeed further research may shed light on some of these effects.

INCENTIVES AND RETENTION

Retention and reenlistments of military personnel respond to many of the same economic factors that affect initial enlistments. There are other forces that affect retention, however. The first-term personnel reenlistment rate rose dramatically in the 1970s because the end of the draft meant that all first-term personnel were truly volunteers. Draftees and draft-motivated enlistees understandably had very low reenlistment rates. In the volunteer era, the services have also made increasing use of the reenlistment bonuses to spur reenlistments and offset sluggish growth in military pay, producing steadily rising reenlistments in the volunteer era.

Figures 3 and 4 show reenlistment and retention rates for first-term personnel and career personnel. Retention measures reenlistments divided by total separation (including reenlistments). The reenlistment rate restricts the denominator only to those said eligible to reenlistment. Because eligibility definition in practice changes frequently, we report both statistics. First-term reenlistment rates are the most important determinant of the future number of career personnel. Because these rates are traditionally low, first-term reenlistment has acted as a choke point on the size of the career force.

Career reenlistments, on the other hand, generally declined in the 1970s. Sluggish growth in pay played a part in this trend. (Career reenlistment rates have also declined because of the growth of first-term reenlistment bonuses. This led to entry in

Fig. 3. First-Term Reenlistment and Retention, 1973–1981.

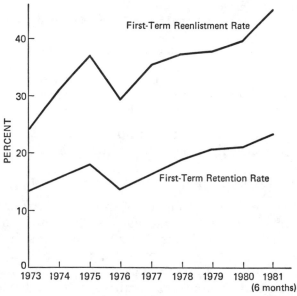

the career force of less career-oriented reenlistees who had remained only because of the bonuses.) In 1979–1981, the pay
climate changed dramatically. The 11.7 percent increase in
October 1980 and the increase of 14 percent in October 1981

Fig. 4. Career Reenlistment and Retention, 1973–1981.

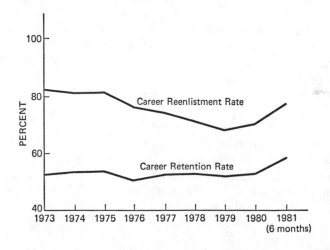

have apparently spurred career and first-term reenlistments by those who are looking ahead to a period of favorable economic trends for military personnel. Career reenlistment rates have risen from 68.2 percent in fiscal year 1979 to 77.1 percent in the first half of fiscal year 1981. The effect on first-term reenlistment rates in 1981 was equally dramatic, rising to 45 percent from 39.1 percent a year earlier. The pay raises and the expectation of a favorable future for military pay have undoubtedly affected reenlistments.

Retention is one of the keys to the success of the AVF in the 1980s. Certainly the favorable trends in this area suggest that increasing manpower requirements can partially be met and unfavorable demographic trends partially offset by improvements in retention.

A SUMMARY OF THE RECRUITMENT DECLINE: 1975 TO 1979

In summarizing the possible reasons for the sharp decline in male high school graduate enlistment rates, we return to the economic incentives to enlist in the military. Over this five-year period, youth unemployment declined significantly. Moreover, pay for the military recruit fell relative to any civilian pay index measured, and, during the same period, a valuable educational benefit was replaced by another far less valuable. Table 7 summarizes the cumulative effects of these changes between 1975 and 1979. Using the median estimates of these economic effects would have predicted a decline in recruits of 21 percent over this five-year period. These estimates themselves are probably somewhat conservative. The reduction in enlistment rates for male high school graduates between 1975 and 1979 is 25 percent. Thus, a high percentage of the observed decline is due to improved employment opportunities combined with reduced financial incentives for military enlistment.

TABLE 7. CUMULATIVE EFFECT OF CAUSES FOR REDUCTION IN RECRUITMENT, 1975–1979

Cause	Range	Midpoint
Reduced youth unemployment	−3% to − 7.5%	− 5.0%
Reduced military pay	−7% to −15.0%	−10.0%
Elimination of the G.I. Bill	−5% to −10.0%	− 7.5%
Cumulative	−14% to −29.0%	−21.0%

A SUMMARY OF THE RECRUITMENT AND RETENTION RESURGENCE:
1979–1981

By fiscal year 1981 military recruiting had plainly rebounded from the depths of fiscal year 1979. Although this period was not marked by such clear movements in pay, unemployment, and other incentives as the earlier period, these have played an important role in the resurgence.

The effects of more liberal pay raises in 1981 and 1982 clearly had a very positive effect on retention. These changes suggest a complete turnaround in the downward trend of career reenlistments in the 1980s and a new high for first-term reenlistments for probably any period since before the Korean War.

The resurgence in military recruitment and retention is the most favorable indicator for the military and the AVF. And the lesson that resurgence is clearly linked to pay incentives is an important principle for managing military personnel in the 1980s and beyond.

PROSPECTS FOR THE 1980s

Figure 5 summarizes graphically the principal variables in military labor supply and demand since the end of the Korean War. As supply, it shows the growth in the population of eighteen-year-old men—the baby boom—that occurred over the past twenty-five years and the decline that will occur over the next dozen years. The eligible line reflects the decrement that may be expected as a result of mental, physical, and other disqualifications. Demand is also shown at two levels. The first is total male accessions, that is, all males, active and reserve, officer and enlisted, who are brought on active duty each year. The second demand line is for active-force enlisted personnel. The peaks on both demand lines represent the Vietnam War.

The ratio of the eligible supply line on Figure 5 to the total demand line (i.e., minimum supply to maximum demand) is shown in Figure 6. A draft was obviously necessary in the 1950s when 1 out of every 1.2 eligible young men was needed. As the population increased and the post-Vietnam drawdown occurred in the early 1970s, the ratio rapidly dropped until only one out of every three young men was needed in 1973 when the AVF became a reality. Today only one out of every four eligible

Fig. 5. Supply and Demand for Young Men.

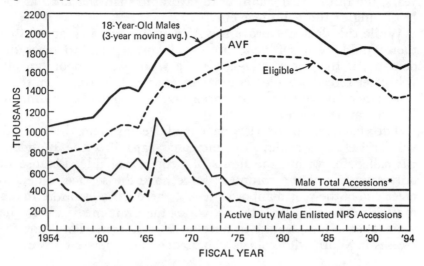

*Officer and Enlisted, Active and Reserve

Fig. 6. Ratio of Eighteen-Year-Old Military Eligible Males to Total Male Accessions.*

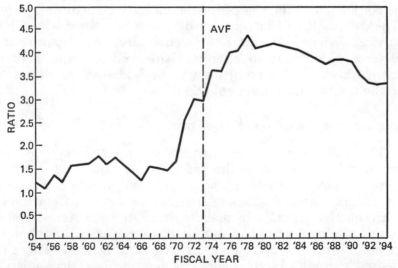

* Total male accessions are active and reserve, officer and enlisted. Ratio equals number of military eligibles per male accession.

young men is needed. While the trend will reverse in the coming years, the ratio will remain more favorable than the ratio at the beginning of the volunteer era.

While this does not prove the AVF will work, it suggests that there could be a sufficient supply of young men to meet the demand, if the American people are willing to support an all-volunteer force with adequate pay incentives. The question, then, is whether one out of every three or four would be willing to join the armed forces.

The challenge to the Department of Defense and the individual services is to achieve the increased capability the President has called for within the limits of people available. Because in only one year of the volunteer force have the services failed to meet end-of-the-year manpower levels, there is no evidence that a draft is necessary. Nor is the return of the draft inevitable in the years ahead. Nor would it necessarily result in significant increases in youth with college experience or higher test scores.

Satisfying the Military Manpower Equation Under the AVF

While the previous section discussed military manpower data in the context of the experience of the AVF, here the data will be considered in the context of the military manpower equation. The data itself will be considered in more detail and by specific services. Whereas the previous section dealt in Department of Defense–wide totals to establish basic relationships, here the more service-specific problems will be addressed as they relate to the military manpower equation.

THE MILITARY MANPOWER EQUATION

The military manpower equation normally is expressed with strength for next year as the dependent variable and this year's strength, next year's losses, accessions, and reenlistments as independent variables. This relationship is shown in equation 1. This equation represents actual peacetime strength. Actual strength is the result of what happens to the other variables; but this equation does not operate on its own in a vacuum. There is a desired strength objective and a plan to achieve that objective.

An analysis of force structure and threat (and available budget)

EQUATION 1:	EQUATION 2:
Normal Manpower Equation	*Planning Manpower Equation*
$S_2 = S_1 + A_2 - L_2 + R_2$	$G_2 = S_2 - S_1 + L_2 - R_2$
S_2 = Strength next year	G_2 = Recruiting goal
S_1 = Strength this year	S_2 = Planned strength
A_2 = Accessions next year	S_1 = Strength this year
L_2 = Losses next year	L_2 = Losses next year
R_2 = Reenlistment next year	R_2 = Reenlistment next year

results in a planned strength for next year. That planned strength is substituted for S_2, and the equation is solved for the number of accessions required to achieve that strength. That number of accessions becomes the recruiting goal (G_2) which the services strive to achieve in the coming year. Equation 2 shows the planning manpower equation.

Losses (or separations) and reenlistments are independent variables in both equations and thus are key to the military manpower equation. They will be considered together as retention and are discussed in the following sections. The recruiting data will also be discussed. Finally, strength data, the bottom line, will be presented, and the resulting representativeness of the force will be discussed.

RETENTION

The first factor to consider in retention is the number of separations or losses. Separations may occur for any of a large number of reasons ranging from honorable discharge at completion of service to dishonorable discharge as a result of sentence of court-martials. It can be a separation after years of honorable service, such as a military retirement, or a training separation in the first days of basic training. Also included in separations are those members who are discharged in order to reenlist. The total number of enlisted separations has declined from almost 800,000 per year in 1972 to a little over 500,000 per year in recent years. Fiscal year 1978 was the lowest year with 516,000. Separation of those in the career category has remained quite steady. First-term separations have dropped from 550,000 in 1972 to about 300,000 to 315,000 per year in recent years. This drop of 40 to 45 percent in first-term separations represents one of the most significant changes occurring during the AVF.

The preceding section has already discussed the trends in Department of Defense retention and reenlistments in the past decade and has shown the relationship to some of the incentives for remaining in the military. This subsection discusses some of the principal differences in retention experience among the services.

The services are each unique and often have different problems. Table 8 presents the data, by service, for the years 1972, 1976, and 1980. Army separations for 1972 through 1973 averaged 265,000 per year, of which 144,000 were eligible to reenlist and 53,000 actually reenlisted. The resulting average retention rate was 20 percent, and the average reenlistment rate was 37 percent. By the end of the decade, average retention had increased to about 51 percent and reenlistments to 69 percent, respectively. In the Army, both career and first-term reenlistments are up. Under the AVF, Army retention has improved significantly in spite of the imposition of stricter reenlistment standards.

The Navy also experienced a decline in separations from 174,000 per year in 1972 to about 119,000 per year in 1980. There have been, however, only modest increases in retention and reenlistment rates. Navy first-term reenlistments have remained about the same over the decade, with the decline in number of separations reflecting significant increases in retention and reenlistment rates from 13 percent to 26 percent in retention and 23 percent to 37 percent in reenlistments.

Career reenlistments in the Navy are down sharply from about 30,000 per year in the early 1970s to fewer than 20,000 at the end of the decade. While there was some increase in 1980 to over 21,000, the problem must be considered serious. In 1972 and 1973 career retention had fallen from 60 percent to 45 percent, and the career reenlistment rate from 90 percent to about 60 percent.

Unlike the Army, which has more experienced enlisted personnel (called noncommissioned officers) than during the draft, the net effect of a small increase in first-term reenlistments and a major decrease in career reenlistments leaves the Navy with a very serious shortage of experience among petty officers (the Navy equivalent of noncommissioned officers). It is unlikely, however, that return to the draft would help. Experience shows that first-

TABLE 8. SEPARATIONS, RETENTION, AND REENLISTMENT

	1972				1976				1980			
First term	Army	Navy	USAF	USMC	Army	Navy	USAF	USMC	Army	Navy	USAF	USMC
Separations*	239	127	115	74	165	97	85	69	123	75	73	40
Eligibles	141	73	77	37	70	53	48	17	50	53	42	19
Reenlistments	14	17	25	4	15	19	18	5	25	20	15	4
Enlistment rate %**	59	58	67	50	42	55	57	25	41	71	42	48
Retention rate %	6	13	22	6	9	19	21	7	21	26	21	11
Reenlistment rate %	10	23	33	12	21	35	37	26	51	37	36	23
Career												
Separations	100	47	85	10	87	46	80	14	119	44	62	19
Eligibles	62	31	57	6	54	30	60	7	83	33	47	16
Reenlistments	28	28	53	5	38	23	49	6	57	22	38	8
Enlistment rate %	62	67	66	60	62	66	74	52	70	75	76	83
Retention rate %	28	61	62	48	44	49	61	41	48	50	62	42
Reenlistment rate %	46	91	95	80	71	75	82	78	69	67	82	50
TOTAL												
Separations	339	174	201	85	252	143	164	83	242	119	135	60
Eligibles	203	105	133	43	123	83	108	25	133	86	89	35
Reenlistments	43	45	78	10	53	41	67	10	83	42	53	12
Enlistment rate %	60	60	66	51	49	58	65	30	55	72	66	59
Retention rate %	13	26	39	11	21	29	41	12	34	35	40	21
Reenlistment rate %	21	43	59	22	43	50	62	41	62	48	60	35

* Personnel figures in thousands.

** Rates in percent.

term reenlistment rates are much lower among draftees and draft-induced volunteers. Since career personnel must reenlist voluntarily at least once to reach career status, there is no reason to believe that the total number of careerists would be improved by drafting first-term personnel.

The Navy already spends over half of the Department of Defense's reenlistment bonus money. The Navy has asked for more ships to reduce the tempo of operations and the length and frequency of deployments overseas. This would appear valid but represents a "Catch 22." How can more ships be manned without pushing the current careerists even harder? This represents one of the major manpower dilemmas for the Navy in the 1980s. The larger pay raises and increased sea pay passed recently by Congress seem to be helping increase overall Navy retention.

Another solution is to broaden the base on which the sea duty burden rests. To open certain ships, such as aircraft carriers, to women as well as men would increase the base. In 1980, the Navy had about 30,000 women in uniform and was taking in about 10,000 per year. While that is less than 10 percent of the 430,000 enlisted men, it would help. Unlike the Coast Guard, women in the Navy currently do not go to sea on any major vessels. Even increasing women's rates at sea, however, would not help in some critical ratings, such as boiler technician, where few men and even fewer women seem to be willing to serve and where the most serious petty officer shortages exist. Special pay for sustained sea duty may be needed for such ratings.

The Marine Corps experience is between the Army and Navy. The number of first-term reenlistments has remained between 4,000 and 5,000 per year with career reenlistments measuring from 5,000 to 8,000 over the period. The Air Force has enjoyed excellent retention throughout the period with retention rates between 35 and 40 percent and reenlistment rates generally near 60 percent.

In summary, while the Navy is having reenlistment problems, there are signs of improvement. A return to conscription for first-term personnel would hurt rather than help. Also, a return to conscription for the Army probably would severely reduce reenlistments and thus cut back on the number of trained and experienced personnel available to man the increasingly complex weapons systems of the Army of the 1980s and beyond. While improvements can and should be made to increase retention, especially in the Navy, the AVF meets the retention test.

RECRUITING

As shown in the planning manpower equation (equation 2), each service recruits against recruiting goals. Those goals are the combination of the strength plan $(S_2 - S_1)$ and the retention experience $(L_2 - R_2)$. During the initial years of the AVF, S_2 often was smaller than S_1, reducing recruiting pressure. In recent years $S_1 = S_2$, and recruiting goals have been met by replacing discharges with reenlistees and new recruits. The planned strength increases of 200,000 discussed by the Reagan administration would actually increase recruiting goals by more than one-to-one because the services must add accessions to offset first-year attrition due to training and other loss factors.

As discussed in the previous section, recruiting goals during the AVF have been challenging but achievable. In the early days of the AVF, large amounts were spent, and perhaps in some cases misspent, to insure success of the AVF. During the last half of the 1970s, successive reductions were made in pay, allowances, and recruiting resources. The result was increased difficulty in recruiting. In late 1979 and 1980 the trend was reversed, with considerable increases in both recruiting and retention rates. The data presented in the following detailed discussion show these factors. The recruiting experience of the 1970s is evaluated in terms of total numbers (the first test of the AVF) and then in terms of measurable quality indicators (the second test).

QUANTITY

Table 9 shows recruiting requirements and percent achievement over the AVF period. Fiscal year 1978 was a very unusual year in that the requirement for accessions was very low. In fiscal year 1979 the requirements for accessions were more normal, but it was a very difficult recruiting year. For the first time under the AVF, all four services fell short of their recruiting objectives. The problems surfaced particularly in the Army and the Navy. Overall, the recruiting shortfall was about 24,000, or some 7 percent of the recruiting objectives. Fortunately, the reenlistment rates were up and the overall strength shortage was only 1.4 percent of required strength as established by the congressional ceiling. At the end of the first two years of the 1980s, each of the armed services met or exceeded recruiting goals, and each was

TABLE 9. RECRUITING SUCCESS, OBJECTIVE AND ACTUAL

Fiscal Year	Army			Navy			Marine Corps			Air Force		
	Obj.	Act.	%	Obj.	Act.	%	Obj.	Act.	%	Obj.	Act.	%
1974	212*	200	94	85	88	104	54	50	93	75	76	101
1975	205	209	102	109	110	101	59	60	102	75	77	103
1976	191	192	101	104	104	98	53	53	100	73	74	101
1977	182	181	99	114	110	96	49	47	96	74	74	100
1978	137	134	98	93	87	94	41	41	100	69	69	100
1979	159	142	89	92	86	93	43	42	98	69	68	99
1980	170	173	102	98	98	100	44	44	100	75	75	100

* Personnel figures in thousands.

about at its strength objective. With the exception of 1978, the services generally met the overall quantity of accessions desired. This was by no means an easy task. Some years it was achieved by exceeding the numbers of prior-service accessions, female accessions, or accessions with lower test scores than desired, but the objective was achieved.

QUALITY

Quality is difficult to define and measure when dealing with any group of people, and it is no easier with military personnel. Honesty, integrity, morality, commitment, and loyalty are all terms that would be associated with quality. Moreover, training and leadership, which are supplied by the service and not the individual, are usually thought to be critical determinants of the efficiency and dedication with which individuals perform. The ultimate quality test of military personnel is success in combat. In peacetime, readiness often substitutes for the ultimate test, but it also is very hard to measure. Current manpower readiness reporting is not very useful as a test of quality. Thus, this chapter, in focusing on recruit quality, considers the measurable attributes of persons who enter military service. The principal measurable attributes are level of education and mental aptitude.

Consequently, these measures of potential, rather than actual capability or readiness, will be discussed here. As mentioned at the outset, the training, equipment, munitions, and command and control, and dedication of the personnel are important in the larger readiness picture and may well overshadow the personnel considerations that are measured. Nevertheless, the services base recruiting decisions on the measurable indications of education and test scores. It is generally accepted that possession of a high school diploma is the best single measure of a person's potential for adapting to life in the military. High school graduates are more likely to complete successfully their terms of service than are their contemporaries who have not received a high school diploma. Thus, active-force recruiting programs have concentrated on enlisting high school diploma graduates. The outcome is shown in Figures 7 and 7A. In fiscal year 1979 the services recruited 73 percent high school graduates compared to 68 percent for fiscal year 1967, the last pre-Vietnam year.

Fig. 7. *Distribution of Department of Defense Total * Active-Duty Nonprior-Service Enlisted Accessions by Education Groups.*

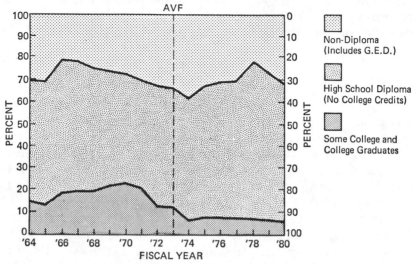

* FY 1964 through 1973 includes inductees.

Fig. 7A. *Active-Duty Nonprior-Service Enlisted High School Diploma Graduate Accessions as a Percentage of Total.*

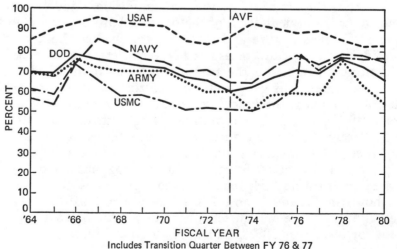

Includes Transition Quarter Between FY 76 & 77

To put these high school graduate accessions percentages in perspective, about 75 percent of the eighteen-year-old youth have graduated from high school, but almost half of these enter college and thus are not prime candidates for enlisted recruiting. The remaining eighteen-year-old high school graduates (not enrolled in college) form the prime market for enlisted recruiting. There are about 1.7 million men and women in this group, or about 40 percent of the eighteen-year-old population.

The situation is complicated, however, by the requirement that nine out of ten of service accessions must be male. There are about 790,000 eighteen-year-old men who are high school graduates not enrolled in college in each eighteen-year-old cohort. In the fiscal year 1980 about 320,000 young men, or 40 percent of the cohort, had to be recruited by the active forces and about 50,000 women, or 5.5 percent of the 910,000 high school young women in the cohort not enrolled in college. Although there have always been some college-bound youth who have enlisted in the service, the ratio of male accession requirements to noncollege-bound young men is a useful measure of the military's recruiting challenge.

While the percentage of accessions who are high school graduates has only slightly increased over the pre-Vietnam period, the percentage of the total active enlisted force with a high school education (including certificates) has reached the highest level ever recorded. In fiscal year 1979, 88 percent of the active enlisted force had a high school education or equivalent, compared to 81 percent in December 1972, the time of the last draft call, and about 75 percent during 1964, the last year before Vietnam draft calls, and a figure of 55 percent in the cold war year of 1956. During the AVF period, the average educational level of persons entering active duty has been greater than the level of those leaving.

The mental aptitude of new accessions has been measured since the beginning of World War II by a series of various psychological tests. Everyone who served in World War II, including officer and enlisted, was classified into five mental categories, with Category I being the highest and Category V the lowest. The fiftieth percentile is near the middle of Category III.

The military services prefer enlisted recruits with above average test scores. This is rather inconsistent with a starting pay scale near (and sometimes in the 1970s below) the minimum wage. One could also question the representatives of a force that precluded half the population for any reason (race, sex, or mental test scores). On the other hand, the increasing complexity of technological weaponry does call for increasing ability. One possibility is that if college graduates are needed for these new jobs, then the positions should be classified in the officer corps instead of the enlisted ranks, as mentioned previously.

With forty years of data, a good historical comparison should be available. Unfortunately, problems in norming of the various tests recently have been discovered that invalidate longitudinal comparisons. The norming problems indicate that many enlistees classified as Category III (percentile range: 31 to 64) were really Category IV (percentile range: 10 to 30). Perhaps up to 40 percent of the Army's enlistees were really in Category IV. Figure 8 illustrates the problem with data taken from our study of 1977 recruits *(America's Volunteers)*.

Figure 8 demonstrates two major conclusions that can be drawn from the test score data. First, the Air Force recruits much more than a proportional share of the youth with better test scores. Second, the high skew in the Army test scores at the boundary between Categories III and IV would result in many Category IVs if the norming moved the scale somewhat to the right.

These data must be put in perspective. In 1980 the Army recruited 44 percent of the total nonprior-service accessions and the Air Force only 20 percent. However, both services received about the same amount (about 30 percent) of the high-quality personnel. The Air Force, however, took only 18 percent of Category III accessions (and most of these were III-A) and less than 1 percent of Category IV. The Army recruited 48 percent of Category III (mostly III-B) and 80 percent of Category IVs, as shown in Table 10.

While historical mental category data may not be reliable for comparisons with the general population, they do permit comparisons among the services. The most significant factors are: (1) the 80 percent of Category IV recruits going to the Army is almost double its fair share of distribution, and (2) every service recruited a significant share of Category I and II accessions.

Mental test scores are not very good measures of the ability of personnel to fight in combat, but do have reasonably good

Fig. 8. Distribution of Fiscal Year 1977 NPS Accessions by Mental Quality.

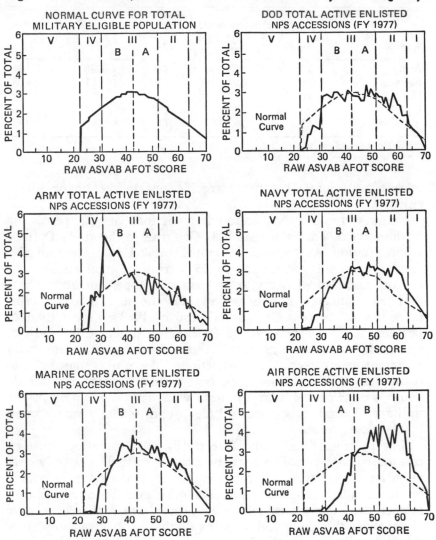

correlations with ability to complete formal training courses in service schools. Instead of using overall mental test scores, the services have developed specific criteria for each school that better predict the ability of the prospective recruit to complete training in that skill. Since recruiting is generally to a specific skill, the

TABLE 10. DISTRIBUTIONS OF NPS ACCESSIONS BY MENTAL CATEGORY IN 1980*

| Service | *Percent of Department of Defense Total* | | | | |
	I	II	III	IV	Total
Army	23	26	48	80	44
Navy	38	33	22	11	25
USMC	10	12	12	9	11
USAF	29	30	18	1	20
Total**	100	100	100	100	100

* Categories before renorming.
** Total may not add due to rounding.

recruit must meet that more specific test before he or she is enlisted.

Congress recently has imposed restrictions on the recruiting of the services. For fiscal year 1981 Congress in the year's Defense Appropriation Authorization limited total Department of Defense Category IV accessions to 25 percent of total enlisted accessions and limited Army to no less than 65 percent high school diploma graduates. For fiscal year 1982 no service may recruit more than 25 percent Category IV and by 1983 no more than 20 percent. If the Department of Defense simultaneously readjusts standards for the norming problems, these combined actions could represent severe recruiting restrictions. There also may be constitutional problems. First, the tests would be used to exclude youth with scores similar to those who have done well in the military. Second, it would exclude proportionately many more blacks than whites.

The previous discussions of recruiting and retention must be considered together. The two are directly related. Not only does retention affect recruiting requirements, but the types of people recruited affect retention. For example, experience has shown that enlisted recruits who have not completed high school have about twice the likelihood of being discharged before completing the first enlistment as do those who have completed high school.

The more high school graduates recruited, the better the first-term retention, thus the lower the number of recruits needed in subsequent years. Fewer recruits leads to lower recruiting and training costs, but higher retention leads to higher salaries and higher retirement costs. In a limited budget situation, one is faced with choices among programs that increase retention and those that facilitate recruiting. Using econometric analysis one can develop policies that represent a least-cost solution for a force of a given size. More sophisticated analysis could address additional parameters that also affect readiness.

STRENGTH

The bottom line of the military manpower equation is strength. To provide perspective, Figure 9 shows military end strength overall and by service from 1964 through 1980. Since 1974, actual military end strength has been within 1.5 percent of the congressionally set ceiling each year. As mentioned previously, 1978 was the poorest year during that period with an overall shortfall of 1.4 percent. Of course, the strength drawdown from the peak in 1968 to the relative steady level set in 1974 helped reduce recruiting needs in the early days of the AVF. The active-force inventories were reduced from over 3.5 million officers and enlisted personnel in 1968 to slightly more than 2 million in fiscal year 1979.

Figure 9 shows that most of the drawdown occurred between fiscal year 1969 and fiscal year 1972 (just as the AVF decision was being made) and that the reduction was concentrated in the Army. Unlike the reserve force, the reductions in active-duty strength were not the result of inability to recruit, but were the result of changes in force structure and weapon systems.

At the end of the first year of the 1980s each of the armed forces was at or above its strength objective, and the combined strength was 5,000 in excess of the objective total of 2,045,000. Table 11 shows the strength in September 1980 against the objective strength set by Congress.

Looking ahead to the rest of the 1980s and beyond, the strength needed will be a major factor in the number of accessions needed. The Reagan administration has announced an intention to build the strength of all services. The size and timing of the increase planned for the Army will be major factors to consider in the decision to continue with an AVF or return to some form of conscription.

An analysis of the strength that results from the military manpower process provides insights into the force itself. The quality analysis of accessions provided insight about new accessions, and

Fig. 9. *Total Active Military End-Strength Trends, 1964–1980.*

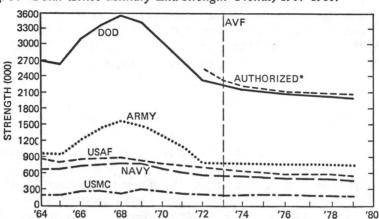

FISCAL YEAR
Includes Transition Quarter Between FY 76 & 77

* Authorized line shows the congressional authorization since fiscal year 1972. Active-force personnel strengths were not specified by congressional authorizations prior to fiscal year 1972. Total Department of Defense actual end-strengths have been within 1.5 percent of the authorized level since fiscal year 1974.

an analysis of retention considered the quality of those being retained. Collectively they represent the quality of the force. Here two measures will be considered: (1) the experience mix of the force and (2) the representativeness of the force.

TABLE 11. TOTAL MILITARY STRENGTH, ACTUAL VERSUS OBJECTIVE

Service	Objective	Actual	Percent
Army	774*	777	100+
Navy	528	527	99+
Marine Corps	185	188	102
Air Force	558	558	100
Total	2,045	2,050	100+

* Figures in thousands.

EXPERIENCE MIX

In the pre-AVF force of 1972, almost 40 percent of military enlisted personnel had less than two years of service. In 1980 that figure had decreased to 33 percent. In the Army the change is most dramatic, shifting from 52 percent in 1974 to 38 percent in 1980. These changes resulted from longer enlistments and more reenlistments. Figure 10 shows the change in enlistment mix under the AVF.

The effect of increased experience is to reduce training costs and provide to the units more man-years per military person. Units with trained military personnel with three or four years experience should be more capable than units with higher turnover every year. However, the Army, in particular, has complained about the effect of longer terms on assignment policies to Europe and Korea and received permission in 1979 to test two-year enlistments under the AVF.

Fig. 10. Distribution of Department of Defense Total * Active-Duty Non-prior-Service Enlisted Accessions by Length of Enlistment.

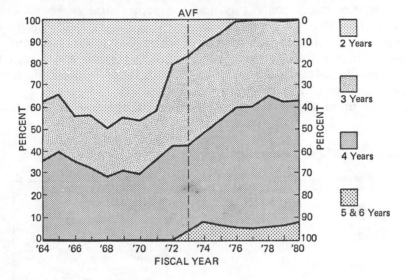

REPRESENTATIVENESS

While clearly the ability to fight is the raison d'être of a military force, issues of societal class and educational representativeness were raised during each period of draft. The upper class, especially college graduates, often was underrepresented. *Society* (March/April 1981) addressed an entire issue to this subject. The upshot of the effort was agreement that the previous Selective Service System had underrepresented the upper class through its exemption and deferment processes and that such problems could be resolved. As White and Hosek point out, representativeness is a significant issue in the AVF, but is one that results from free decisions in an open marketplace.

As Charles Moskos points out, representativeness in the military of all parts of society is important, especially in a democracy. Before World War II, the military was almost exclusively a white male organization with the sons of established families serving as officers, and the sons of white workers and immigrants in the ranks. After World War II, the major representative issue was racial integration to bring blacks into the military.

During the AVF, the concern reversed with noted military sociologists questioning if the military could experience a tipping phenomenon where few, if any, whites would enlist. During the 1970s, the black content passed the representative level. Black accessions exceeded representative percentages, and black re-enlistment rates were higher than white. Figures 11, 12, and 13 show these results in terms of strength, accession levels, and re-enlistment rates. In the early part of the 1980s, white enlistments increased as did minorities other than black.

The other major representativeness change was an increased,

Fig. 11.   Blacks as a Percentage of Active-Duty Enlisted End Strengths.

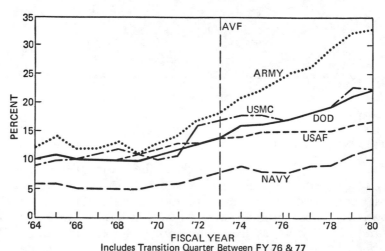

Fig. 12. *Distribution of Department of Defense Total * Active-Duty Non-prior-Service Enlisted Accessions by Racial Groups.*

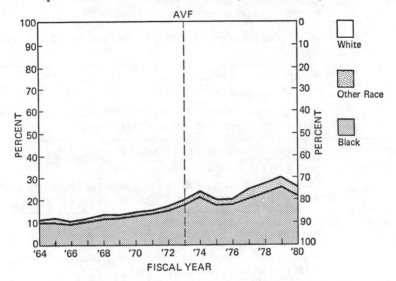

Fig. 13. *Comparison of Reenlistment Rate, Black versus Nonblack.*

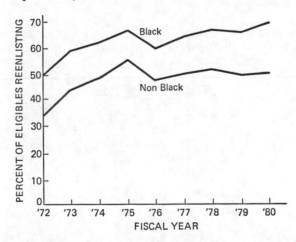

though far from representative, role for women. The number of women in the military, the occupations open to women, and the willingness of women to serve in what had previously been all male jobs and units reflected the change as shown in Figures 14 and 15 and Table 12.

TABLE 12.   MILITARY OCCUPATIONS OPEN TO WOMEN

Army	$\dfrac{\text{MOS* open to women}}{\text{Total MOS}}$ $\dfrac{323}{345} \times 100 = 94\%$
	MOS closed include infantry MOS, artillery MOS, and armor MOS.
Navy	$\dfrac{\text{Ratings open to Women}}{\text{Total ratings}}$ $\dfrac{83}{99} \times 100 = 84\%$
	Ratings closed include fire control technicians, some aviation crewmen, sonarmen, and gunnersmates.
Marine Corps	$\dfrac{\text{Occupation fields open to women}}{\text{Total occupation fields}}$ $\dfrac{34}{38} \times 100 = 89\%$
	Occupation fields closed include infantry, artillery, tank and amphibious tractor, and flight crews.
Air Force	$\dfrac{\text{AFSC** open to women}}{\text{Total AFSC}}$ $\dfrac{226}{230} \times 100 = 98\%$
	AFSC closed include B-52 gunners, pararescue recovery, radio operators with infantry.

* Military Occupational Specialty.
** Air Force Specialty Code.

Fig. 14. Women as a Percentage of Total Department of Defense Active-Duty Enlisted by Department of Defense Occupation Group as of End of Fiscal Year 1971 and 1980.

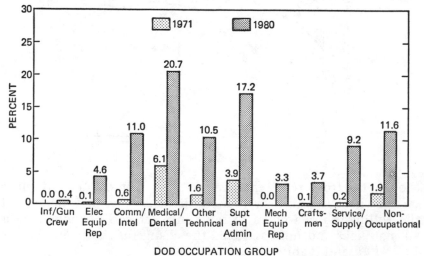

While there are economic and social factors that contribute to these changes in representativeness, the voluntary nature of the force and the relative high pay for serving must be considered important. Since Congress has specifically excluded women from the draft, and the Supreme Court has upheld that decision, a return to the draft would act against increases in the representativeness of women.

It is not so clear what would happen to the level of black representation in a draft since both blacks and whites would be drafted. One could assume that a draft would move toward representativeness, especially if recruiting standards are tightened at the same time; but in low-draft years with many volunteers the results could be essentially the same as under the AVF.

Fig. 15.   Active-Duty Enlisted Women End Strengths.

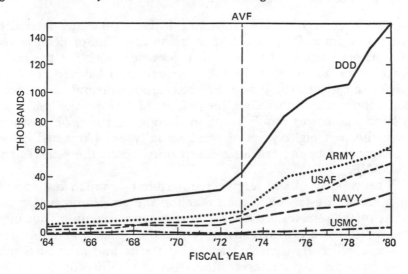

THE EQUATION IN THE 1980s AND BEYOND

The Reagan administration has announced plans to increase military strength by 200,000 from 1981 through 1986. This means an increase in S_2 over S_1, and a corresponding increase must be made in recruiting and retention. Some military planners have hinted that this increase will force a return to conscription, but the administration has remained committed to the continued use of volunteers. As shown in the previous section, there are incentives available that support that assertion. In spite of a smaller youth population over the decade of the 1980s, there are reasons to be optimistic that the AVF can continue to meet the three tests of strength, quality, and experience; but such success is not automatic. The services will need to continue to work hard at recruiting and retention, to develop improved incentives, and to manage compensation resources in order to remain within the combined constraints of the military manpower equation and the fiscal limitation set on defense spending levels. The competing demands for resources within the defense budget undoubtedly will keep manpower costs for the volunteer system an active issue in the years ahead.

RESERVE FORCES

This chapter has concentrated exclusively on issues related to the active force. The active force is the first line of defense and the primary test of the AVF. If it does not work for the active force, some action must be taken to correct whatever problems have been identified. While the reserves are integral to the total force concept and, therefore, the defense of Europe and constitute a large manpower requirement in their own right, observations over the past eight years of what actually has happened causes one to pause before reaching conclusions about the reserves and the AVF.

The validity of the reserve requirement is much less specific and less well established than that for the active forces. Certain units in the reserves are needed to support active units, but most reserve forces are programed to enter the theater well into any major conflict. By then shortages of material and munitions may well have already set severe limits on the ability of even fully manned units to contribute. Until these shortages are eliminated, the ability to utilize reserve forces must be seriously questioned.

In each of the eight years under the AVF, there have been serious shortages in reserve personnel resulting in strength below the established requirements. While precise figures vary from report to report, there are about 250,000 too few trained reserve personnel to meet the NATO scenario, to say nothing of the skill mix problems. This "paper shortage" has been widely discussed since 1977, yet very little has been done to bridge the gap between people and requirements. When resources are identified to address the problem, they soon are diverted to other purposes. These observations lead to the conclusion that the reserve forces (Selected Reserve, National Guard, and Individual Ready Reserve) are not manned to perform their primary mission.

As it is now structured and managed, the AVF is not going to provide the hundreds of thousands of reservists that seem to be needed to sustain a prolonged high-intensity conventional war in Europe. In addition, increased active-force retention, reduced active-force recruiting, and other active-force factors that are considered desirable under an AVF tend to aggravate reserve shortages. In spite of these facts, no administration, past or present, has ever suggested reinstating a draft to provide reserves for any purpose.

One is left to conclude that if active-force issues result in continuation of the AVF, as seems likely, the reserve problem must be addressed separately. To fix the reserve problems calls not only for people, equipment, and munitions, but also for fundamental changes in organizational structures, compensation systems, and training procedures. As a minimum, trained individuals should be able to enlist in the Individual Ready Reserve. Addressing the full scope of the reserve issues could fill additional books. Here it is sufficient to observe that the active-force issues, not reserve issues, are likely to continue to control decisions about the all-volunteer force.

Conclusions

From the analysis of the active forces during the first eight years under the AVF, two types of conclusions can be drawn. The first relates to the experience itself. What actually happened? The second relates to prospects for continuing the AVF through the 1980s and beyond.

EXPERIENCE

While not without problems, during the first eight years the AVF generally has met the three tests established to measure its viability.

Strength—The AVF has met peacetime active-duty military manpower strength requirements on a regular and sustained basis. Active end strength has never been more than 1.5 percent below the congressionally imposed ceiling. In 1980 and 1981 end strength was essentially at the ceiling.

Quality—The AVF has attracted persons of adequate quality to meet the specific skill requirements for the full range of military jobs. Many critics have attacked the AVF for not producing more middle- and upper-class youth with college aspirations, and that is true. Others have identified quality, training, and disciplinary problems and asserted that these problems establish failure to meet the quality requirements. Certainly the problems exist; but, as the Steiger quote in the first section illustrates, the problems predated the AVF. As shown in the second and third sections, quality of accessions can be influenced by the incentives available and the conditions of the labor market. The problems became serious when the economy was strong, youth unemployment was low, military compensation had not kept up with the growth in the general economy, and significant benefits to service had been reduced or eliminated.

Experience—The AVF has retained the trained and qualified personnel necessary to provide the leadership for the enlisted force. While the Navy has serious problems in retaining career petty officers, retention under the AVF probably is better than it would be under the draft. Army retention has increased dramatically under the AVF.

PROSPECTS

Looking to the future, the military services do face significant labor supply problems in the 1980s.

1. The population of youth of prime recruiting age will decline by 15 to 20 percent in the latter part of this decade.
2. Active-force requirements are likely to rise, as the Reagan administration seeks to augment all four military services.
3. The Congress has placed limits on recruits without high school diplomas and those with scores below the thirty-first percentile of the population due to concerns with the quality of recruits in 1979 and 1980.

The recruiting and retention of adequate supplies of quality manpower is no less a management problem than developing military weapons, receiving adequate supplies of war reserves, or maintaining the readiness of our military forces. This chapter has suggested some important management principles.

1. Competitive pay levels for recruits will maintain and possibly increase the level of military recruits.
2. The turnaround in reenlistments and retention in the past two years due in large measure to better pay suggests that this source of fully trained manpower may offset adverse population trends and help, in particular, in meeting requirements for larger forces.
3. The use of bonuses and targeted forms of pay (such as extra sea pay for sustained sea duty) will help in meeting spot shortages and difficult-to-fill occupations.
4. The use of women in technical and noncombat roles may raise the overall quality of military personnel and alleviate the pressure to find additional male recruits.
5. The careful husbanding of trained resources through minimizing losses, such as through attrition, can reduce the need for new recruits.
6. Highly attractive military service, e.g., the Air Force, can likely help recruiting of high-quality personnel in the Army and Marine Corps by taking its share of recruits across the full spectrum, instead of exclusively from the higher mental categories.

Although the full force of economic incentives is only now being realized, these tools have generally been known throughout most of the volunteer era. New management tools can be and need to be developed. For instance, if the technology of modern war requires more people from the mental Category I–IIIA levels with high school or better educations, then new programs to attract such individuals will be needed. The largest source of such people, that now rarely join the armed forces, are graduates of two-year colleges. Their educations and expectations pull them out of the market for the junior enlisted force, but they do not qualify for officer commissions. A creative new program to bring these people into certain, or perhaps all, skills in one or more services in a warrant officer, midlevel noncommissioned officer, or similar status should be examined. The military has persisted with an outmoded system that utilizes only college graduates or untrained enlisted instead of adopting its personnel systems to utilize persons with education and skills gained outside of the military.

The net result drawn from the analysis for this chapter is that the AVF has had problems but has met active-duty military quantity, quality, and experience requirements and, with good management and the support of the American people, can continue to do so through the 1980s and beyond.

Charles C. Moskos

4

Social Considerations of the All-Volunteer Force

Since 1973 the United States has sought to accomplish what it has never attempted before—to maintain a large active-duty force with world-wide commitments, along with an expanded reserve force at home, on a voluntary basis. In the early years following the end of conscription, the all-volunteer force (AVF) was hailed as a success by its proponents, notably within the officialdom of the Department of Defense. Official assessments reported that not only was the AVF working well, but, indeed, was attracting a quality of youth as good if not better than that of the draft era. At most, it was argued, only incremental changes in management policies and recruitment incentives were required to continue an effective AVF.

By the early 1980s, however, it was becoming increasingly apparent that the AVF was in serious difficulty. One effect of the shift to the AVF was the sharp decline in active-duty force levels, from over 2.6 million in the early 1960s to slightly over 2 million in 1981. To man an active-duty force even at this reduced level,

CHARLES C. MOSKOS *is professor of sociology at Northwestern University. During 1980–81 Dr. Moskos was a fellow at the Woodrow Wilson International Center for Scholars. A recognized authority in military sociology, his books include* The American Enlisted Man, Public Opinion and the Military Establishment, *and* Peace Soldiers: The Sociology of a United Nations Force.

NOTE: A version of this chapter is published in *National Service: Social, Economic and Military Impacts* edited by Michael W. Sherraden and Donald J. Eberly, Pergamon Press, Inc., 1982.

the military must recruit between 350,000 and 400,000 enlisted persons annually. All four services have been hard pressed to meet recruitment goals since the end of conscription. To compound matters, one in three service entrants does not complete initial enlistments for reasons of job inaptitude, indiscipline, personality disorders, and the like. On top of this attrition, desertion rates are double those of pre-Vietnam levels. A growing number of skilled technicians have been leaving the military; retention of qualified people in the career force has become an acute problem. Army reserve components are hundreds of thousands below the manpower requirements set by Congress. These problems have led to renewed talk of bringing back the draft.

Describing the AVF in starkly negative terms can be misleading, however. The armed forces of the early 1980s were noticeably improved over the military of the early 1970s by many indicators, whether in unit effectiveness, disciplinary rates, or race relations. But to place the all-volunteer experience in a more balanced light, it would be better to use the immediate pre-Vietnam period as a benchmark rather than 1970–73, the worst times in modern American military history. And even though military recruiters have accomplished a task of immense proportions in the all-volunteer era, it has become evident that enlistments based sheerly on marketplace competition cannot insure a sufficient number of qualified entrants.

To raise serious questions about the viability of the AVF is not to advocate restoration of conscription. The choices before us are not limited to either tinkering with the all-volunteer status quo, on the one hand, or bringing back the draft, on the other. An informed discussion of the real choices must be supported by careful social analysis, organizational insight, honest presentation of data, and, yes, even common sense.

The purpose of this chapter is fourfold. First, background information is presented on trends in the social composition of the AVF with particular reference to the enlisted ranks of the Army, the largest of the services and the one that most directly relied on the draft. Second, there is a discussion of the controversial issue of "representativeness" and how this relates to soldierly performance and the standing of the military in society. Third, there is an overview of organizational developments within the military during the AVF era. Finally, in an effort to counterbalance prevailing econometric analyses of the AVF, military service in the ranks is linked to broader questions of citizen participation and national service.

Social Composition

EDUCATIONAL LEVELS

Over the course of the all-volunteer era, the number of male recruits with a high school diploma has averaged 86 percent for the Air Force, 71 percent for the Navy, 65 percent for the Marine Corps, and 55 percent for the Army. There are studies which show, moreover, that among high school graduates who do enter the military the tendency is to come from the lower levels of their graduating class, especially for those entering the Army. Trends in mental aptitude levels, as measured by entrance tests, are also a concern. In 1964, the last year before the war in Vietnam, 38 percent of Army recruits placed in the top mental categories of I and II (a figure higher than the national distribution) compared with 14 percent in 1980.

Even if we look only at the high school completion rates, it is indisputable that the educational level of male enlistees in the all-volunteer Army is far lower than either the equivalent civilian population or the Army entrants of the peacetime draft era. Since the start of the AVF, an average of 45 percent of male recruits have not had a high school diploma, compared with 29 percent of draftees and 39 percent of volunteers in 1964. The contrast between the educational levels of the all-volunteer Army and the peacetime-draft Army is even greater when considered in light of the proportional increase in male high school graduates in the population as a whole, from 65 percent of males aged eighteen to nineteen years in 1964 to 80 percent in 1978. Thus while the national trend has been toward a higher percentage of high school graduates, the percentage of graduates among Army enlistees has been dropping.

There has been an even sharper decline in the proportion of

Army entrants with some college from the pre- to the post-Vietnam periods. Whereas about one in six of the draftees and one in eight of the enlistees in 1964 had some college, the corresponding figures in the all-volunteer Army have been around one in twenty-five.

RACIAL CONTENT

The various services differ in their racial composition. The pattern has been for the Army to have the highest proportion of blacks, followed in order by the Marine Corps, Air Force, and Navy. In 1980, blacks in the enlisted ranks accounted for 32 percent of the Army, 22 percent of the Marine Corps, 16 percent of the Air Force, and 11 percent of the Navy. Among Army senior sergeants, blacks have become considerably better represented over the course of the AVF. In 1981 one in four master sergeants was black. This reflects the black reenlistment rate being 1.6 times greater than that of whites. At the noncommissioned officer level, we can expect blacks to play an increasingly important and positive role. Blacks continue, however, to be underrepresented in the officer corps. A disproportionately white officer corps with a disproportionately minority enlisted component will be one of the sociological considerations in the Army leadership of the 1980s.

It is a well-recognized fact that the educational levels of blacks in America have trailed behind that of whites. But the intersection of race and education is quite different among entrants in the all-volunteer Army. Since the end of the draft, the proportion of male black recruits with a high school diploma has been 65 percent compared with 53 percent for whites. In point of fact, today's Army enlisted ranks are the only major arena in American society where black educational levels surpass those of whites, and by a significant degree. Whereas the black soldier seems fairly representative of the black community in terms of educational and social background, white entrants in the all-volunteer Army have been coming from the least educated sectors of the white community. In other words, the Army has been attracting not only a disproportionate number of minorities, but also an unrepresentative segment of white youth, who are more uncharacteristic of the broader social mix than are our minority soldiers. Though put far too crassly, there is an insight in the assessment given me by a longtime German employee of the U.S. Army in Europe. "In the volunteer army you are recruiting the best of the blacks and the worst of the whites."

WOMEN

No change in the make-up of the AVF has received as much media attention as the growing number of women service members. An argument could be made that the margin of success in AVF recruitment has been in the sharp rise of female entrants, virtually all of whom until 1979 were high school graduates. Before the Vietnam War, the utilization of women as military personnel was essentially token. In 1964, only 1.6 percent of all recruits were female; by 1975 the figure had risen to 7.5 percent. In 1980 females accounted for 12.7 percent of all enlisted entrants, ranging from 18.6 percent in the Air Force to 5.2 percent in the Marine Corps.

The role of females expanded rapidly in the first phase of the AVF. That many male soldiers believe women shirk full responsibilities, and that the men end up with added workloads and late night shifts, speaks more to informal policy and personal preference than to innate capabilities. But in the years ahead the increase in female utilization will in all likelihood be much slower than anticipated. One important factor in this regard is the emotionally laden decision as to whether women will be recruited for combat; there has already been an undeniable movement of females into roles where they would suffer casualties during hostilities.

There have also been difficulties in incorporating enlisted women into nontraditional assignments even outside the combat arms. These include rates of attrition much higher than for comparably educated males, the reluctance on the part of many women to accept permanent assignments outside clerical and health settings, and the incidence of pregnancies (one in eight Army enlisted women is pregnant at any given time). There is also the fact that women in the military, as is true for all service members, are paid according to rank, not whether they are in traditional or nontraditional roles. Thus the appeal of higher salaries in nontraditional work that occurs for females in the civilian economy does not apply to military women.

This is not to argue that the ceiling on female military personnel has been reached, but that further expansion into nontraditional tasks will be very gradual at best, and may even be reversed. The 1979 policy change to accept female high school dropouts will only further complicate the utilization of women soldiers.

MARITAL STATUS

Though usually neglected by students of all-volunteer trends, there has been a significant change in the marital composition of the junior enlisted ranks. Since the draft's end, the proportion of marrieds at grade E-4—the modal junior-enlisted pay grade— has about doubled, to around 45 percent. The high incidence of junior-enlisted personnel who are married is all the more noteworthy in that it runs directly counter to national patterns, where the clear trend is toward later marriage. In the all-volunteer era just about every major military base in the United States is ringed by trailer camps or shoddy apartment complexes where many of the young enlisted marrieds live an existence close to or below the poverty line. Overseas—such as in Germany, where young military couples live "on the economy"—they face cultural isolation as well as financial distress. Moreover, the new phenomena of intraservice marriages and fraternization between officers and enlisted personnel of the opposite sex have hardly been acknowledged, much less appraised for their effects on organizational readiness.

Is a Representative Force Desirable?

There can be no question that since 1975 the Army has undergone a social transformation in its enlisted membership. It is difficult to understand how high-powered commissions, well-financed studies, and Department of Defense assessments come up with the opposite conclusion. It is, however, another kind of question as to whether a representative enlisted force is good, bad, or irrelevant.

The strongest evidence bearing upon the effects of social background on soldierly performance deals with enlisted attrition. The striking finding is that high school graduates are twice more likely than high school dropouts to complete their enlistments.

More revealing, this finding is virtually unchanged when mental aptitude, as measured by test scores, is held constant. High school graduates from the lower aptitude levels are actually much more likely to finish their tours than high school dropouts in the higher aptitude levels. Overall attrition rates between the races are comparable, with the main exception that blacks in the lower aptitude levels do better than their white counterparts. Possession of a high school diploma, it seems, reflects the acquisition of social traits (work habits, punctuality, etc.) which make for a more successful military experience.

Examination of enlisted evaluation reports shows the same pattern. High school graduates significantly outperform high school dropouts; high mental levels tend to do better than lower mental levels, but education is a much better predictor than mental level. Studies of unauthorized absences and desertions show such behavior is most likely to occur among those having the least education, coming from broken homes, and having been in trouble with the law before service entry. The facts are also unambiguous that higher educated soldiers do better across the board—in low-skill jobs as well as in high-skill jobs.

The crucial aspect of military manpower is the effect of social composition on combat performance. From a historical standpoint, the evidence is clear that military participation and combat risks in World War II were more equally shared by American men than in either the wars of Korea or Vietnam. (The draft per se is thus no guarantee that there will be class equity in military participation.) In fact, soldiers in World War II reflected a higher socioeconomic background than that of the general population. More to the point, careful studies of combat soldiers in World War II and the Korean War showed that, in the aggregate, soldiers with higher education were rated as better fighters by peers and immediate superiors. Surveys of AVF soldiers report high levels of disaffection from the military system (comparable to what was found among military prisoners in World War II!). One researcher concluded that the AVF was drawing from the most socially alienated segments of the youth population, thereby raising questions of soldierly commitment in the event of hostilities.

By no means does being middle class or educated make one braver or abler. There are many outstanding members of the

AVF who come from impoverished backgrounds. But our concern must also be with the chemistry of unit cohesion which requires an optimum blend of talents and backgrounds. Research evidence confirms the observations of commanders and NCOs who remember the draft period; middle-class and upwardly mobile youth helped enrich the skill level and commitment of military units in peace as well as in war.

The distinctive quality of the enlisted experience starting with World War II was the mixing of the social classes and, starting with the Korean War, the integration of the races. This gave poor youth an opportunity to test themselves, often successfully, against more privileged youth. Such enforced leveling of persons from different backgrounds had no parallel in any other existing institution in American society. This was the elemental social fact underlying enlisted service. This state of affairs began to diminish during the Vietnam War when the college educated avoided service; it has all but disappeared in the all-volunteer era.

The military has always recruited large numbers of youth, white and black, who had no real alternative job prospects. It will always continue to do so. But present trends toward labeling the Army as a recourse for America's underclasses are self-defeating for the youth involved, precisely because they directly counter the premise that military participation is one of broadly based national service. From the 1940s through the mid-1960s, the military served as a bridging environment between entering low-status youth and eventual stable employment. Whatever successes the military had as a remedial organization for deprived youth were largely due to the armed forces being legitimated on other than overt welfare grounds, such as national defense, citizenship obligation, patriotism, even manly honor. In other words, those very conditions peculiar to the armed forces which serve to resocialize poverty youth toward productive ends depend directly upon the military not being defined as a welfare agency or an employer of last resort. It will be increasingly difficult for the Army to avoid such characterization, even if unfair, unless enlisted membership reflects more of a cross section of American youth.

The rising minority content in the Army actually masks a more pervasive shift in the social class bases of the lower enlisted ranks. To what degree the changing racial composition of the Army reflects white reluctance to join an increasingly black organization is unknown, though it is surely a factor. Yet, I am unpersuaded that any significant number of middle-class youths of any race would join the Army, under present recruitment incentives, no matter what its racial make-up. That the disproportionately white Navy and the racially balanced Air Force also face recruitment problems indicates that there is more than racial content at work in attracting a cross section of youth to serve in the AVF. It is a social reality that the combat arms especially will never draw proportionately from middle- and upper-class youth. But to foster policies that accentuate the tracking of lower-class youth into such assignments is perverse. To rationalize the outcome as the workings of the marketplace is duplicitous. This is not to argue that the make-up of the enlisted ranks be perfectly calibrated to the social composition of the larger society, but it is to ask what kind of society excuses its privileged from serving in the ranks of its military.

The AVF: Institution or Occupation?

The military can be understood as an organization which maintains levels of autonomy while refracting broader societal trends. It is from this standpoint that two models—institution versus occupation—are presented to describe alternative conceptions of the military. The basic hypothesis is that the American military is moving from an institutional format to one more and more resembling that of an occupation. To describe the move toward occupationalism is not to hold that such a trend is inevitable. In point of fact, recognition of this trend has focused attention on the consequences of policies that affect military social organization.

The contrast between institution and occupation can, of course, be overdrawn. To characterize the armed forces as either an institution or an occupation is to do an injustice to reality. Both elements have been and always will be present in the military system. But our concern is to grasp the whole, to place the salient fact. Even though terms like institution or occupation have descriptive limitations, they do contain core connotations which serve to distinguish each from the other.

An *institution* is legitimated in terms of values and norms, i.e., a purpose transcending individual self-interest in favor of a presumed higher good. Members of an institution are often seen as following a calling, captured in words like "duty," "honor," and "country." They are commonly viewed and regard themselves as being different or apart from the broader society. To the degree one's institutional membership is congruent with notions of self-sacrifice and primary identification with one's institutional role, one usually enjoys esteem from the larger society.

Military service has traditionally had many institutional features. One thinks of extended tours abroad, the fixed term of enlistment, liability for twenty-four-hour service availability, frequent movements of self and family, subjection to military discipline and law, and inability to resign, strike, or negotiate working conditions. All this is above and beyond the dangers inherent in military maneuvers and actual combat operations. It is also significant that a paternalistic remuneration system has evolved in the military corresponding to the institutional model: compensation received in non-cash form (e.g., food, housing, uniforms, medical care), subsidized consumer facilities on the base, payments to service members partly determined by family status, and a large portion of compensation received as deferred pay in the form of retirement benefits. Moreover, unlike most civilians, for whom compensation is heavily determined by individual expertise, the compensation received by military members is essentially a function of rank, seniority, and need.

An *occupation* is legitimated in terms of the marketplace, i.e., prevailing monetary rewards for equivalent competencies. Supply and demand rather than normative considerations are paramount. In a modern industrial society, employees usually enjoy some voice in the determination of appropriate salary and work conditions. Such rights are counterbalanced by responsibilities to meet contractual obligations. The cash-work nexus emphasizes a negotiation between individual and organizational needs. The occupational model frequently implies priority of self-interest rather than that of the employing organization.

Traditionally, the military has sought to avoid the organizational outcomes of the occupational model. This is in the face of repeated governmental commissions and studies advocating that the armed services adopt a salary system which would incorporate all basic pay, allowances, and tax benefits into one cash payment and which would eliminate compensation differences between married and single personnel, thus conforming to the equal-pay-for-equal-work principle of civilian occupations. Nevertheless, even in the conventional military system there has been some accommodation to occupational imperatives. Reenlistment bonuses have been a staple incentive to retail highly skilled technical personnel. Off-scale pay has been a feature of military compensation for physicians for many years. Since the advent of the all-volunteer force, bonuses have been used to recruit soldiers into the combat arms.

Despite certain exceptions, the traditional system of military compensation reflected not only the so-called "X-factor"—the unusual demands of service life—but the corporate whole of military life. The military institution is organized "vertically," where an occupation is organized "horizontally." To put it in as unpretentious a manner as possible, people in an occupation tend to feel a sense of identity with others who do the same sort of work and who receive about the same pay. In an institution, on the other hand, it is the organization where people live and work which creates the sense of identity that binds them together. Vertical identification means one acquires an understanding and sense of responsibility for the performance of the whole. In the armed forces the very fact of being part of the services has traditionally been more important than the fact that military members do different jobs. The organization one belongs to creates the feeling of shared interest, not the other way around.

Although antecedents predate the appearance of the AVF, the end of the draft might be seen as a major thrust to move the military toward the occupational model. The selective service system was premised on the notion of citizen obligation—a "calling" in the almost literal sense of being summoned by a local draft board—with concommitant low salaries for junior enlisted personnel. Furthermore, it is estimated that about 40 percent of "volunteers" in the peacetime pre-Vietnam era were draft motivated. Even though the termination of the draft in 1973 has been one of the most visible changes in the contemporary military system, it must be stressed that an all-volunteer military in and of itself need not be correlated with an occupational model. It is only that the architects of the present AVF have chosen the occupational model as their paradigm.

The marketplace philosophy clearly underpinned the rationale of the 1970 Report of the President's Commission on an All-Volunteer Force, better known as the "Gates Commission Report." The Gates Commission was strongly influenced by a laissez-faire economic thought and argued that primary reliance in recruiting an armed force should be on monetary inducements guided by marketplace standards. This dovetailed with the systems analysts who had become ascendant in the Department of Defense under both Democratic and Republican administrations. Whether under the rubric of econometrics or systems analysis, such a redefinition of military service is based on a set of core assumptions. First, there is no analytical distinction between military systems and other systems, especially no difference between cost-effectiveness analysis of civilian enterprises and military services. Second, military compensation should as much as possible be in cash (rather than in-kind or deferred) and be linked as much as possible to skill differences of individual service members (thereby allowing for a more efficient operation of the marketplace). Third, social cohesion and goal commitment are essentially unmeasurable (thereby an inappropriate object of analysis). Fourth, if end-strength targets are met in the AVF, notions of citizenship obligation and social representativeness are incidental concerns. This mind-set has contributed to moving the American military toward an explicitly occupational format.

Other indicators of the trend toward the occupational model can also be noted.

COMPENSATION AND ENTITLEMENTS

The move toward making military remuneration comparable with the civilian sector preceded the advent of the AVF. Since 1967 military pay has been formally linked to the civil service and thus, indirectly, to the civilian labor market. During the late 1960s and early 1970s, military compensation, especially at recruit levels, increased at a much faster rate than civilian rates. Toward the latter part of the 1970s, it appears that military pay lagged behind civilian levels, although this point is not without dispute. In the early 1980s, "catch-up" pay raises were given to military personnel. Precisely because military compensation was being redefined as comparable to civilian rates, increased attention was given to actions and proposals to reduce a number of military benefits and entitlements (notably, a restructuring of the retirement system). A widespread concern with "erosion of benefits" became evident among military members since the advent of the AVF.

A kind of "devil's bargain" may have been struck when military pay was geared to comparable civilian levels. Institutional features of the military compensation system may have been unwittingly traded off for the relatively good salaries enjoyed by military personnel in the early years of the AVF. It is highly unlikely that service entitlements can be maintained at past levels if military salaries are to be competitive with civilian scales. Discontent with the erosion of benefits was intensified by the fact that the major pay increases of the late 1960s and early 1970s preceded the reduction in benefits. The pay increases, that is, were not seen as part of a package which would also entail some reductions in benefits.

Another major outcome of the AVF has been a dramatic compression of pay scales within the military. In the 1960s, the basic pay of an E-9 (the senior enlisted grade) with twenty-six years of service was better than seven times that of an entering recruit. Since the end of the draft, that same E-9 makes only 3.5 times the pay of the recruit. The paradox is that this "front-loading" of compensation toward the junior ranks and changes to improve lower enlisted life cannot be appreciated by those newly entering the service—they did not experience the old ways. Instead, junior enlisted members see little monetary or "life style" improvement over the course of a military career, thereby reducing the likelihood of their choosing to remain in the service. Once upon a time sergeants measured their incomes and perquisites against those of the soldiers they led and felt rewarded; now they see a relative decline of status within the service and compare their earnings against civilians and feel deprived.

MILITARY UNIONS

The possibility that trade unionism might appear within the armed forces of the United States was once unthinkable. Reliance on marketplace models to recruit and retain military members and the blurring of the line between military service and civilian occupations is quite consistent with the notion of trade unionism. Several unions indicated an interest in organizing the military during the 1970s. This led to statutory prohibitions on organizing activities or job actions in the armed forces. The constitutionality of the 1978 law banning union activity has yet to be tested, and the situation of full-time reservists who are already unionized remains unclarified.

Another development has been the trend toward representation activity or "creeping unionism" on the part of service associations. The Association of the United States Army, the Fleet Reserve Association, and, especially, the Air Force Sergeants Association (AFSA) have taken an increasingly active role in lobbying Congress for servicemen's pay and benefits. Significantly, the AFSA has grown from a membership of 23,000 in 1974 to over 120,000 by 1981. Whatever the degree or form representational activity may take in the armed forces, it is important to note that only in the public sector, where there are no owners to oppose, is ' labor union membership growing as a percent of the American work force.

ATTRITION

In the pre-Vietnam military it was considered aberrant for an enlisted man not to complete his initial tour of duty. Since the end of the draft, however, about one in three service members was failing to complete initial enlistment. From 1973 through 1981, over 600,000 young people have been prematurely discharged from the military. Attrition varies by service with the rate being highest in the ground forces, lowest in the Air Force, and the Navy in-between. When education is held constant, however, the attrition rates between the different services are essentially the same.

The attrition phenomenon reflects changing policies of military separation—the "easy-out" system of the AVF—as well as changes in the quality of the entering enlisted force. Put in another way, the all-volunteer military, like industrial organizations, is witnessing the common occurrence of its members "quitting" or being "fired." In time, it is possible that a general certificate of separation will replace the present discharge classification system. Unlike an older era, there would no longer be a stigma for unsuccessful service. Such a development would make the military that much more consistent with the civilian work model. In all but name, the AVF has already gone a long way down the road toward indeterminate enlistments. Yet it is symbolic that the word "honorable"—a term not found in occupational evaluations—is still used in classifications of military discharges.

WORK AND RESIDENCE SEPARATION

A hallmark of the traditional military has been the adjacency of workplace and living quarters. As late as the mid-1960s, it was practically unheard of for a bachelor enlisted man to live off base. Not only was it against regulations, but few could afford a private rental on junior enlisted pay. By 1980, although precise data are not available, a reasonable estimate was that about one in four single enlisted members in stateside bases had apartments away from the military installation.

To the increasing proportion of single enlisted members living off base, one must add the growing number of married junior enlisted people, nearly all of whom live on the civilian economy. Like civilian employees, many junior enlisted members are now part of the early morning and late afternoon exodus to and from work. One of the outcomes of the large salary raises for junior enlisted personnel needed to recruit an all-volunteer military has been the ebbing of barracks life.

MOONLIGHTING

One striking manifestation of the occupational model is found in the growing numbers of military personnel who hold outside employment. According to military surveys, about one in four enlisted members reported themselves as holding a second job.

Moonlighting is often attributed to the service member's need for additional income in an inflationary economy. This undoubtedly is a factor for many of the junior enlisted marrieds (though the increase in junior enlisted marrieds is itself an outcome of the AVF). Yet the anomaly exists that moonlighting also increased among single members of the junior enlisted force, even though their buying power far exceeded that of the prevolunteer era. In any event, moonlighting, virtually unheard of in the draft era, clearly runs contrary to the institutional premise of a service member's total role commitment to the armed forces.

MILITARY SPOUSES

In a manner of speaking, the role of institutional membership in the military community extended to the wife of the service husband. Wives of career personnel were expected to initiate and take part in a panoply of social functions in the military environment. Military wives and their clubs contributed time and raised funds for a wide range of volunteer projects. In recent years, there has been a perceptibly growing reluctance of wives at both non-com and junior officer levels to participate in such customary functions. With the rising proportion of service wives working outside the home, moreover, there were bound to be fewer women with either the time or inclination to engage in the volunteer work which has structured much of the social life of military installations. Moreover, even those military wives who were not gainfully employed began to regauge their commitment to volunteer work in light of their perceptions of the lower effort put forth by employed wives. It is not so much that female liberation has arrived among career military wives, though this is not absent, as it is the growing tendency for wives to define their roles as distinct from the military community.

CIVILIAN PERSONNEL

The increasing proportion of civilian workers in total defense manpower—from 27 percent in 1964 to 32 percent in 1980—reflects another trend in the American military establishment. The diminution of the proportion of uniformed personnel within the defense establishment is projected to continue and its impact on institutional commitment deserves attention. Interviews and observations of military personnel working in units with civilians indicate a detrimental effect on morale. The narrow definition of the work role among civilians can increase the work load (such as overtime and holiday work) of military personnel. This, along with the higher pay civilians may receive for doing seemingly the same kind of work as military members, can generate resentment. The point here is that feelings of relative deprivation are unavoidable when the diffuse responsibilities of the military institution coexist with more limited work roles found in civilian occupations.

Another manifestation of organizational change departs entirely from the formal military organization. This is the use of civilians hired on contract to perform jobs previously carried out by active-duty servicemen. These tasks range from routine housekeeping and kitchen duties, through rear-echelon equipment and weapons maintenance and civilian-manned oilers and tenders, to quasi-combat roles such as "tech reps" aboard warships, operators of missile warning systems in remote sites, and air crews of chartered aircraft in war zones such as occurred in Vietnam. From 1964 to 1980, contract-hire civilians rose from 5 percent to 15 percent as a proportion of total defense manpower. Presumably considerations of task efficiencies and costs bear upon decisions to substitute contract civilians for uniformed personnel. Nevertheless, the increased reliance on civilian employees, whose institutional affiliation with the military is attenuated, is yet one more indication of the direction of organizational change in the defense establishment.

The sum of the above and related developments would seem to confirm the ascendancy of the occupational model in the emergent military. This presentation can be faulted for presenting too monolithic a picture of trends. There are, of course, always countervailing forces in effect. Indeed, it is the tension and interplay between institutional and occupational tendencies that characterize organizational change within the armed forces. Moreover, not all of the described trends can be attributed to the AVF. The point remains, however, that the shift toward an occupational format is reinforced by the econometric designers of the present AVF.

Saving the AVF: A National Service Approach

The central issue remains: is there a way to meet military manpower needs without conscription or excessive reliance on cash inducements for recruits? Or, to put it another way, can we obtain the analogue of the peacetime draftee in the all-volunteer context? I believe we can. First, link federal aid for higher education to a program of voluntary national service to include military reserve duty or civilian work. Second, introduce a G.I. Bill for the AVF. Third, construct a two-track military personnel and compensation system which differentiates between a short-term volunteer and one who makes a long-term commitment. The interactive effect of these proposals deals with the "three Rs" of military manpower: recruitment, retention, and the reserves. Most important, such a program would counter the trend toward an occupational definition of military service.

EDUCATIONAL BENEFITS IN CONFLICT WITH THE AVF

Under the Veterans Educational Assistance Program (VEAP), which replaced the G.I. Bill in 1976, the government matches, within prescribed limits, voluntary contributions made by service members. It has been estimated that governmental expenditures for VEAP will be under $90 million annually. But, for 1980 alone, federal aid to college students in the form of grants and loan subsidies exceeded $5.2 billion. Legislation passed in 1978 removed or loosened need requirements for the bulk of federal aid to college students. Even if budget cuts to reduce student aid are implemented, we will still confront an immense sum in competition with the educational benefits offered to military members. A system of educational benefits has been created which offers more to those who do not serve their country than to those who do. In effect, we have created a G.I. Bill without the G.I.

It is surprising that no public figure thought to tie such student aid to any service obligation. A program of voluntary national service should be introduced in which participation becomes a prerequisite for federal postsecondary school assistance. Indeed, the educational establishment should take the lead in proposing such a linkage in order to legitimate current student aid programs.

The preferred conditions of such national service should be broad but light, rather than narrow but heavy. The aim is for inclusiveness in youth participation, but maximum decentralization and minimum costs. The following is set forth as one way to meet these standards.

To be eligible for federal postsecondary educational aid, a youth would be required to serve a short period—say three to six months—in an unpaid capacity. Most likely, recruitment would be handled by voluntary associations, welfare agencies, nonprofit institutions, schools, recreational facilities, and the like. The range of such tasks could include grooming care for the aged in nursing homes, teachers' aides, escort services for the aged, monitors on public transit systems, and even museum cataloguing. National service could also entail self-selected tasks, for example, driving the aged to medical or shopping facilities. Military reservists would be preeminent examples of those meeting the national service requirement for federal student aid. To go a step further, one can envision a state of affairs whereby persons who complete national service will have priority in public employment.

Determining whether or not a specific task would meet service criteria would be the responsibility of local national service boards, whose members themselves would be volunteers (albeit not youth). Salaries would be received only by clerical help at regional board levels and staffers at a national headquarters office. The decentralized system of the old selective service boards is the obvious parallel.

From the viewpoint of the national server, the educational benefits would be substantial. Let us assume an annual outlay of $5 billion (approximately the 1980 federal expenditure for student aid) and 1 million national servers (a figure most likely way too high). This would mean $5,000 in potential educational benefits to each recipient. (In 1980, some 2.2 million college students received federal aid for an average of about $2,500 each.)

PROVISIONS OF A G.I. BILL FOR THE AVF

Along with linking federal educational assistance beyond high school to voluntary national service, we should introduce postservice educational benefits for members of the AVF along the lines of the G.I. Bill following World War II. A person who enlists in the armed forces and completes his or her two-year obligated period of active duty would be entitled to educational assistance as follows: (1) the costs of tuition up to $3,000 per academic year up to a maximum of three years, (2) a monthly stipend of $300 up to a maximum of twenty-seven months, (3) eligibility to be limited to those who receive honorable discharges or separations, and (4) such entitlements being dependent upon an appropriate reserve obligation. In this way, maximum federal educational benefits would be allotted to those who serve in the active-duty military.

The maximum direct costs of such an AVF G.I. Bill would probably be under $1.25 billion a year. There would be, however, substantial offsetting savings in net costs. Cutting the attrition rate in half would alone result in manpower savings in excess of $.6 billion annually. Substantial savings would occur in lowering recruitment outlays required to enlist high school graduates. Cost reductions would also result from less loss time in unauthorized absences and desertions, the elimination of combat arms enlistment bonuses, the end of VEAP, and, most likely, fewer lower-ranking service members with families. With these savings, the net costs of an AVF G.I. Bill would probably be well under $.4 billion annually—a sum much smaller than proposed increases in recruit pay and enlistment bonuses.

One argument against the AVF G.I. Bill is that it will reduce retention among those first termers the military would like to remain in the service. It should be noted, however, that career retention problems have been aggravated since the end of the G.I. Bill in 1976. Special career provisions in conjunction with a G.I. Bill would complement, not undermine, retention incentives. There should be no cutoff date for G.I. Bill eligibility, thereby allowing career service members to take advantage of it. A cash-out feature in the form of a reenlistment bonus might be offered in lieu of G.I. Bill benefits. A career soldier might take out educational loans for college-age dependents which can be forgiven at certain rates in return for reenlistment commitments. Or, a career soldier could use educational entitlements to take a "sabbatical" involving an engineering curriculum for future technical work in the military. By no means do educational benefits define innovative measures necessary to retain the required career force.

Two general principles should always be kept in mind when appraising recruitment and retention proposals. First, recruitment incentives must be kept as simple as possible—as much for the recruiter's sake as for the recruit. Second, reenlistment incentives can be fairly complicated; one will never go wrong overestimating the grasp career service members have of compensation packages.

CITIZEN SOLDIER AND CAREER SOLDIER: COMPLEMENTARY ROLES

The definition of military service in the all-volunteer context needs overhauling as much as does the machinery of military recruitment. The armed services can set up a two-tier personnel and compensation system recognizing a distinction between a "career soldier" and a "citizen soldier." (Soldier as used here refers, of course, to sailors, airmen, and marines.)

The career soldier would initially enlist for a minimum of four years. He or she would receive entitlements and compensation in the manner of the prevailing system, but there would be significant pay increases at the time of the first reenlistment and throughout the senior NCO grades. Many career persons would be trained in technical skills, though others would make up the future cadre in a variety of military specialties. Along with improvements in the quality of service life, steps such as these would go a long way toward retaining the experienced personnel needed for a complex and technical military force.

The citizen soldier would enlist for two years of active duty (the term of the old draftee) and be assigned to the combat arms, low-skill shipboard duty, aircraft security guards, routine maintenance, and other labor-intensive positions. These are the kinds of assignments in the present AVF where recruitment shortfalls, attrition, and desertion are most likely to occur. Because there would be no presumption of acquiring civilian skills in the military, the terms of such service would be honest and unambiguous. Active-duty pay for the citizen soldier would be lower—say by one-third—than that received by the career soldier of the same rank. Other than a generous G.I. Bill, the citizen soldier would receive no entitlements such as off-base housing or food allowances.

A college or graduate education, or vocational training, in exchange for two years of active duty would be the means to attract highly qualified soldiers who can learn quickly, serve effectively for a full tour, go on to the reserves, and then be replaced by similarly qualified recruits. It is important to note that surveys of high school youth and college undergraduates consistently show that G.I. Bill–type incentives hold greater appeal than does higher pay for those youth not presently inclined to

join the service. The main point is that the citizen soldier concept would reintroduce the national service ethic into the format
of military manpower.

The AVF in Perspective

The national service framework advanced here departs from
the prevailing systems analysis and econometric approaches to
the AVF. The starting point is not how are empty spaces to be
filled, but rather how can a substantial number and cross section
of American youth serve their country. To stretch a little and
to borrow from the fashionable economic terms of the day, I
am suggesting a supply-side rather than demand-side model of
military manpower. Or, to put it yet another way, how can we
introduce a large dose of genuine volunteerism into the all-volunteer military? The AVF, if it is to survive, must attract middle-
class and upwardly mobile American youth who would find a
temporary diversion from the world of school or work tolerable,
and perhaps even welcome.

To avoid the present trend toward defining the military in
occupational terms accompanied by a policy of recruiting at the
margin, the choice comes down to a return to the draft or a comprehensive program of voluntary national service. The dominant
economistic model of the AVF relies on the mistaken premise
that long initial enlistments are always to be preferred over short
enlistments. In 1964, 36 percent of all enlisted entrants signed
on for four or more years compared with 61 percent in 1980.
Yet with the high attrition rate, the personnel turnover is greater
now than it was in the peacetime draft era!

We do not want to be so bedeviled with rival sets of numbers,
so overwhelmed with data, that the key policy choices are hardly
understood, much less addressed. It appears that as the technical
competence of the Department of Defense to deal with personnel
data expands, its actual ability to deal with manpower issues
declines. The grand design is to make governmental subsidies of
higher education consistent, not contradictory as presently, with
the ideal that citizen obligation ought to become part of growing
up in America. Such a realization would also clarify the military's
role by emphasizing the larger calling of national service.

Richard V. L. Cooper

5

Military Manpower Procurement Policy in the 1980s

Introduction

For more than eight years, since the draft was ended in 1973, the nation has relied on the all-volunteer force (AVF) to fill the ranks of the military. The magnitude of this undertaking should not be underestimated, for never before in modern history has a nation with such global military responsibilities or such a concern about national defense left itself without the authority to conscript young men into military service. The AVF accordingly represents one of the largest and most important "experiments" of its type ever conducted.

Perhaps not surprisingly, the success of this endeavor has been and continues to be widely debated in public circles. Just as the volunteer force was born amidst some controversy, it has continued to attract considerable public attention throughout its eight-year history. Editorials, media horror stories, and public

RICHARD V. L. COOPER *is a partner in the Management Consulting Services division of Coopers and Lybrand. Dr. Cooper was formerly director of the Defense Manpower Studies program at The Rand Corporation. He has written extensively in the fields of military manpower requirements and procurement.*

debate continued throughout the 1970s, fueled in part by such factors as manpower shortages, recruiting scandals, and rising manpower costs, as well as by more general concerns about American military preparedness. The debate gained added momentum in 1979, when for the first time since the draft was ended, all four military services fell short of their recruiting quotas.

Thus, if one thing has become clear from the experience since the termination of the draft, it is that military manpower procurement policy will likely continue to be a major policy issue in the years to come. Although improved recruiting performance by the military services during 1980 and 1981 may have at least temporarily slowed down some of the AVF critics, the declining size of youth population cohorts will make it difficult for the military to attract the requisite numbers and kinds of personnel during the 1980s, even if force sizes remain constant, let alone increase. This, combined with the almost naturally controversial nature of military manpower procurement policy, will thus likely keep the AVF in the mainstream of public concern.

Yet for all the expressed concern, interest, and rhetoric, the debate itself has lacked completeness in its treatment of the issues, problems, and alternatives. There has been a tendency to focus on issues and problems out of context and to confuse what might be termed as general manpower or defense problems with the AVF. Perhaps even more significant, the debate has failed to put forth a comprehensive assessment of the AVF, as compared with its alternatives. While it is true that a return to the draft would solve certain problems that have beset the volunteer force, for instance, such a policy change would create new problems, some of which might be worse than the problems that were solved. What is therefore needed is a comprehensive assessment of the various military manpower procurement policy alternatives, in their entirety.

The purpose of this chapter is to lay the foundation for making such an assessment, so that we might gain a better understanding of the full consequences that would result from any of the various policy alternatives that confront this nation. The following section presents an analytic framework for examining the implications of alternative military manpower procurement policies. The next three sections then examine in some detail the implications of the three main categories of procurement policies: volunteer force, universal service, and selective service. What problems do the different alternatives have? Which do they solve? Conclusions are then presented at the end of this chapter.

Analytic Framework

The development and specification of an analytic framework is an important first step in any analysis. It is especially so here, since a fundamental problem with much of the previous literature and discussion regarding military manpower procurement policy has been the failure to specify adequately the terms of reference, bases of analysis, policy alternatives, and methods of evaluation.

This section begins with a brief discussion of the basic framework, including the components of the problem and the method of analysis. It then reviews, first, the issues and considerations that need to be taken into account; second, the potential policy options; and, third, the policy environment.

METHODOLOGY

Broadly speaking, the framework employed here consists of four distinct parts. The first is the set of issues and considerations that must necessarily be addressed by any military manpower procurement policy. It will be argued later in this section that there are two broad classes of such issues and considerations: (1) national security considerations and (2) other concerns, including economic, equity, social, and political considerations. In a sense, these various concerns might be thought of as the criteria against which military manpower policy alternatives must be judged.

The second component of the analytic framework consists of specifying a realistic set of policy alternatives, since the choice of a military manpower procurement policy cannot be made in the abstract, but must rather be made in the context of the available policy options. In other words, we must view military manpower procurement policy in comparative terms—comparative in the sense of how the various alternatives stack up against one another.

The third component consists of the policy environment within which the policy choices must be made. Not only must the various policy alternatives be compared against one another, as previously noted, but also these comparisons must be made in the context of the particular policy environment. In other words, there is no system that is "right" in absolute terms. What may be "right" under one set of circumstances may be inappropriate for another set. For example, the manpower procurement policy that is appropriate to staff a military force of 2 million personnel may not be the most appropriate to staff one of 3 million personnel. In short, we need to understand the policy context in order to determine the appropriateness of the various potential policy alternatives.

The final part of the analytic framework is the methodology for integrating the policy concerns (i.e., criteria), policy alternatives, and policy environment. That is, we need a methodology for evaluating *in total* the various policy options in terms of the criteria and constraints.

Although the above framework may seem obvious, it is in this regard that the literature and debate about military manpower seems most wanting. The tendency has too often been one of focusing on particular issues and policies out of context, not recognizing the full consequences of the various alternatives put forth. Specifically, one needs to recognize that changing manpower policy to solve one problem frequently creates another. Thus, policy changes must be evaluated in terms of all their effects, both positive and negative.

The point is not that manpower problems are hopelessly insoluble, but rather that manpower policy represents a series of trade-offs. What is needed, then, is a methodology for weighing these various effects, so as to arrive at a reasonable compromise among the many and sometimes conflicting policy objectives.

Theoretically, such a methodology can be envisioned as a "matrix scorecard," with one side of the matrix consisting of the various policy criteria and the other consisting of the particular policy alternatives. Although the detailed development of such a scorecard is beyond the scope of this chapter, the analysis presented here will be based on the general scorecard approach. Specifically, each of the various military manpower procurement alternatives will be examined with respect to the various policy criteria outlined in the next section.

ISSUES AND CONSIDERATIONS

The complexity and controversy surrounding the military manpower procurement policy problem stem in large part from the fact that so many different factors must be taken into account: not only military effectiveness, but also a myriad of economic, social, political, and equity considerations as well. In short, military manpower procurement policy is a military problem, an economic problem, and a social/political problem all rolled into one.

Dealing effectively with the military manpower procurement problem thus requires that we systematically examine each of these individual policy concerns and considerations. As noted earlier, these issues and considerations in turn serve as criteria against which the various policy alternatives must be judged.

To facilitate the analysis, it is useful to think of these issues for criteria in two broad groupings: (1) military or national security concerns and (2) nonmilitary concerns such as cost, equity, and social/political considerations.

MILITARY CONSIDERATIONS

A nation has an armed force for the protection of its interest— i.e., national security. In this country, that means defense against other nations, since internal security is left primarily to the various civilian law enforcement agencies, except for the use of the National Guard for certain emergency and disaster situations. Thus, our armed force must be able to provide a sufficient level of national security: to deter war if possible and, that failing, to wage and win a war.

From a manpower perspective, we can think of national security objectives in three main components: first, manning the peacetime active forces; second, manning the reserves; and third, providing sufficient manpower to meet military mobilization requirements in the event of war or a national emergency. Each of these represents a separate and distinct problem that must be addressed by whatever military manpower procurement policy is used.

Manning the peacetime active forces involves the following

specific issues and considerations, among others: recruiting for the enlisted ranks, both quantity and quality; recruiting officers, again both quantity and quality; postenlistment behavior, such as attrition and indiscipline; retention; and unit effectiveness and productivity. Similar kinds of concerns must also be taken into account when evaluating how various policies fare with respect to manning the Selected Reserves. Policy concerns that must be addressed with respect to mobilization capabilities include manning the Individual Ready Reserve (IRR), as well as the ability to increase force sizes rapidly in the event of war.

NONMILITARY CONSIDERATIONS

Three broad categories of nonmilitary issues stand out: cost or efficiency, equity, and social/political concerns. Efficiency, or cost, is clearly an important criterion for judging various different military manpower procurement policy options. Less expensive is obviously preferable to more expensive, other things being equal. In this regard, however, although budget costs are the most visible measure, "real resource" costs are an equally, if not more important measure from an overall public policy perspective. For example, it is generally acknowledged that the budget cost of military personnel understates the real resource cost of manpower during a draft, both because the wages paid to draftees understate the economic value of these individuals in alternative civilian pursuits and because military personnel costs do not capture the large amount of resources expended for draft avoidance. The discussion here will focus on budget costs and, to the extent that they differ from budget costs, the real resource costs of the different policy options.

The "fairness," or equity, of various policy alternatives is likewise always an important criterion. Defining precisely what is "fair," and what is not, is of course impossible. Nevertheless, society must regularly make judgments of this sort with respect to a variety of different issues. It is not that society should not impose "burdens" on its citizens, for it must, usually in the form of taxes. Rather, the issue is one of trying to distribute these burdens equitably.

Finally, social and political concerns include such specific considerations as the representativeness of the military, military/

civil relations, social conflict, responsibilities of citizenship, and political perceptions of the military, both domestic and international.

To the extent possible, military manpower procurement policy should be consistent with the nation's other economic, social, and political goals. In fact, one can go one step further and argue that, to the extent possible and reasonable, military manpower procurement policy ought to further the nation's economic and social goals. For example, the military helped pave the way for racial integration in the 1950s.

At the same time, we must be careful to avoid having "the tail wag the dog." For example, adopting a policy of universal service solely to encourage a "socialization" of American youth would seem to be a great waste of the nation's resources. Alternatively, if such a policy was useful for military purposes, then this socialization might be a useful and positive by-product.

Thus, it must be remembered that the primary purpose of military procurement policy is to provide the needed manpower to the military. It should not conflict with the nation's broader economic, social, and political policy objectives, but it should not also be the prime agent to achieve social or economic change. Except in some few instances, military manpower procurement policy is simply a very inefficient way for effecting social and economic change. Moreover, using it in this fashion may have very undesirable military effects. To illustrate, it may be very sensible, both from the military viewpoint and from society's viewpoint more generally, to attempt to enlist successful "graduates" of various social and economic action programs such as CETA. At the same time, using the military instead of CETA is likely to be both inefficient and detrimental to national security.

POLICY OPTIONS

Although it is typical to think of military manpower procurement policy in terms of the choice between volunteerism and conscription, it is perhaps more useful to categorize the policy options into one of three classes of systems: volunteer, selective service, and universal service. Selective service and universal service, while both forms of conscription, differ in an important respect. Whereas all or nearly all of the eligible population is required to serve under a policy of universal service, this is not the case with selective service. Rather, when the eligible population exceeds the military's requirements for conscripts, only some will be required to serve—hence, the *selective* nature of selective service.

All military manpower procurement systems can be grouped under one of the above three general headings. There are, however, many different variations on each of these as described below.

UNIVERSAL SERVICE

Three general types of universal service policies immediately come to mind: Universal Military Training (UMT), Universal Military Service (UMS), and Universal National Service (UNS). Under UMT, all qualified individuals in the eligible population (usually male youth) are required to receive military training, except for conscientious objectors who are generally assigned to alternative civilian service. This training can range from just basic military training to basic training plus some unit training. Upon the completion of such training, those individuals who do not remain in the military are generally assigned to the reserve forces. (In the case of the United States, this could be either or both the Selected Reserves or the IRR.) The period of active service (i.e., training) under UMT could thus range anywhere from as little as eight or ten weeks to as much as nine months or so; the period of reserve service could range from as little as a year to perhaps many years.

There are at least two main variants of the basic UMT model: UMT-draft and UMT-volunteer. Under the latter, individuals would be conscripted only for military training; the standing forces would be filled by volunteers from the trained conscript pool. Under the UMT-draft model, some of the trained conscript pool could be drafted into the standing forces. This approach is thus a combination of UMT and Selective Service.

UMS goes one step beyond UMT, in that all qualified eligibles not only receive military training, but are also required to serve in a substantive capacity in the active forces. In order to make productive use of these conscripts, the active-duty tour for UMS, including training, probably cannot be less than a year, with two years representing a more reasonable minimum tour length. After this period of active service, UMS conscripts will generally be assigned to some form of reserve service that can last anywhere from one to several years.

UNS is like UMT and UMS in that all qualified eligibles must serve, but differs from these two in one important respect: whereas UMT and UMS conscript individuals to serve in the military, UNS conscripts individuals to perform other public service as well. Individuals can satisfy their obligation by performing either military service or some other public service that is designated as being in the "national interest." The tour length for UNS is typically envisioned as one to two years.

SELECTIVE SERVICE

Selective Service represents the other main form of conscription. It differs from universal service in that not all eligibles are required to serve. It is thus the form of conscription used when the size of the qualified and eligible population base—e.g., eighteen-year-old males—exceeds the military's requirements for new recruits. In other words, when this situation prevails, the military or its agent (the Selective Service System in the case of the United States) must *select* only a portion from among the qualified eligibles to serve in the military.

As with universal service, there are many possible variations of the basic Selective Service concept. We can think of these variations in several dimensions: (1) for what purpose individuals are to be conscripted, (2) the method of selection used, (3) the policy toward volunteers, and 4) other manpower policies. With respect to the first, conscription can be to fill the active forces, the reserve forces, or both. (It is typically not necessary to have a reserve draft, however, if a draft is used for the active forces. The reason for this is simply that when an active-force draft is used, there are usually long queues of individuals waiting to join the reserves, since reserve service typically excuses these individuals from further military obligation.) It should be noted that there have also been proposals to use a Selective Service draft to conscript individuals for both the military and public service jobs.

There are likewise many different kinds of selection methods. A random process, such as the lottery introduced in the late 1960s, can be used to select which individuals will be conscripted into the military. Alternatively, deferments and exemptions can be used to channel which individuals will ultimately serve, as in fact was the case in the United States before the lottery draft. An extreme example of this channeling process can be found in the World War I draft, where individuals were classified and drafted according to their "value to society."

The third important factor in the Selective Service draft is the policy toward volunteers. For example, during the postwar draft, the United States relied on a mixed draft-volunteer system, using the draft only to fill the gap between the military's requirements for new recruits and the number of volunteers. Alternatively, policy could be changed to reduce or eliminate voluntary enlistments. A version of this policy was used during much of World War II, and has again been proposed for use by the Association of the United States Army.

While the above discussion has focused on such obvious draft specific issues as the method of selection, it is important to recognize that other manpower variables, such as pay and quality standards, are also a key part of military manpower procurement policy. To the extent that military pay is reduced or quality standards raised, for example, there will be fewer volunteers, and therefore a greater need for conscripts.

Despite these many possible variations, all Selective Service Systems have one thing in common: they conscript only a portion of the qualified eligible manpower pool. Specific versions of Selective Service then differ according to where conscripts are to be used, according to what type of selection process is used, the policy toward volunteers, and other related manpower policies.

VOLUNTEER SYSTEMS

As the name implies, volunteer systems rely *solely* on individuals who join the military for voluntary reasons. The operative phrase in the above statement, however, is the word "solely," for other than the fact that a draft uses coercion to force some individuals into the military, draft and volunteer systems are otherwise conceptually similar. Both rely on a host of incentives to fill the ranks: pay, education, job training, patriotism, pride and prestige, a sense of adventure, and so forth. And both tend to rely exclusively on volunteers to fill the career ranks.

Although not generically different in the sense of some of the different conscription models just described, there are a number of variations of the basic volunteer model. These variations differ from one another with respect to the particular incentives employed, and how they are employed. For example, the military relied largely on pay incentives in converting from a draft-based system to volunteer system in the early 1970s. In addition to pay incentives, one might also think of tying certain societal benefits, such as educational assistance, to successful service in the military.

THE POLICY ENVIRONMENT

As noted earlier, we need to understand the general policy environment in order to determine the appropriateness of the various possible military manpower procurement alternatives. Two factors in this regard particularly deserve mention here: defense requirements and the population base.

Defense Requirements—Perhaps the single most important factor governing the choice of military manpower procurement policy is force size: the larger the required force size, the more difficult it becomes to sustain a volunteer military. Present policy calls for about 2.1 million active-duty personnel, about 900,000 personnel in the Selected Reserves, and several hundred thousand individuals in the Individual Ready Reserve. This, in turn, means that the military has to obtain in the neighborhood of 400,000 to 500,000 recruits (or inductees) each year (active and reserve, officer and enlisted) in order to meet military manpower strength objectives.

Also important is the kind of defense effort that is needed. In this regard, the U.S. armed forces are structured primarily as an expeditionary force, not to provide territorial defense of the U.S. mainland. Combined with the highly sophisticated technology embodied in the U.S. military, this means that it is not a home guard or militia that is sought by the United States, but rather a well-trained, large standing force capable of fighting both on a quick response basis and for a sustained period of time outside the U.S. mainland.

In the event that these requirements change substantially, then so will the desirability of the various manpower procurement policy alternatives. For example, changing active-force strength requirements from the present 2 million to, say, 3 million would almost surely necessitate a return to some form of conscription for the active forces. Alternatively, doubling Selected Reserve strengths without changing the size of the active military would probably require a draft explicitly for the reserves.

Population—The population base from which the military must draw its manpower is the second important environmental factor. This population base—actually the ratio of the military's manpower requirements to the population base—is an important determinant of the attractiveness of the various military manpower procurement options. For instance, when manpower requirements are large relative to the population base, countries are drawn closer to some form of universal service. Conversely, universal service becomes impractical when manpower requirements are very small relative to this population base.

When the issue is one of sustaining a military force, it is useful to think of comparing the military's annual accession requirements with the number of eighteen- or nineteen-year-old males, this being the definition of the "relevant" population base. For the United States, the number of eighteen-year-old males increased from about 1.1 million in the mid–1950s to more than 2.1 million in 1980. Because of the "baby bust" in the late 1960s and 1970s, this number will decline to about 1.8 million in the mid–1980s and 1.6 million or so by the early 1990s. By the mid to late 1990s, however, the number of eighteen-year-old males will once again increase to somewhere between 1.6 and 2 million. Assuming that about 75 percent of these individuals could qualify, the military will thus have a male youth population of some 1.2 to 1.7 million each year to draw upon over the remainder of this century.

All-Volunteer Force

With the exception of a short hiatus in the draft following World War II, 1973 marked the first time in more than three decades that the U.S. military was without the authority to conscript young men into the nation's armed forces. What has been the experience since the removal of the draft in 1973? And, what does this experience tell us about the future? These are questions that must be addressed in order to assess adequately what military manpower procurement policy ought to be in the 1980s and 1990s.

ORIGINS OF THE VOLUNTEER FORCE

It is useful to begin a review of the volunteer force with a consideration of why the draft was terminated in the first place. Not only does such a consideration provide the historical context, but more importantly, it helps to put into perspective the problems and trade-offs that must be faced today in evaluating military manpower procurement policy, for the conditions that resulted in the removal of the draft will in all likelihood persist throughout the remainder of this century.

Although the demise of the draft is frequently attributed to the Vietnam War, the volunteer force was actually the result of far more fundamental concerns. To be sure, the Vietnam War clearly served to dramatize the draft issue and indeed acted as a catalyst for the debate. But, the root cause was a growing concern about the inequity of the Selective Service draft.

There are two parts to the equity issue: the burden of conscription and the selective way that this burden was applied. Those individuals subjected to the draft were forced to bear a burden that other members of society were able to avoid. The specific burdens were many, including low pay, risk to life and limb, personal hardship, arduous working conditions, and disruption in their personal and working lives, among others.

The issue of inequity arose because of the selective way that these burdens were applied. As the numbers of young men reaching military age each year increased substantially during the 1960s, a smaller and smaller proportion was required to serve. As a result, the vast majority of military-age youth would never have to serve. For every young man forced to serve, three or four were not. Thus, no matter how fair or equitable the selection process could be made in an *ex ante* sense, such as using a random lottery, there was no escaping the fact that a selective service draft would be inequitable *ex post*—i.e., to those unfortunate enough to be drafted.

The Selective Service draft turned out to be even more inequitable than implied above, since "who serves when most do not serve?" turned out to be those least able to spend the resources to avoid induction—namely, the poor and the black. Even after the draft reforms of the late 1960s, lower income persons stood a much greater chance than their more affluent counterparts not only of serving, but of being inducted. The reason for this is that there were still legal ways of avoiding induction, which were generally more available to the more affluent. These included serving in the reserves, using medical excuses such as orthodontia, filing legal claims, entering some of the few exempted occupational areas such as the ministry, etc.

Recognizing the above, the President's Commission on an All-Volunteer Armed Force concluded in 1970 that, at a minimum, those serving in their nation's military should not have to pay a large financial penalty in addition to the other burdens of service. The commission thus recommended that the pay for junior military personnel be raised from the then poverty wage to a level commensurate with that earned by their peers in civilian employment. The commission determined further that raising pay in this fashion would provide enough impetus to sustain an all-volunteer military. In other words, a volunteer military would not require a large pay premium, but merely the comparable wage due for equity reasons alone. Thus was born the all-volunteer force.

PERFORMANCE OF THE VOLUNTEER FORCE

For all the debate and rhetoric, however, it remained for the draft actually to end to determine whether the AVF would work in fact as well as in theory or, in the view of its skeptics, be doomed to failure. In this regard, it will be argued below that despite some specific problems along the way, the first eight years of the volunteer force proved to be generally successful. Although this success has not been entirely uniform in the sense that the reserves, for instance, have not fared as well as the active forces or the Army not as well as the other services, the volunteer force by and large accomplished what was intended.

Enlisted Recruiting—Despite some modest recruiting problems during the first year of the volunteer force and again in 1979, the military services did quite well in meeting their quantitative recruiting objectives for the active forces during the first eight years of the AVF. Equally important, the services were even more successful in maintaining total manpower strengths during this period. With the exception of 1979, when the 25,000 strength shortfall left the military about 1.2 percent below its targeted level, the services were well within 1 percent of their strength objectives since the draft ended. In fact, they finished fiscal 1980 with 5,000 above the targeted level.

The magnitude of this achievement should not be underestimated. Recruiting 350,000 to 450,000 new recruits each year and sustaining an active military force of more than 2 million members without a draft, as the services have in fact done since 1972, is clearly an accomplishment of major proportions, and one that has not been duplicated elsewhere.

(It is interesting to note that even having a guaranteed supply of new recruits, as would be the case under a draft, does not guarantee that the services will always meet their end-strength objectives. This is amply illustrated by the experience in fiscal 1972, when, despite the presence of the draft, the services collectively fell more than 50,000 short of their programed strength objectives—twice the size of the fiscal 1979 strength shortfall under the AVF.)

The "quality" of new recruits has been a more controversial issue. Because it is difficult to even define quality, let alone measure it, debate about the quality of volunteers has been more anecdotal in nature. Unlike the quantitative performance of recruiting, where reliable numerical evidence exists, there is no universally accepted measure of quality.

The problem was compounded, and the controversy exacerbated, by the discovery in 1980 that the written tests used to screen applicants for enlistment had been misnormed. The result was that some individuals previously thought to be of average mental aptitude were instead found to belong to the below average group—so-called Category IV. Although the studies identifying this problem focused on the mental aptitude tests that had been in use since 1976, it appears that this misnorming problem existed, though perhaps to a lesser extent, well back into the 1960s.

The above problem notwithstanding, the statistical evidence that is available suggests that, in the aggregate, the "quality" of enlisted accessions is broadly similar to what it was during the draft years. For example, about 67 percent of all enlisted accessions during the first eight years of the volunteer force were high school graduates, as opposed to about 70 percent during the last twelve years of the draft.

With respect to mental aptitude, whereas the numbers of Category IV accessions—i.e., those classified as below average mental aptitude—were previously thought to have been about 6 percent during the volunteer force, the renorming suggests that this figure was probably closer to 30 percent during the first eight years of the AVF. However, this 30 percent is about the same as that experienced during the last eight years of the draft, if one likewise attempts to correct for the presumed misnorming in the tests used then. (Although the officially reported Category IV figure is 21 percent for the 1965 to 1972 period, correcting for this presumed misnorming suggests that the true figure was closer to 32 percent.) Moreover, the figure dropped to 17 percent in 1981. To put these figures into some historical perspective, it is interesting to note that the officially reported Category IV figures ranged from a high of 40 to 45 percent during and immediately following the Korean War to a low of 14 percent during the 1960 to 1964 period.

In the aggregate, the volunteer force has also not evidenced much change with respect to the other end of the mental aptitude spectrum. Category I and II classifications together comprised about 35 percent of enlisted accessions during the period of the lottery draft, as opposed to 33 percent during the first eight years of the volunteer force.

The one exception to the above generally optimistic assessment of quality under the AVF concerns the Army, since, according to most measures, the Army has experienced a decline in quality since the removal of the draft, especially during the 1977 to 1980 period. For example, the proportion of Army recruits with a high school diploma fell from 67 percent under the draft to 57 percent under the volunteer force. Similarly, the Army's Category IV intake was more than 40 percent during the late 1970s, using the renormed test results, and hit a high of 52 percent in 1980. This was at least 5 to 10 percentage points above what the Army experienced during the lottery draft. Equally striking, although the Army managed to maintain its combined Category I and II intake at about 30 percent of enlisted accessions during the first four years of the AVF, which was near the rate experienced during the draft era, this rate declined substantially during the second four years of the AVF. In 1977, it dropped to 20 percent; in 1979, to 17 percent; and in 1980, it hit a low of 15 percent.

This generally negative trend in the quality of Army recruits during the late 1970s showed a marked turnaround in 1981, however. For a variety of reasons, including congressionally imposed quality constraints, improved pay and benefits, and what appears to have been a generally improved attitude, the Army achieved a significant improvement in the various measures of quality. Its high school graduate intake increased to 65 percent or so in 1980; its Category IV intake dropped from 52 percent in 1980 to 27 percent in 1981; and its Category I and II intake increased to 24 percent in 1981 from 15 percent a year earlier.

To summarize the AVF experience with quality, the other services generally seem to have at least maintained, if not actually improved somewhat, the quality of enlisted accessions under the volunteer force, but this performance appears to some extent to have come at the expense of the Army. Although the quality of Army recruits during the first four years of the volunteer force does not appear to have been too much below that experienced during the draft, it did drop significantly during the 1977 to 1980 period. The results for 1981, however, provide the basis for cautious optimism, since the various measures of quality improved significantly for the Army, and in some cases exceeded those experienced during the draft years.

One final note with respect to quality is warranted. The above discussion has been couched in terms of comparisons of quality under the volunteer force with that experienced during the draft. While these comparisons are certainly relevant, nothing has been said about how quality, under either the AVF or the draft, compares with some absolute standard. The reason is simply that no one has yet determined what quality ought to be. As a result, we are forced to a large extent to rely on comparisons of the sort used here.

Retention—Improved retention was one of the principal arguments that proponents of the volunteer force used in their initial advocacy of the AVF. By bringing in individuals who wanted to be there, rather than who were forced to be there, it was argued, the military would evidence much higher retention, which in turn would lead to a more capable force, a more cost-effective force, and a more highly motivated force.

With one notable exception, the prediction of higher retention rates under a volunteer force has by and large proved correct. First-term reenlistments rates have improved dramatically under the AVF, from about 18 percent during the period 1965 to 1972 to 33 percent under the first eight years of the AVF. As a result of these improvements, the career content of the enlisted forces—i.e., the proportion of the force with four or more years of service—has likewise improved, from 39 percent in 1972 to 43 percent in 1979.

The only exception to the above concerns first-term enlisted attrition—that is, the failure of enlisted recruits to complete their first tour of duty. Proponents of the volunteer force apparently failed to recognize that first-term enlisted attrition rates would increase in the absence of a draft. During the draft, the services were forced to hold down enlisted attrition rates, lest attrition become too much of an "easy out" for those serving involuntarily.

Once the draft was ended, the pressure to hold down attrition rates was correspondingly lessened. Indeed, a number of specific programs, such as the Training Discharge Program and the Expeditious Discharge Program, were developed with the express purpose of identifying and separating early those individuals found not suited to the military, thereby improving the overall readiness and morale of the forces. By most accounts, these programs contributed to this goal, as the numbers of malcontents and the various measures of indiscipline, such as rates of incarceration, seem to have generally declined following the removal of the draft. But the price was high, as first-term enlisted attrition rates soared, from 26 percent for the fiscal 1971 cohort to 37 percent for the fiscal 1974 cohort of young men entering the military.

Recognizing the magnitude of the problem, the Department of Defense began to focus its efforts in the late 1970s on reducing enlisted attrition. These efforts appear to have been quite successful, as attrition rates for fiscal 1979 dropped to about 29 percent, only three percentage points above the fiscal 1971 rate and only one percentage point above the fiscal 1972 rate.

Overall, then, the volunteer force seems to have accomplished what it was designed to accomplish with respect to improving retention and, correspondingly, raising the experience level of the enlisted ranks.

Representation—Perhaps the single most controversial AVF issue concerns social representation in general and the racial composition of the forces in particular. By 1980 minority personnel accounted for about 30 percent of all enlisted manpower— 22 percent were black, 8 percent Hispanic and other minorities. For the Army, 41 percent of enlisted personnel were minorities.

The increased minority participation in the armed forces is attributable to both increased minority enlistments and increased minority reenlistments. Whereas blacks, for example, comprised about 10 percent of enlisted accessions historically, and about 14 percent during the last four years of the draft, they made up roughly 20 percent of all new recruits during the first eight years of the AVF. Blacks have also historically reenlisted in larger percentages than whites, about 1.6 times higher during both the draft and AVF years.

Although concern has been expressed that the volunteer force has thus resulted in the nation placing a disproportionate share of the defense burden on the least advantaged segment of society, it is important to recognize that the increased minority participation in the armed forces is largely unrelated to the AVF. Rather, the present racial composition of the military can be traced in large part to two factors, the first being that increased numbers of young blacks now qualify for military service. This can be seen, for example, by the fact that only 27 percent of eighteen- to nineteen-year-old black males were high school graduates in 1967, as opposed to 42 percent in 1974. Similarly, only about 12 percent of black youth were classified as Category I–III in the mid–1950s; by the mid–1970s, this number was well over 40 percent. Second, young blacks faced particularly severe economic prospects in the civilian job market during the 1970s. In other words, the number of blacks serving in the military would probably be about the same whether or not the draft had ended unless, of course, blacks were explicitly or implicitly discriminated against and not allowed to join.

Similar concerns have been raised with respect to the numbers of middle- and upper-income youth serving in the military. The charge most frequently levied against the volunteer force in this regard is that "the American middle class has deserted the military." Yet, a comparison of the draft and AVF shows little difference in the composition of enlisted accessions according to the average family income of their home address ZIP code. The reason for this, of course, is simply that middle- and upper-class youth have always been underrepresented in the enlisted ranks. To the extent that they have served, they have been more likely to do so as officers; but, more often than not, they have not served at all.

The main difference between the draft and volunteer force, then, is not in the numbers of blacks and poor serving, but rather that, by paying a fair wage, the AVF has not discriminated against these young men the way that the draft did.

Reserves—If the active forces can be regarded as having fared reasonably well in the absence of a draft, the reserves have clearly had a far more difficult time. The long queues of young men waiting to join the reserves in order to avoid being drafted all but disappeared upon the removal of the draft. As a result, the Selected Reserves—i.e., those units that train regularly—fell in strength by nearly 200,000 between 1970 and 1978, from 987,000 to 788,000.

The picture for the reserves improved substantially between 1978 and 1980, however, as strength levels increased by nearly 60,000 in that two-year span. Continued strength increases are projected through the early to mid–1980s, when strengths are expected to once again reach 925,000 or so, about what they were in 1972 when the draft was ended.

In retrospect, the performance of the reserves during the late 1970s is not particularly surprising. The six-year obligation for enlisted members of the reserves meant that the last of the draft-motivated enlistment cohorts had not completed their period of obligated service until 1978, which, in turn, kept reserve re-enlistment rates very low until then. And, in marked contrast to the active forces, which actively promoted the AVF from the outset, the reserves did little to promote themselves until three or four years after the draft had ended. (In fact, the reserves actually undertook a number of counterproductive measures during this period, such as temporarily reducing the length of the reserve obligation.)

Finally, although the quality of reserve enlistments when viewed in terms of mental aptitude and educational attainment has fallen since the end of the draft—indeed, 56 percent of reserve enlistments in 1970 were college educated—the reserve forces of the 1980s may actually be stronger and more capable than their counterparts of the 1960s. The reason for this is twofold. First, with the fall-off in nonprior-service enlistments, the reserves have been forced to rely more on recruiting individuals with prior service, who thus bring more experience and knowledge to the reserves. Second, because the reserves during the 1960s were, for many, a "gentlemanly" way to dodge the draft, they were populated by large numbers of well-educated youth whose principal purpose for being there was to avoid serving in the active military. Nevertheless, the quality of reserve enlistments continues to be an important policy concern.

Similar improvements have been made in the IRR, where strengths, which declined to a low of 340,000 in 1978, increased to about 410,000 by the end of 1980. Although still short of mobilization requirements, the Department of Defense projects continued IRR strength improvements through the early 1980s.

PROSPECTS

The foregoing, although far from a complete analysis of the AVF experience, nevertheless highlights some of the key issues, problems, and successes since the removal of the draft. In the aggregate, the above discussion suggests that the services have fared reasonably well under the volunteer environment. They have almost certainly done better than the most pessimistic forecasts of the late 1960s and early 1970s, but not as well as the most optimistic assessments of that period indicated.

What does this experience tell us about the prospects for AVF in the 1980s and beyond? The answer to this question depends critically on force strength objectives. So long as force strengths stay near the present levels—i.e., 2 to 2.3 million in the active forces, 800,000 to 1 million in the Selected Reserves, and 400,000 to 500,000 in the IRR—the AVF has a reasonable chance. If, on the other hand, manpower requirements increase substantially beyond these levels—say, to 2.7 million for the active forces or 1.5 million for the reserves—the AVF will clearly have a very difficult time, unless such force size increases are accompanied by large military pay increases.

Assuming for the moment that manpower requirements do not in fact change appreciably, the overriding problem to be faced by the volunteer force clearly concerns how the military can recruit enough young men (and women?) without seriously degrading quality from a manpower pool that will decrease some 15 percent between 1980 and 1985, and by another 10 percent between 1985 and 1992. This is certainly a major and difficult challenge. The services' success in this regard will depend in a large part on their success in continuing to reduce enlisted accession requirements, which have already declined from a high of 450,000 in 1975 to 375,000 in 1981. In other words, retention is likely to be the key to the success of the volunteer force in the 1980s.

Universal Service

Of the various possible types of military manpower procurement policy, universal service is in many ways the most intuitively appealing. The notion of every young man (and woman?) serving his nation has a certain instinctive appeal. Since all would serve, by definition, universal service would be representative. And, there would thus presumably be a great mixing of the various social, ethnic, and racial segments of society.

Despite their intuitive appeal, however, it will be argued below that the various forms of universal service are simply very impractical for the United States, given the combination of population demographics, military requirements, and budgetary constraints that comprise the policy environment for the remainder of the twentieth century. The discussion below reviews in more detail the three main forms of universal service: universal military service (UMS), universal military training (UMT), and universal national service (UNS).

UMT AND UMS

The concepts of both UMT and UMS have as their roots the notion of the "citizen soldier"—the idea that to be a citizen of the nation state is to have the right and obligation to bear arms in the defense of that nation state. Perhaps George Washington's view is most representative of this concept:

> It may be laid down as a primary position, and the basis of our system, that every Citizen who enjoys the protection of a free government owes not only a proportion of his property, but even of his personal services to the defense of it.

Although it can be argued that both UMT and UMS conform to this ideal, neither is particularly well suited to today's policy environment. The issue in both cases is simply that there does not appear to be the need for the numbers of military personnel that would be generated by either UMS or UMT.

In the case of UMS, two years is probably the minimum active duty tour length that would be acceptable from a military standpoint. Exclusive of *any* female participation in the armed forces, UMS would thus lead to an armed force of some 3.5 to 6 million members.

The basic question then is "what would the United States do with a military force this large?" Moreover, such a force would be expensive: another $10 billion to $20 billion per year for manpower alone, not counting the additional expenditures that would have to be made for equipment to effectively use and support this manpower, for base construction and maintenance, and for training. Given the questionable need for an armed force this size, UMS would thus appear to be highly wasteful of the nation's resources.

Like UMS, UMT does not appear to be practical for the United States for the foreseeable future. Under UMT, all able-bodied males (and females?) would receive some military training, after which time some would be routed to the active forces, some to the Selected Reserves, and the remainder to the IRR. To be effective, such training would at a minimum probably have to include both basic military training and some individual specialty training, which would mean twelve to sixteen weeks of training for each UMT conscript. (Even this, however, is not very much.) Assuming that the active forces would take about 400,000 new recruits each year, and the Selected Reserves about 100,000, UMT would thus put 600,000 to 1 million newly trained UMT conscripts into the IRR each year. Assuming only a one-year obligation in the IRR for each UMT conscript, and

recognizing that 300,000 or so active-duty separatees would enter
the IRR each year (for one or two years), the IRR would have
between 1 million and 2 million members at any point in time,
exclusive of any female participation.

The first question, then, concerns the usefulness of an IRR
this size. Even under the most demanding scenarios considered
by the Department of Defense, there does not appear to be a
justification for an IRR this large. Second, unlike many European
countries, where territorial defense is paramount, the United
States envisions a largely overseas war. Yet it is precisely for this
type of expeditionary force where UMT conscripts (serving in
the IRR or its equivalent) are of the least use. Thus, because the
greatest value of UMT conscripts lies in territorial defense, UMT
does not provide the kind of manpower needed by the U.S.
military.

Third, UMT by itself would appear to do little to solve any
of the problems that the volunteer force will face over the 1980s.
The services would still have to recruit volunteers much as they
do now. Although it can be argued that the military might be
able to recruit more volunteers because UMT would expose
larger numbers of young men to military service, it can just as
well be argued that this exposure could discourage some enlistments from individuals who would have enlisted in the absence
of UMT. The only area where UMT would seem to be un-
ambiguously advantageous is with respect to enlisted attrition.
On the one hand, the military would have more information with
which to screen potential volunteers, while on the other, the
period of UMT service would help individuals determine their
preferences with regard to serving in the military. Together,
these factors would likely lead to lower attrition than would be
expected from a volunteer force and less indiscipline and morale
problems than would be expected from a drafted force. Attrition
aside, however, UMT would thus appear to do little with respect
to manning the active peacetime forces, and could actually prove
harmful.

Finally, although not as expensive as UMS, it should be recognized that UMT would be costly. Training costs alone would
probably add another $3 to $6 billion to the defense budget,
not counting the additional capital expenditures that would be

required to develop the military installations and facilities required to train this volume of new recruits.

As envisioned by its supporters, a national service draft would serve two principal purposes. It would help to supply the manpower required to staff the nation's armed forces, and it would provide a means for utilizing the remainder of young men (and possibly young women) in nonmilitary functions designed to benefit the national purpose.

Philosophically, national service is seen by some as a vehicle for encouraging a new "sense of commitment" to the country—a hoped-for result of the direct labor contribution that each young national service participant would make. Ideally, this would be accomplished in part through the "meaningful" activities that would comprise a national service program. Youth would be more effectively brought into the mainstream of American society, and society in general would become better acquainted with the aspirations, needs, and ideas of youth. National service is also seen as a means for encouraging a certain "socialization" process among the nation's youth—specifically, a mixing of individuals from different backgrounds and with different interests that might not otherwise take place under a strictly market economy. Moreover, participants in a national service program would perform a number of tasks and duties that would presumably benefit society as a whole.

National service is also seen by its advocates as having certain practical advantages. Not only would a national service draft reduce youth unemployment rates directly—approaching 30 percent or more for certain minority groups—but a possible side benefit would be decreased future unemployment rates for national service participants, a result of the skills and maturity presumably gained during their period of service. Thus, compulsory national service is seen as a tool for making youth more "employable."

Although the above objectives are clearly laudable, it is important to recognize that they are only a possible outcome of compulsory national service, *not a certainty*. Indeed, a national service draft could do far worse than the current system in achieving these objectives. For example, resentment among those subject to a national service draft might reduce rather than increase the "sense of commitment" to the country.

Not only are these supposed benefits uncertain, but compulsory national service has some severe shortcomings. First, there is the equity question concerning how national service workers would be distributed among the various national service jobs—especially between military and nonmilitary assignments—given that the distribution of individual preferences would be unlikely to match the distribution of jobs. In general, an excess supply of applicants for nonmilitary assignments would be expected.

Second, a national service draft would be enormously expensive. Total program cost would depend on a number of factors, including the number of young Americans serving in the program (which in turn depends on disqualification rates and the extent to which young women would participate), the length of the service commitment, the pay for national service, the costs of accession and training, and the costs of administering the program. Although it is difficult to pinpoint the exact costs of a national service draft, it can be expected that a men-only national service program of this sort would add $15 to $25 billion to the federal budget. Including both men and women would about double this figure. (Moreover, the more one attempts to reduce these costs, such as by reducing training, the more such a program would take on a "make work" appearance, thus reducing whatever benefits might be expected.)

Third, a national service draft would likely displace some currently employed workers. In fact, because national service workers would tend to be less educated, less trained, and less experienced, the individuals most likely to be displaced from their current employment would be the black, the poor, and the undereducated—those with the most difficulty in finding alternative employment opportunities.

Fourth, the removal of 1.5 to 3 million young men and women from the work force and/or student rolls for one or more years each could cause possibly severe economic dislocations. For example, since about half of all graduating high school seniors go on to college, compulsory national service would create difficult transition problems for the nation's colleges, universities, and trade schools. In addition, the high youth unemployment rates during the 1970s are clearly cause for concern, but the fact that 80 percent or more of those in the youth work force find employment means that a national service draft would deprive the economy of many productive workers.

Fifth, finding and managing the 1.5 to 3 million jobs needed to support universal national service would be an administrative nightmare. Many, if not most, of these jobs would likely be "make work," since the fact that government and industry do not presently support these kinds of jobs suggests that the value to society of the tasks that would be performed by national service members is less than their cost.

Sixth, there is considerable doubt about how well a program of compulsory national service would work, since the "need" for this type of conscription is unlikely to be seen by many of those subject to this type of conscription. One only has to look back to the Vietnam War to see the effects of an "unpopular" conscription. Whereas the importance of defense may be well recognized by the American population—thus providing a certain credibility for a *military* draft when needed—drafting for "nonessential" purposes might seriously dilute support for nonmilitary draft. In other words, the same arguments used in support of a military draft—e.g., a youthful fighting force and the necessity of defense—cannot be used to justify conscripting young men and women for nonmilitary purposes. As a result, imposition of compulsory national service would almost inevitably generate a considerable amount of social conflict. Even if a majority of American youth were to support such a program, which in itself is a big "if," there would almost certainly be a vocal minority in very strong opposition, thus serving to undermine the overall program.

Finally, compulsory national service would seem to directly contradict the long-held principle of individual freedom. Indeed, it is not clear whether a nonmilitary draft is even constitutional.

Selective Service Draft

Should the United States ever return to a draft, it would almost certainly be a selective service–type draft. The reason is that universal service is simply not very practical for the United States, given the present and foreseeable policy environment.

Specifically, the number of draft eligibles would far exceed the military's requirements for recruits, even should peacetime standing forces be expanded substantially.

What would be the implications of returning to a selective service draft? This question is addressed below in the context of some specific policy alternatives. Although these do not represent a comprehensive list of the available policy alternatives, they do illustrate the kinds of effects, good and bad, that would result from a return to selective service conscription. The specific options examined below include the following: (1) a simple lottery draft, (2) a lottery with reduced military pay, (3) a lottery with raised quality standards, (4) an oldest-first draft, (5) a McCloskey-type draft (which would incorporate nonmilitary service as well), and (6) a reserve only draft.

SIMPLE LOTTERY

By itself, and given present manpower strength requirements, a lottery draft of the sort used just prior to the AVF would likely have little impact. The reason, of course, is simply that the services have demonstrated that they can meet or come very close to meeting recruiting objectives without conscription. As a result, even if the authority to draft were reestablished, there would be few, if any, draftees.

Quantitatively, the main thing that a draft would do would be to ensure an adequate supply of manpower, even when the manpower pool declines in size during the 1980s. Although present indications are that the volunteer force can also provide sufficient manpower during this period, it is not assured of doing so.

Otherwise, simply reinstating the draft would do little. For example, a comparison of the quality of enlisted accessions during the AVF with that just prior to the volunteer force suggests that a draft by itself would do little to improve quality. (The implications, both positive and negative, of coupling a lottery draft with raised quality standards are addressed explicitly later in this section.) Such a draft would similarly have little or no impact on the racial composition of the enlisted forces. The reason in both cases is that a simple lottery draft, by itself, would bring in only a few individuals not already serving. To illustrate the above, the Selective Service System recently estimated that even if draft calls amounted to 50,000 per year, which is in itself unlikely, the military services' Mental Category I intake would increase from 3 to 3.1 percent, hardly a significant difference.

The imposition of a draft would probably force the services to reduce attrition rates, although the results presented in the section on the AVF indicate that the services have already reduced attrition rates almost to the level experienced during the last stages of the draft. Moreover, to the extent that the services would be forced to keep individuals who otherwise should be separated, indiscipline would probably increase, as would the population in the brigs and stockades. In this regard, a return to conscription would create an additional problem for the services, one that concerns their policies toward homosexuals. On the one hand, the services would be most reluctant to change their policy of forbidding homosexuals, but on the other, continuation of the present policy would provide a ready exit route for those individuals seeking to leave.

A draft of this sort would also do little to aid the reserves. The reserves benefit from an active-forces draft only to the extent that there are many draftees. If there are few draftees, as would be the case for the draft described here, individuals have little incentive to join the reserves.

Mobilization capabilities would not be much affected either. In both cases, the volunteer force and the draft, the services would have to rely on new draftees to fill mobilization manpower requirements—that is, draftees not already in the system. Assuming fourteen weeks for processing and training new draftees, the first draftee would appear in the theater ninety-eight days after M-day in the case that a draft was already in place, versus one hundred days for the volunteer force. This is hardly a significant difference.

Perhaps the greatest difference between AVF and a draft concerns not either extreme, peacetime or war, but rather the scenario in between—that is, rising tensions which call for a steady, but substantial force build-up. It is in this regard that the AVF has only limited flexibility, since it is difficult to increase force sizes substantially in the short run without a draft. Under a draft, by way of contrast, all that needs to be done is to increase draft calls.

Budgetary costs would similarly be little affected by a return to conscription. Assuming that military pay would not be reduced, the only cost savings would come from the elimination of enlistment bonuses and a reduction in recruiting effort, although it should be noted that the services maintained a sizable recruiting establishment even during the draft. The magnitude of those cost savings would probably be less than $500 million per year. Partially offsetting these savings would be certain cost increases, such as the costs associated with reactivating the Selective Service System (which alone would increase by $100 million per year or so) and with the establishment of an alternative service program for conscientious objectors. Moreover, a return to the draft would also likely result in a reinstatement of some type of G.I. Bill, which would more than wipe out any cost savings from less recruiting and fewer enlistment bonuses.

Finally, a return to conscription would not be without its adverse social consequences. An alternate service program for conscientious objectors would need to be established. And the draft would have to be enforced, which would mean pursuing and punishing draft evaders.

Thus, so long as force sizes are not increased substantially, simply returning to the draft would thus have little military or economic benefit, at least through the mid–1980s. It would, however, have possible adverse social consequences. In the event that a reevaluation of defense requirements calls for a substantial increase in force sizes, however, then some form of conscription, such as the lottery draft described here, may be needed. In other words, the benefit to the military of a draft in the event of a large force build-up could well outweigh the adverse social consequences.

LOTTERY DRAFT WITH REDUCED PAY

Coupling a return to the draft with reduced pay for junior military personnel would accomplish two things relative to the simple lottery draft previously described. First, it would lead to some budgetary savings, although it will be argued later that such savings would likely be considerably less than is commonly assumed. Second, because lower pay would mean that fewer volunteers would join, the military would have to make greater use of the actual draft mechanism.

Making greater use of the draft mechanism itself would probably lead to a modest improvement in the quality and representativeness of enlisted recruits, since "randomly" selected draftees are on an average likely to be of somewhat higher quality and to be somewhat more representative than the volunteers they would replace. The emphasis in the above statement, however, should be on the word "modest," since history tells us that even a seemingly fair lottery does not result in a random cross section of American youth. First, large numbers of true volunteers would continue to serve—i.e., basically the same individuals serving under the volunteer force. Second, if previous experience is a guide, about half of the difference between the numbers of true volunteers and total manpower requirements would be filled by draft-motivated volunteers—that is, individuals who voluntarily enlist, but who would not have done so in the absence of a draft. History tells us that these individuals would not be a random cross section, but rather would more closely resemble true volunteers in terms of their socioeconomic characteristics. Third, draftees themselves would not be a random cross section, as illustrated by the fact that individuals from high-income areas stood only about half the chance of being drafted as did individuals from lower income areas during the lottery draft of the early 1970s. As described earlier, even after the use of deferments and exemptions had been largely curtailed, legal methods for avoiding inductions were still available, but were more readily available to the more affluent.

Although increased numbers of draftees might be thought of as a modest advantage in terms of quality and representation, they would clearly be a disadvantage in terms of retention. Even with the substantial improvements in reenlistment rates that have taken place under the volunteer force, the services are still concerned about the adequacy of reenlistment rates. A draft would only serve to worsen the problem, and the more that volunteers are replaced by draftees, the more that the problem would be worsened. In contrast to volunteers, who reenlisted at a rate exceeding 30 percent during the first eight years of the AVF, draftees have historically exhibited reenlistment rates of 5 to 10 percent. Thus, replacing large numbers of true volunteers with draft-motivated volunteers and draftees would likely have a serious adverse impact on retaining adequate numbers of non-commissioned officers (NCOs).

Turning to costs, a return to the draft is frequently seen as a way of holding down the ever increasing defense manpower budget. Yet it can be shown that reducing the pay for junior military personnel would have a relatively small budgetary impact. Even taking such a drastic step as reducing even the pay for those in their first two years of service by half, the Department of Defense would save less than $2 billion per year, which is only about 1 percent of the defense budget!

The above savings are so small basically because the draft provides very little leverage over the defense manpower budget. The manpower budget is driven largely by the costs of career personnel, retired personnel, and civilians, none of which can be reduced by a return to the draft. In fact, the costs of career personnel would probably have to increase under a draft, in order to counter the otherwise lower retention rates than a draft could be expected to produce. In sum, the draft provides little or no control over costly elements that collectively make up more than 95 percent of the defense budget, and only limited control over the remaining 5 percent.

Not only does a draft provide only limited leverage over manpower budget costs, but it would actually increase the real resource costs associated with military manpower. The reason for the deceptive appearance is, of course, that many of the costs of a drafted force are hidden from public view, while those of a volunteer force appear in the budget.

A selective service draft is more expensive than a volunteer force for three reasons. First, individuals who have a higher valued use outside the military in fact end up serving in the military. Second, enormous resources were, and would again, be spent on draft avoidance activities. And third, a draft encourages the military to misallocate its resources—e.g., too much labor, relative to capital; too many uniformed personnel, relative to civilians; and too many junior personnel, relative to more experienced service members.

Finally, reducing the pay for military recruits would reintroduce the worst inequities of the selective service draft. Not only would just a small proportion of American youth be forced to serve in the military, but those so forced would have to pay a large financial penalty in addition to the other burdens of service. This hardly seems to be enlightened social policy, especially since these burdens would fall disproportionately on the most disadvantaged segments of American society—the poor and the black. In other words, because the "conscription tax" is regressive, returning to a poverty wage for military recruits would have the most adverse effect on the least affluent members of society.

LOTTERY DRAFT WITH RAISED QUALITY STANDARDS

To the extent that there are major concerns about the "quality" of enlisted recruits, the military could consider making quality an explicit part of draft policy, since this is the only way that the services can be assured of a substantial increase in quality. For example, the services could limit Category IV accessions to 10 to 20 percent of total accessions. Alternatively, they could limit voluntary enlistments to, say, high school graduates falling in the upper half of the mental aptitude spectrum, using the draft to fill the remainder of manpower requirements. At the extreme, one could even envision setting specific quotas by mental category, using the draft to fill recruiting shortfalls on a category-by-category basis.

Although coupling a return to the draft with raised quality standards would almost certainly raise the average quality of first-term enlisted manpower, the overall effects might not be as advantageous as would at first appear. For example, simply putting a cap, say 20 percent, on Category IV accessions would improve the average quality in the Army but would probably have little impact on the other services, since their Category IV accession rates have been either below or only marginally above the 20 percent rate, even using the renormed standards.

Imposing stricter limitations on the Category IV intake would obviously further reduce the numbers of Category IV accessions, but would in fact deny the service many potentially useful volunteers. For example, a 1974 survey of enlisted manpower productivity showed that Category IV high school graduates rated only about 3 percentage points lower than Category III high school graduates, and about 15 percentage points *above* Category III high school dropouts, for the one-third of military occupational specialties classified as low skill. Would the services really be better off replacing Category IV high school graduate volunteers with individuals scoring somewhat higher on the written tests who, first, do not want to be there and, second, perform no better and perhaps worse in actual job assignments? Whereas one might be able to rationalize, say, a 20 percent ceiling on Category IV accessions to benefit the Army, it would thus seem questionable whether stricter limitations would be warranted.

Moreover, simple caps on the numbers of Category IV accessions would likely do little to solve what some see as an equally important quality problem, too few recruits with above average mental aptitude. That is, the reduction in Category IV accessions would most likely be made up from individuals in the middle of the mental aptitude spectrum, not from the upper end. The only way of increasing appreciably the numbers of enlisted personnel from the upper end of the mental aptitude spectrum is to impose much stricter quality standards, either by raising substantially the cutoff for volunteers or by implementing specific quotas according to mental category. There are important problems with both kinds of approaches, however. Both would be difficult to implement because of the imprecision in the methods for measuring "quality." For example, individuals would have a strong incentive to perform poorly on the screening tests. Both approaches would also result in denying some qualified individuals the opportunity to serve as volunteers while simultaneously drafting other individuals who would in fact be less qualified.

Perhaps the greatest military disadvantage of coupling a return to the draft with raised quality standards is the adverse effect that such a policy would have upon enlisted retention. The more that quality standards are raised, the more that true volunteers will be replaced by draftees and draft-motivated volunteers, both of whom it was argued earlier exhibit much lower reenlistment rates than do true volunteers. Thus, although raising quality standards for enlisted accessions would almost certainly improve the measured quality of the first-term enlisted force, such a policy change would at the same time have a disadvantageous effect on the enlisted career force.

OLDEST-FIRST DRAFT

Many of the advantages that some AVF critics foresee from a return to conscription would accrue not from the youngest-first lottery-type draft instituted in the late 1960s, but rather from the oldest-first local board-type draft used prior to the lottery.

The two models differ in several respects. The first, as the names imply, is the age at which individuals are inducted. In essence, twenty-year-olds were drafted first under the youngest-first versus twenty-five-year-olds under the oldest-first. Second, under the youngest-first policy, the individual's period of prime vulnerability was reduced to one year. After the individual passed that one-year period—the year in which he turned twenty-years old—he could be drafted only in the event of war or a national emergency. In contrast, the oldest-first policy kept the individual subject to the draft from the time he turned eighteen until his twenty-sixth birthday.

Third, under the draft reforms of the late 1960s, a single lottery was used to replace local board discretion. After the lottery was held, the individual would know almost immediately his chances of being inducted. Those drawing lottery number 1, for instance, could be certain that they would be drafted, while those drawing lottery number 365 could be equally certain of escaping. This replaced the system where the individual was deliberately kept uninformed about his chances of having to serve. Finally, the prelottery draft relied extensively on deferments and exemptions to "channel" youth into approved pursuits and vocations.

It should be noted that the reforms which together comprised the lottery draft were instituted primarily for social reasons, not military reasons. Indeed, it can be argued that, although it made the draft less inequitable, the lottery system was inferior to its predecessor on military grounds. Thus, many of the historical advantages that proponents of the draft frequently cite would simply not happen in the event that the nation returned to lottery-based conscription.

To illustrate, the youngest-first policy would mean that no college graduates would be inducted, since very few people graduate from college by the age of twenty. Similarly, a combination of the youngest-first policy with the single year of prime vulnerability means that there would be less incentive for otherwise nonmilitary-bound college graduates to join the officer corps through ROTC or OCS. By reducing the uncertainty about the chances of being inducted as happens with a lottery, individuals would have less incentive to join the reserves than they had under the prelottery system. And, finally, the youngest-first lottery system would do nothing to broaden the age mix of individuals serving in the enlisted ranks, a sometime criticism of the volunteer force.

Though far from advocating a return to the inequities of the prelottery system, the above discussion makes it clear that these reforms were not accomplished without a price. More to the point, many of the presumed benefits of the draft would fail to materialize, so long as the youngest-first lottery system were to again serve as the basic draft model.

MCCLOSKEY-TYPE DRAFT

Representative Paul ("Pete") McCloskey introduced legislation in the Ninety-Sixth Congress that called for a type of selective service conscription. Although not enacted into law, the McCloskey bill is nevertheless an interesting variant of the basic selective service model, and is thus examined here as illustrative of a more general approach to a selective service draft. Briefly, upon registering at the age of eighteen, individuals would be required under the McCloskey bill to elect one of the following four options, although the individual could postpone the first and third options for a few years if he so chose: (1) serve in the active military for at least two years; (2) serve in the reserves for six years, six months of active service and five and a half years in a reserve unit; (3) perform one year of civilian public service; or (4) none of the above. Individuals choosing option (4) would then be put into a draft pool, where they would be liable for induction should the need arise.

Although the McCloskey bill contained a number of other specifics, such as pay levels, it is not the specifics that are of interest, but rather the basic concept. The avowed purpose of the McCloskey proposal was to encourage a sense of commitment to the nation on the part of American youth. Whether or not the bill would achieve this lofty goal is of course open to question.

Perhaps the most interesting consequence of the McCloskey proposal, however, would be to lessen the inequities of a selective service draft, since the individual's prospects of having to serve in the military would not be left entirely to chance. Rather, the individual could legitimately excuse himself from two years of military service by performing one year of civilian public service.

This improvement with respect to the inequity of selective service conscription would not, however, come without a price. In general, the military would be expected to fare much less well under a McCloskey-type draft than under more traditional selective service, since the high-quality recruits that the military might hope to gain under a more traditional selective service draft would have a ready alternative to the military. Thus, although a McCloskey-type draft could guarantee the military adequate numbers of personnel, quality might actually decline, especially if pay were lowered as proposed in the specific McCloskey bill. Moreover, the McCloskey proposal would also increase costs, since in addition to military personnel, civilian service workers would have to be paid.

Thus, what a McCloskey-type draft would gain in the form of reduced inequities, it would likely lose in the form of a less effective military draft and higher costs.

RESERVE DRAFT

Historically, there has been little need to consider drafting personnel for the reserve forces. The reason, of course, is that the presence and use of an active-forces draft was enough to guarantee a more than adequate supply of manpower for the reserves. Indeed, the postwar draft was characterized by long queues of young men waiting to join the reserves so that they might avoid being inducted into the active forces.

The notion of drafting for the reserve forces began to be considered seriously during the 1970s for two reasons. First, the reserve forces generally fared much less well during the first several years without a draft than was the case for the active forces, as described earlier. Thus, as viewed by some, the active forces might be able to survive without a draft, but perhaps the reserves could not. Second, it was argued earlier in this section that simply introducing a draft for the active forces in the 1980s would do little to aid the reserves. The reason for this is that, unlike the 1960s where large active-forces draft calls guaranteed an adequate supply of manpower for the reserves, the absence of large draft calls for the active forces in the 1980s would provide correspondingly less incentive for young men to join the reserves.

Despite the above, it would appear that a reserve draft would have little impact, given present reserve strength objectives. Between 1978 and 1980, the reserves increased in strength by some 60,000, as noted earlier, and further increases are anticipated through the early 1980s. Thus, a draft would do little with respect to strengths, so long as reserve strength requirements remain in the neighborhood of 900,000 to 950,000.

The main advantage of a reserve draft would appear to concern quality, since the quality of nonprior-service accessions in the reserves has generally been below that experienced by the active forces. Thus, combining a reserve draft with a limit, say, on Category IV accessions would likely improve the quality of nonprior-service enlisted accessions. (It should be noted, however, that the quality of nonprior-service and prior-service reserve enlistments together is roughly equivalent to the quality of enlistments in the active forces.)

The main disadvantage of a reserve draft, other than the general problems with a draft that have been previously described, concerns the mix of nonprior-service and prior-service enlistments. One of the major achievements of the volunteer force has been to force the reserve components to increase their prior-service enlistments, thus taking advantage of the skills, experience, and expertise developed by the active forces. Implementing a reserve draft would enable, or perhaps force, the reserves to once again emphasize nonprior-service accessions, which would probably have an adverse impact on reserve readiness and capabilities.

To summarize, a reserve draft would probably end up having little impact, so long as Selected Reserve strengths remain in the neighborhood of 900,000. If, on the other hand, Selected Reserve strengths are to be increased substantially, say to 1.5 million, then a reserve draft might be needed.

Conclusions

The all-volunteer force has, from its inception, been the subject of an often heated public debate. Indeed, scarcely one week after the authority to draft had expired in 1973, former Army Chief of Staff General William Westmoreland declared that "as a nation we moved too fast in eliminating the draft." During the period since then, the volunteer force has been criticized, among other things, for being too costly, for producing low-quality recruits, for leading to a force that is unrepresentative of the American public, for destroying the unique character of the military, and, in general, for providing a military force that is not capable of meeting U.S. defense needs.

The results presented in this chapter thus stand in considerable contrast to the often grim assessment put forth by AVF critics, since, for the most part, it was argued earlier that the volunteer force has generally accomplished what was originally intended. The military services, for example, have met or come close to their quantitative targets throughout the AVF period. The quality of new recruits does not seem too different from that experienced during the draft era. And the volunteer force seems to have evidenced clear improvements relative to the draft in terms of such factors as retention and indiscipline.

Racial composition is one of the few areas where the AVF has differed significantly from what was originally predicted, since minority participation in the armed forces is in fact substantially higher than initially estimated by proponents of the volunteer force. The reasons for this change, however, are largely unrelated to the volunteer force per se, but rather concern economic and demographic factors that would have had a similar impact whether or not the draft had been ended.

The above should not be taken to mean that the volunteer force has been without problems, for that is clearly not the case. The reserves, for instance, fared much less well during the initial AVF period than did the active forces, although even the reserves have begun to evidence significant improvements during the past several years. The services have also had difficulty recruiting adequate numbers of physicians. Attrition was likewise a major problem during the first few years of the AVF. Perhaps most important, however, the military services will face a very difficult recruiting environment beginning in the mid–1980s, when the numbers of military-age youth begin to decrease significantly.

Given this generally optimistic assessment, the above problems notwithstanding, why then has so much of the AVF debate come to a different conclusion? There are several reasons. The first is that AVF critics have tended to focus particularly, and perhaps disproportionately, on the Army, as opposed to the services as a whole. Whereas the other services generally seem to have at least maintained, if not improved upon, the positions they enjoyed during the draft, most measures indicate that the Army has not fared as well under the volunteer force as it did under the draft.

The Army has the most difficult recruiting task, since it is the largest of the services and is viewed by many as the least glamorous. Even in the case of the Army, though, the picture is not as bleak as has sometimes been portrayed.

Second, many criticisms of the volunteer force are based on comparisons that are either not really relevant to the policy environment of the 1980s or that reflect an overly optimistic appraisal of the past. To illustrate, the volunteer force is frequently compared to a draft where Harvard and Princeton graduates, for instance, served alongside youth from less affluent backgrounds. This phenomenon, which did occur during the 1950s, was, however, the result of force sizes that were large relative to the then small youth population cohorts and of the oldest-first draft, neither of which would likely prevail in the 1980s.

Third, the AVF debate has often confused general manpower problems with the volunteer force—that is, critics of the AVF have often blamed the volunteer force for problems that are largely unrelated to military manpower procurement policy. The frequent references by AVF critics to the large exodus of skilled manpower from the military is one of the more striking examples, since, if anything, retention would likely be worsened by a return to conscription. Cost is another example, since rising manpower costs are mainly a result of the increased costs of civilian personnel, retired personnel, and career military personnel, not the volunteer force.

Finally, and perhaps most significantly, general defense problems are often confused with AVF problems. In this respect, it is not one, but rather two parallel debates that have been taking place for the past five to ten years: one concerning military manpower procurement policy and the other concerning U.S. defense posture in general. Concerns about the United States having a "hollow army," as voiced by the Army Chief of Staff in 1980, are much more a question of "how much is enough?" than of what military manpower procurement policy to use. Although the two issues are not entirely separable, it is important to keep these two debates in perspective. One cannot blame the AVF for all supposed inadequacies of U.S. defense posture, just as all the ills of the Vietnam-era military cannot be attributed to the draft.

The point of the above is not to make excuses for the volunteer force, but rather to emphasize that simply returning to a draft would do little by itself to solve most of the problems that have been raised during the course of the AVF debate. In many ways, the AVF debate has served as a watershed for the whole array of defense and manpower issues and concerns. To the extent that this has helped focus attention on the broader problems confronting the U.S. military, the debate has served a useful purpose. Unfortunately, by dwelling so exclusively on the AVF in the narrow sense, the debate may have done more to focus attention away from the important issues than toward them. As a result, the more fundamental problems with the military manpower system have gone largely unaddressed.

In this regard, the AVF debate of the 1970s and 1980s almost seems to be a replay of the draft debate of the 1960s. Just as many then draft critics saw a volunteer force as the solution to most military problems, too many AVF critics see the draft as the solution to today's manpower problems. Both groups are almost necessarily destined to be wrong. Although military manpower procurement policy clearly has effects beyond the narrow confines of recruitment, military manpower procurement policy cannot by itself solve the myriad of manpower and personnel problems that confront any large organization, let alone one as unique in character and mission as the American military.

Turning to the specific issue of military manpower procurement policy, perhaps the most important conclusion that can be drawn from the discussion and analysis presented here is that military procurement policy cannot be viewed in terms of absolutes. To begin with, military manpower procurement policy necessarily consists of a series of trade-offs, or compromises. There is no single policy that is uniformly better than all others in all dimensions.

An oldest-first draft, for instance, has certain advantages relative to other policies. It results in some college graduates serving, to the extent that it is found desirable; it results in more high-quality college students entering ROTC and OCS; it results in a broader range of age groups serving; and it is probably most beneficial with respect to manning the reserves. But, it is also one of the most inequitable draft policies and causes the greatest personal inconvenience to those few unfortunate enough to be drafted. Deferments and exemptions likewise offer certain advantages, relative to other conscription policies. They make conscription more efficient in the narrow sense, in that they result in youth being channeled into "socially approved" pursuits. But a policy with extensive use of deferments and exemptions is also the most discriminatory. The lottery draft was implemented in the late 1960s so as to lessen the worse social consequences of the then draft policy—i.e., oldest first, local discretion, and wide use of deferments and exemptions. But the youngest-first lottery draft was less attractive from a purely military viewpoint. These examples thus illustrate some of the kinds of trade-offs that must be made.

The choice of a military manpower procurement policy likewise depends critically on the policy environment. What may be "right" for one set of circumstances may be altogether inappropriate, and perhaps not even feasible, for another. For example, universal military service has many intuitively appealing attributes. All young men (and women?) would serve their nation, the military would be representative, and there would be a large cadre of trained military manpower in the event of a war or national emergency. But universal military service is simply not practical for the United States, given the very large youth cohorts of the 1980s and 1990s.

Military manpower procurement policy is thus best viewed in comparative terms, comparative relative to the policy environment and comparative relative to the various specific attributes inherent in each policy alternative.

In looking at the military manpower procurement situation for the United States over the next ten years, the single overriding determinant of that policy is force size. In the event that the nation decides to increase force sizes substantially, a draft would almost surely be required, since the taxpaying public would not be likely to be willing to pay the large additional costs that a volunteer force of that size would entail. If, on the other hand, force sizes are to be kept at or near their present levels, a volunteer force becomes a much more viable alternative.

Assuming that force sizes do not in fact increase appreciably, the choice is between a volunteer force and a selective service draft, since universal service is not very practical for the U.S. policy environment. Yet it was argued earlier that simply imposing a selective service draft would have little impact. About the only thing that a simple lottery draft would do would be to ensure an adequate supply of recruits, something that the volunteer force cannot be guaranteed of doing, but can probably accomplish if properly managed. Otherwise, a simple lottery would do little. It would have little impact on the quality of new recruits or on representation, unless significantly raised quality standards were to accompany the draft. But these would be difficult to implement.

The reason that simply introducing a draft would have so little impact is that the vast majority of young men (and women?) who would be serving in that force are the very same ones who would serve in a volunteer force. Absent a large build-up in force sizes, the only way to change the make-up of the force substantially is to replace large numbers of today's volunteers with draftees. Not only would that deny many qualified volunteers the opportunity to serve, but it would also have an adverse impact on retention, just when the military has come to recognize the importance of improving retention. In short, a draft would do little to aid the military so long as force sizes remain at or near their present levels. Thus, it is not that a volunteer force is intrinsically better than other alternatives—indeed, it was argued earlier that no single policy is intrinsically superior. Rather, given the present circumstances, there does not appear to be another alternative that is any better, and most would be worse.

At the same time, it must be recognized that the volunteer force faces a very difficult challenge in the years ahead. During the first eight years, the AVF muddled through on a more or less "business as usual" basis. Demographics tell us, however, that that will not work as well for the next eight. The services barely made their recruiting quotas during the last part of the 1970s, when the size of the recruiting pool was at an all-time high. What will happen when there is a much smaller manpower pool from which to recruit?

From a technical viewpoint, the answer rests in the military making improvements with respect to both the supply side and the demand side of the problem—that is, finding ways to attract a greater proportion of the qualified and available youth and reducing the need for new recruits. Important progress has been made in the past few years—increased military pay, reduced attrition, and increased reenlistment—but more is needed.

Perhaps far more important than these technical solutions, though, is the need to revitalize the American military and the general public's attitude toward its armed forces. That is something that neither a volunteer force nor a draft can accomplish by itself. And, yet, it is critical to the success of either policy.

James L. Lacy

6

The Case for Conscription

Anticipating the outcome of a debate that has not yet been engaged in in earnest is always a hazardous undertaking. With respect to one issue, however, the ground is not quite as perilous as with other matters of national policy: it is a near-certain prospect that the United States will resume a peacetime draft in the 1980s.

The reasons for this have little to do with the agreeableness of conscription per se, however, for a draft in any form is a cantankerous proposition for the United States:

1. it entails involuntary service, and this invariably rankles in a political culture, economic heritage, and legal tradition that so keenly aspire to both cherish and safeguard personal freedoms and individual choices;
2. it is inevitably selective (in even its "universal" versions), and, because it is selective, it seems inherently inequitable; and

JAMES L. LACY *recently completed a book on the details of resuming a military draft while he was a senior fellow at the National Defense University. Previously he was special assistant to the assistant secretary of Defense for Manpower, Reserve Affairs, and Logistics and special assistant to the deputy assistant secretary of Defense for Program Development. Between these two Defense positions, Mr. Lacy served as principal assistant to the secretary of the Department of Energy. A member of the New York bar and a former assistant director of the Police Foundation, he has also consulted several judicial, police, educational, and corporate organizations.*

3. the principles by which we would aspire and require that it be conducted are essentially discordant; a fair draft, a compassionate draft,
an economical and militarily effective draft, a conscription policy that
is certain in its terms but flexible to respond quickly to changed
military requirements are not self-evidently one and the same thing.

Instead, the outcome is fairly well assured for the same reasons
that produced military drafts in the past: the absence of credible
alternatives makes conscription indispensable; the case for resuming a draft becomes persuasive precisely because the case for
not doing so is perilously implausible. It is this essential fact, and
not vague sentiments about the wonders to be worked by a draft,
that leads to both the high probability and the correctness of the
draft's resumption. The exact timing may be debatable; the stern
reality is that the conclusion is not in great doubt.

That this is so derives from several related factors. Despite
many great efforts to put draft-free armed forces on a permanent
footing, the all-volunteer force (AVF) was sustained in the 1970s
chiefly by the convergence of compatible, but unenduring, circumstances. A sharp (although not entirely understandable) drop
in military manpower requirements, coupled with auspicious
demographics (the legacy of an earlier "baby boom"), had provided a distinctively favorable context for switching from inductions to inducements in the early seventies. Manpower supply
relative to military requirements seemed too large to draft from
equitably, but in the view of some, large enough to recruit from
competitively. In the 1950s, the armed forces had need for close
to 80 percent of America's healthy young men. By 1970, that
requirement was down to 25 percent.

Transient favorable circumstance is nevertheless a slippery
slope on which to construct national policy, and, in this instance,
reversal was in store within a decade. By 1980, American force
strength had slid to its second-lowest ebb since June 1950. (The
lowest was in 1979.) It was not self-evident how much more
shrinkage prudence would allow, but, short of a radical alteration
of the nation's defense commitments, these force reductions had
probably already bottomed out. At the same time, new pressures
to revert to larger forces in the eighties coincided with new limitations on the available manpower supply. Few but the most
ardent advocates of a draft-free defense seriously contended that
force size can be substantially increased in peacetime by reliance

on volunteers alone, without much greater dependence on women recruits (and this has many and much the same limitations on volunteering as does reliance on young men) or a drop in general enlistment standards. Yet by 1981, the Reagan administration was firmly committed to such a substantial force bolstering by mid-decade; the military services were conspicuously resistant to relying any more heavily on women (who by then comprised 8 percent of the enlisted force); the Congress, if anything, seemed of a mind to raise, not lower, enlistment standards. At the same time, the fruits of the baby boom had peaked and passed—by 1987 there would be 15 percent fewer males turning age eighteen than in 1978. The agreeable context of the seventies had shifted mightily, and probably irrevocably. In the eighties, military man-power requirements would most likely go up at the same time that manpower supply would most certainly go down.

It is not only the march of events, however, that points to a return of conscription. The underlying vision of a draft-free force had a range of little more than a decade. In execution, the con-cept was heavily mortgaged at the outset. The essential compro-mise tilted toward starting an all-volunteer force and away from sustaining it. Compromises along the way merely added to the mortgage and to the limited life span. In its final character, the AVF was an opportunity for the 1970s (probably a politically necessary one, and in several respects a remarkably successful one), but not an enduring alternative. The source of subsequent falterings was structural, rather than a mere matter of manage-ment and execution. In light of this, a draft was bound to follow.

Still, an outcome is not necessarily correct simply because it is unavoidable. It is not the sureness of the prospect alone that makes compelling the case for resuming conscription (although the draft's indispensability is an essential element of its appeal). While to speak of conscription admits a host of possibilities (from universal military training to selective military service to universal "national service"), to speak of no draft allows only two prospects: a substantial reduction in standing forces, on the theory that their size and significance need not be matters of concern, or a draft-free, all-volunteer force of credible military dimensions. The first of these "no draft" alternatives is unlikely as well as unwise; the second is devilishly imprecise in numerical particu-lars, but it is also the only plausible alternative to conscription.

Yet there are essential limitations in the all-volunteer concept that make it quite debatable whether it is a serious and durable policy alternative. Despite its allure as a political aspiration, the all-volunteer force has remained a risky and conceptually hazy matter of national policy. It is not merely the gap between the AVF's ruling assumptions and its everyday existence that has been worrisome. The idea itself permits little flexibility for crisis, or for adjusting force levels to respond to changing world conditions. In part this derives from ambiguities in the concept itself, in part from thoroughly implausible force augmentation schemes that have been attached to it, and in part because attention has focused less on whether the AVF can be expanded and sustained in armed conflict and more on whether it can be maintained in the domestic economy. By contrast, and in spite of its politically cranky heritage, conscription is a potent alternative, precisely because, in matters of defense preparedness, it is the more relevant and reliable alternative.

The Draft and Political Principle

It is nevertheless useful to distinguish at the outset two manners of debate, for their muddling has much to do with the historical intractability of the subject matter. On one level, the choice of an AVF or a draft is a great question in the most proper sense of the term, a matter of high political drama, in which two unalterably opposed political philosophies clash, and from which no obviously "correct" conclusion can emerge. On this level, it is more philosophical predilection than analysis that molds opinion. It is not a matter of conflicting evidence, for data command no loyalty as does a great principle. Nor is it a matter that admits the relevance of necessity or practicality. In 1814, Daniel Webster thought it hardly necessary to suggest a plausible alternative to the draft as he excoriated James Monroe's scheme for conscription; the republic might lose its sovereignty along with its raggedly undermanned army (and so it surely seemed at the time), but it would not, for Webster, surrender its principled virginity. Similarly, in 1910 the great philosopher William James would have had the nation conscript an entire generation for national service for their own good. That the republic had little use for a few million youthful indentured servants seemed to matter not at all; for James, the principle was persuasive.

For long stretches in the nation's history, the draft had not been much of a factor; volunteers filled the ranks of the national forces, although never in quite formidable numbers. In 1789, the regular army consisted of all of 718 officers and enlisted personnel; the largest volunteer army before World War II was a mere 190,000 in 1939, and ranked seventeenth in size in the world.

A national draft had been proposed as early as 1786, and had been vigorously debated in 1814, but it was not attempted until the 1860s (first by the Confederacy, later by the federal government), and, at that, was used sparingly thereafter: in World War I, in 1940 in anticipation of America's entry into World War II, and in the wake of the communist coup d'état in Czechoslovakia in 1948. All were of short duration, save the last: it endured for close to a quarter of a century. All were contentious in inception, save again the last; it was not until the late 1960s that America's fourth draft joined in the stormy political heritage of its first three.

For those who favored it, the draft was, variously, a necessary evil, a temporary expedient, an enlightened distribution of the burdens of common defense. For those who feared it, a greater evil was virtually unimaginable; they thundered at it with an apocalyptic foreboding. For young Daniel Webster, conscription was a "horrible lottery" based on a "throw of the dice for blood" and a foul libel on the Constitution. The outspoken senior senator from Ohio, Clement F. Vallandigham, saw in the Lincoln administration's draft nothing less than an attempted coup d'état —to retain political control "by bringing the majority under the iron heel"—and warned with innocent portent that "free men have always expelled or killed such conspirators and tyrants." Woodrow Wilson's draft impressed Wisconsin Senator Robert La Follette as a scheme

> to clothe one man with power, acting through agents appointed by him, to enter every home in our country, at any hour of the day or night, using all force necessary to effect the entry, and violently lay hold of 1,000,000 of our finest and healthiest and strongest boys . . . and, against their will, and against the will and wishes of their parents or family, deport them across the seas to a foreign land . . . and require them to wound and kill. . . .

For social commentator Norman Thomas and Senator Robert Taft, the World War II draft was unalterably "the first essential to the totalitarian state." A critic of the 1948 measure warned the Congress that the issue was not merely a draft law, but "the actual fate of western civilization." Few national policies, it seems, provoked as much commotion or inspired so much flatulent rhetoric.

There were rejoinders, of course. James Monroe thought it not only preposterous, but repugnant, that a nation could not conscript its citizens for the common defense. Echoing George Washington, John C. Calhoun warned of the villainy of a non-conscripted military: "It draws from society its worst materials, introducing into our army, of necessity, all the severities, which are exercised in that of the most despotic government." Former Army Chief of Staff Leonard Wood would complain of the voluntary system in 1914:

> It is uncertain in operation, prevents organized preparation, tends to destroy that individual sense of obligation for military service which should be found in every citizen, costs excessively in life and treasure, and does not permit that condition of preparedness which must exist if we are to wage war successfully with any great power prepared for war.

And Harvard President Emeritus Charles Eliot saw great social purpose in conscription:

> All the able-bodied young men in the country would receive a training in the hard work of a soldier which would be of some service to them in any industry in which they might afterward engage. They would have been accustomed to a discipline under which many men cooperate strenuously in the pursuit of common objects.

In these terms, the fundamental issue never did get resolved, nor is it likely to be. The case for a draft, no more so and no less so than the case against the draft, is difficult to deduce from great principle. It is a stubborn, wonderfully enduring and characteristically American debate, with heroes and heroic arguments on both sides.

Still, a nation cannot permit itself to be paralyzed by embalmed philosophical disagreement in matters of national defense, and it is on an altogether different level that America has engaged the fundamental choice in practice. Here the arguments have tended to center on the draft's necessity, rather than on its theoretical virtues and defects. And it is here that the case for a draft has been made most powerfully in the past, and where it again reposes in the 1980s. The difficulty with the clash of great principles is not that it is trivial or irrelevant; it is rather that it is unending.

The Transient Alternative

To appreciate why a draft would be necessary in the eighties when it seemed conveniently dispensed with only a decade earlier, it is helpful to first note the fragile durability of the AVF's early undergirdings.

With great fanfare America had embarked on what enthusiasts touted as a "new era" in defense policy in 1973. A quarter century of partly conscripted military forces was done with; henceforth, the United States would rely entirely on volunteers. On its face, the proposition was simple: increased levels of compensation would be substituted for compulsion to fill the ranks. If military compensation were kept competitive with that of relevant sectors of the labor market, there would be no need for inductions; sufficient incentive to serve voluntarily would exist.

The idea was hardly new, but the scale was unprecedented. The largest previous all-volunteer American force had been 1.4 million in early 1948, had faltered for lack of recruits, and had succumbed to the draft's resumption before that year was out. Thereafter, ardor for draft-free forces cooled discernibly. An all-volunteer force did not factor prominently in the struggles over defense manpower policy in the fifties and early sixties; the chief alternatives to selective service promised more, not less, conscription, in terms such as universal military training and compulsory "national service."

In sharp contrast to the late forties, the AVF of the 1970s would be in the range of 2 million, and could, according to some, top 3 million if need be. All that was required was decent pay and service conditions for recruits, it was argued. The earlier baby boom would provide an abundant universe of seventeen- to twenty-one-year-olds from which to recruit.

It was a bold undertaking, and in several respects a remarkably successful one. While there were many doubters and doubts, the great fears of the AVF's critics were not realized. Democratic instincts and institutions handily survived the volunteer force;

mercenarism did not materialize in discernible fashion; and, while the racial composition of the enlisted force shifted noticeably, the armed forces by 1980 were still far from becoming an army of the poor, the black, and the socially disadvantaged. Court-martial and desertion rates were kept at manageable levels, and recruiting results generally approximated objectives. An active force of some 2 million, and a reserve of some 1 million, were maintained through the seventies.

Perhaps as importantly, the conversion from draft to AVF allowed the nation to recoil from and reflect upon its experience in Vietnam without drastically or precipitously altering its military capabilities, by removing from center stage a matter of intractable political divisiveness—the draft. By 1970, conscription seemed hopelessly mired in its own bizarre history and conceptual confusion: reforms had come incrementally, reluctantly, late, and with ambiguous results. The "best" draft reform, particularly since the opportunity was present, was probably to put the draft to rest. A nation bogged down in an uncertain and unpopular war seemed incapable of making sense of a conscripted military.

Still, the nation's considerable success in maintaining larger forces in the 1970s than it had ever previously attempted without a draft masked several fundamental frailties that would spell terribly bad prospects for continuing the experiment much into the 1980s. Indeed, the true "test" of the AVF as a viable and durable policy was not the 1970s at all; unusually favorable circumstances, plus a small measure of intellectual shenanigans, could get it through the first decade. The telling was in the period beyond, when these circumstances would no longer underwrite the AVF's performance or convincingly explain away its growing misfortunes. And here the obstacles were enormous. It was apparent that the AVF could be made to function in the 1970s, but it was difficult to see how it could be made to work much beyond, let alone permanently.

Foremost was the fact that the abundant manpower supply on which the volunteer force was predicated had a predictably short life. After a peak of 10.8 million in 1978, the number of seventeen- to twenty-one-year-old males began a decline that would last through the early 1990s. The drop was modest from 1979 to 1982— less than 1 percent per year—but it would increase to 2.5 percent per year between 1983 to 1987. By 1987, the number of males in the prime recruiting pool (seventeen to twenty-one) would be 15 percent less than the 1978 level; by 1990, 17 percent less; by 1992, 20 percent less. In short, the crucial favorable circumstance was transient.

At the same time, the military demand for manpower was kept in check in the seventies by several, but again short-lived, crutches. First, the AVF met quantitative manpower requirements that were steadily, and inexplicably, reduced throughout the decade. The "correct" size of the armed forces is, of course, endlessly disputable; but importantly, the winnowing of strength in the seventies happened incrementally and without reference to any understandable change in strategic circumstance or vision. Active-force manpower authorizations—already lowered at the AVF's inception to a point smaller than at any time since mid-1950—dropped in the aggregate by 236,000 between 1973 and 1980. The prescribed strength of the drilling reserves (the "Selected Reserve") dropped by 93,000 in the same period. Detente with the Soviet Union and lessened tensions in Asia may have explained the baptismal downturn in force size at the AVF's inception, but they were unconvincing in terms of the subsequent, steady annual decline. And, while lessening manpower requirements would abet the AVF's performance for a while, it was improbable that the decline could go on indefinitely. Still, to arrest it, let alone reverse it, would place the AVF in a new circumstance of military manpower demand at precisely the time when manpower supply would be less favorable.

Second, despite the great pronouncements of the day, there was a certain coyness in the way the nation had moved from draft to no draft, such that the true consequences of an AVF would be postponed by several years. The initial conversion had not been quite as bold as its proponents made it out to be. When in 1971 the nation ended its special "doctor draft," it did so with the third largest induction call for physicians since 1951, handily filling the ranks for another few years. So, too, with general inductions. Between the AVF's inception in January 1973 and the expiration of the President's authority to induct six months later, some 35,000 individuals subject to induction were indeed drafted. Moreover, persons already conscripted were not released; they would serve their full tours (two years) and incur their full reserve service obligations (which, in most cases, amounted to

four additional years in call-up status). Individuals who had
avoided the draft by enlisting in the drilling reserves would be
kept for their full obligation, six years in most instances. And the
cutback in force size as the nation "drew-down" from Vietnam
would simply add thousands of G.I.s to reserve call-up rosters for
up to four more years. In short, the draft would indirectly work
its wonders on force strength—especially reserve force strength—
for several years (as many as six) after conscription's formal
demise: a "true" AVF was not to be a matter to contend with
until 1977 or 1978.

These two factors found agreeable expression in a third AVF
feature: the volunteer force was married at the outset to a
companion policy—the "total force concept"—which helped to
rationalize a smaller active force than in pre-AVF times by shifting more of the defense burden to the reserves. The idea was not
new (theoretically, the reserves had always had some such responsibilities), but in the era of the draft it had had no practical
significance. With the AVF, however, the "total force" was to
take on a critical, if not altogether plausible, role both in making
the case for a volunteer force and in explaining its smaller force
levels.

While, with the possible exception of World War II, the draft
had not quite produced large surges of manpower rapidly, it had
been a trusted medium for increasing force size in a relatively
short time frame. A critical concern about an active force comprised entirely of volunteers was that it might not be able to
expand quickly enough in time of threat or emergency. One
solution—which flowed from the idea of draft-free forces with
compelling but painful logic—would be to maintain a larger active
force in peacetime (larger, that is, than one that would be needed
with a draft in operation), and thereby obviate the need for
quick expansion. This, however, would not only increase defense
manpower costs, it would also upset the fragile relationship of
manpower supply to military demand so essential to the AVF's
feasibility in the 1970s.

Instead, the nation turned to the reserves, or, as the theory
went, to the concept of the "total force." The AVF active force
would be promptly supplemented in an emergency by the part-
time, drilling Selected Reserve and by the nondrilling Individual
Ready Reserve (a pool of former active-duty members still liable

for call-up in a national emergency for several years beyond their active service). Furthermore, certain programed wartime requirements would be shifted to the reserves in peacetime as well, thereby lessening the numbers of active-force members needed in peacetime.

Indeed, such a role for the reserves had been critical in the arguments about ending the draft. AVF critics had argued that only conscription provided the means for emergency force expansion and that a force stripped of this flexibility would be perilously vulnerable and conceivably unusable. AVF advocates countered that military preparedness in contemporary circumstances depends on forces in being, not fresh inductions; that the reserves could fill the bill for augmentation; and that, in the context of quick force expansion, the draft provides only inexperienced civilians who need to be organized, trained, and equipped before they can be militarily effective, a process, according to this view, which takes several months.

The "total force concept," nevertheless, scoffed several historical facts. The nation had little experience in calling up reservists. When the forces required either quick or steady expansion, the normal course had been to increase draft calls, not turn to the part-time reserves. Compared with 4.9 million inductions between 1951 and 1973, there had been only 870,000 reservists involuntarily activated for full-time duty, two-thirds of them in the first year of Korea. Nor was this limited experience especially reassuring. The Korean call-up had been a haphazard affair. Individuals who had not drilled in peacetime were called before units that had; why some units and not others were called was a great mystery; most who were called were discharged within a year and replaced with conscripts. The largest post-Korea reserve call-up (150,000 reservists in the Berlin crisis of 1961-62) had been similarly chaotic. Some reservists "were not cognizant of the responsibilities which they incurred as obligated reservists," according to a 1962 evaluation by the secretary of the Army, and "there had been defects in the distribution of equipment, troop housing, unavailability of medical care at many installations." More importantly, the reserves had been fretfully undermanned in the 1950s until a change in the draft law made reserve service a draft exemption, and, accordingly, gave an enormous boost to reserve force manning. In practical circumstance, a solidly-sized reserve force seemed possible (and, at the same time, unnecessary) precisely because of a draft. On this count, total force policy begged an essential question: without the draft, how would this new linchpin of national defense secure adequate and dependable levels of manpower? The answer was uncertain, but the decision to avoid a large standing active force made the policy unavoidable. At the same time, the draft had already fueled reserve manpower for several years beyond conscription's termination.

Still, the total force rationale was predicated on *maintaining* this reserve strength. Beyond the transitory prop given reserve manning by the draft, an all-volunteer reserve force of credible dimensions was no more certain a prospect than an all-volunteer active force. In fact, both active and reserve strength dropped in the seventies. Between 1973 and 1980 the active forces declined by 9 percent, the Selected Reserve by 10 percent, and the pool of individual reservists (who in wartime would round out undermanned units and serve as casualty replacements) by 66 percent. Yet a reduction in active forces would seem to logically demand a raising, not lessening, of strength in the Selected Reserve, if the concept of a total force is to have any substance. And, if the Selected Reserve declines in strength, a credible individual reserve would seem an essential fall back. By late 1979, however, the steep decline in the individual reserve alone contributed to a 16 percent shortage in the Army's manpower inventory for its most demanding wartime scenario—a conflict in Central Europe.

These declines forced the Department of Defense to dip deeper into its contingency mobilization well in the late 1970s, a circumstance that would lead to the great and curious irony of the AVF: its eventual dependence on the draft for wartime needs in order to offset the declining numbers of peacetime active and reserve volunteers.

The draft had never been eliminated. With the AVF, it had merely been placed in stand-by status, for reactivation as a last resort were future circumstances to require the mobilization of large numbers of men. If the reserves were the second line of defense, the stand-by draft was a distant third. Yet as the total force had earlier shifted some wartime manpower requirements from the active force to the reserves, so, too, would it eventually shift them from the reserves to the draft.

At the AVF's inception, no one had seemed quite certain or specific about the purpose or characteristics of a draft in stand-by. At first, the Selective Service System was left largely intact: an annual draft lottery was held, males were required to register, and the system classified draft registrants in terms of their eligibility for induction, even though the power to actually induct no longer existed. Between 1975 and 1977, however, this stand-by apparatus was virtually scuttled by the Ford administration in a series of budget-related moves. Under the early total force concept, it seemed in theory an acceptable risk to postpone preinduction steps (registration, classification, physical examination) until after a declaration of war or national emergency. The reserves would provide the first wave of force augmentation in an emergency; if a second wave were required at all, the draft could be reinstated rather leisurely. Accordingly, for wartime purposes, the draft—reconstituted from a cold start—need simply produce its first conscript within 110 days of the onset of armed conflict and 300,000 inductees by the 150th day.

The particularly sharp drop in individual reserve strength worked its own considerable pressures, however. In order to be prepared for a major conflict, the stand-by draft accordingly would have to produce manpower more quickly in an emergency. In 1977, the Department of Defense mandated a tighter production schedule: 100,000 conscripts to be delivered to Army bases within two months of a declared mobilization. In early 1980, the Carter administration reinstated draft registration (but no other draft measures) in peacetime. In late 1980, Defense quickened even further its requirement for conscripts in a national emergency. From a cold start in stand-by status, Selective Service was now to deliver 100,000 inductees to Army training camps within thirty days of mobilization. Conscripts would still be the second wave of force augmentation (after the reserves), but in a major war they would be in battle a lot sooner, and probably much more surely, than had been contemplated in the original AVF blueprints. Still, this production schedule would lessen some of the pressures for rebuilding active and reserve strengths in peacetime, by shifting a greater burden of force augmentation into the indefinite future.

Coupled with auspicious demographics and the lingering effects of the draft, these several policy shifts cushioned the AVF's early years, but superficially, and only with a growing mortgage on the years beyond. While the AVF was hardly in danger of collapse by the turn of the decade, it was running short of cushions. Force size could not drop indefinitely; the total force concept was a transient blessing, as much an explanation as a doctrine; the stand-by draft's production schedule required a great act of faith, at even the more leisurely points in its tightening. Nor were the results of these maneuverings especially reassuring. By 1980, the defense capability for a major war had taken on the following characteristics:

1. slightly over 2 million strong, the smallest active-duty force in three decades;
2. to be quickly augmented by the smallest reserve force in three decades, in a nation that has not fully mobilized since the early 1940s, and that has scant experience in reserve force activation;
3. to be further augmented by a cold-start draft that would have to produce more inductions in a shorter period of time than any ongoing draft had produced since World War II, and at the same time to reconstitute from scratch virtually all the machinery (save registration) required to do so.

Still, it is not merely the implausible ring of the scenario that makes continuation of the AVF a dubious prospect in the decade beyond. In an odd respect, the draft had already returned by 1980. In a span of eight years, the nation had come to rely on the stand-by draft to do what no peacetime draft had done before. Apart from its doubtfulness, the proposition posed a remarkable dilemma: either active and reserve strengths had to be increased to shore up the logic of the total force, or the nation had to rely on an untested stand-by to meet its most dangerous contingency. With respect to the first, however, the abundant manpower supply from which to draw volunteer recruits had already peaked and was on the decline, and few of even the AVF's most consummate defenders would maintain that force size could be significantly increased without a draft. With respect to the second—reliance on the stand-by draft—conscription was now required to do what the AVF's proponents had argued all along it was incapable of: rapidly bolstering force size. Either way, it seemed, the nation had a draft to deal with. The question by the early eighties concerned not whether a draft, but, simply, what kind of draft.

The March of Events

At the same time, the Congress and the Reagan administration seemed committed to compounding the equation further: the Congress, in 1980, by imposing restrictions on the numbers of lesser quality recruits the AVF could take in for the remainder of the decade, a stern obstacle to maintaining even the low force levels of the seventies; the administration, by promising a sweeping increase in force levels by mid-decade. As Winston Churchill once remarked, "You cannot ask us to take sides against arithmetic," and the arithmetic seemed terminally disagreeable for the AVF much beyond its first decade.

The Matter of Flexibility

It is not merely the numbers, or victimization by circumstance, however, that create doubt about the AVF's durability as a functioning defense policy. Once past questions about whether a volunteer force of a given size can be sustained in peacetime at a tolerable cost, there is the matter of its military dependability in time of crisis or changing world conditions. Structurally, the AVF is designed to produce military manpower for the bipolar extremes, but with stunted capability for circumstances that might fall between. In a conflict of short warning and short duration, forces-in-being would be all that matter. In a conflict of major proportions and longer duration, the reserves could be fully mobilized and a stand-by draft reactivated. But between the two, and in contingencies of different characteristics, there seems perilously little flexibility to expand. This arises from several limitations and ambiguities in the structure of the volunteer force itself.

First, an AVF is premised on one of two assumptions: either that certainty of manpower supply is not an important value, or that compensation can be confidently substituted for conscription in this respect. Few would seriously argue the first in matters of national defense (although the Nixon-appointed Gates Commission, which reported favorably on the AVF, conceded that if taxpayers balked at the expense, the nation just might have to do with a smaller defense force). Most AVF supporters have trusted in the second. Yet with respect to the second, the fall backs without conscription are necessarily unstable. If enlistments fall behind objectives, the only recourse is to either lower objectives, lower enlistment standards, increase pay, provide additional bonuses, or live with an acknowledged shortfall, all but the last of which take time and lag behind the shortfall (and all, including the last, to which the AVF has resorted in practice at one time or other). For AVF purists, these may seem tolerable discomforts in normal circumstances, but they do subordinate force manning to cyclical whims. The hazard, however, does not lie in the normal circumstance. Even assuming that high enough compensation levels could generally produce a steady manpower supply in peacetime and quiescence, it requires something of a suspension of reason to assume that compensation alone would continue to produce a secure supply of manpower in times of escalating international tensions, limited emergencies, or actual conflict. In such circumstances, where the risk to personal safety increases, would not the attractions of military service diminish at precisely the time when a sure supply of manpower is most critical? If the international threat were unambiguous, if pay were raised rapidly to take account of increased danger, and if patriotism ran unusually high, conceivably not, but this would be a cheerfully rare conjunction of favorable circumstances, hardly a prudent premise for defense preparedness.

This, indeed, seems a fundamental drawback in the vision and practice of volunteer force manning. The AVF was fashioned as a *peacetime* volunteer force, constructed on analogies to the pushes and pulls of labor supply and demand in civilian industry. Yet while the analogy may hold in peacetime, it is misplaced when it comes to military emergencies in two respects: there is seldom quite the risk to life and limb in the civilian labor market as there is in a military emergency, and the failure to produce manpower confidently in such an emergency is much graver than a labor shortage in peacetime industry. AVF theory would seem to pertain only so long as the force is not likely to be used. Were the likelihood of use to come about quickly, volunteers already in the ranks could be held in place in anticipation of use in conflict, but the prospect of additional volunteers would be uncertain. And in an extended period of international tension, even the normal flow of volunteers would probably be affected.

This peacetime limitation of the AVF was underscored implicitly by the Carter administration's renewal of emphasis (and reliance) on the stand-by draft. It was made explicit in 1981 by Lawrence Korb, the Reagan administration's senior defense manpower official:

> [the] worry that, once combat starts, casualties would discourage volunteers is somewhat misplaced: the premise of the AVF is that it is essentially a peacetime force; in time of a large scale war, conscription would be resumed and we would not have to rely only on volunteers to fight.

How "large scale" war would need to be before casualties discourage volunteers is debatable, but the point underscores a certain ambivalence about the draft in the logic of volunteer force manning. The case in favor of the AVF rested in no small part on a case against conscription: the draft was a bad proposition, a hidden and an unfair tax. Still, the draft was retained in stand-by, as an increasingly essential wartime measure. Yet, if a draft is an unfair tax in peacetime (when the tax at worst amounts to inconvenience for those upon whom it is levied), it is not evident what transforms it into something less obnoxious in time of armed conflict (when the consequences of being drafted are presumably more severe).

That the question need be raised at all derives from a quirk in the fundamental vision: the assumption that the nation could endure with both a volunteer force and a force that is smaller than any previous draft era force. The draft had provided a means for force expansion in circumstances short of a full mobilization, both at times when American forces were already engaged in conflict (Korea, Vietnam) and at times of tension when force bolstering was a measure of both precaution and resolve (the Berlin crises of 1948 and 1961). The AVF was to locate this flexibility in the reserves. Yet beyond the temporary boost the Vietnam drawdown had given the reserves, reserve strength was not programed to increase in the AVF. Furthermore, the difficulties in relying on the reserves for such purposes lie in more than numbers. One, it has never been done on a significant scale. Two, the problems of distributing a reserve call-up are probably as severe, in terms of equity and control, as those associated with activating the stand-by draft. Three, once the reserves are committed, what does the nation do for reserves? One obvious risk is that forces might not be expanded in time. The more probable risk is that a President and Congress, faced with such uncertainties, would rush the stand-by draft into existence even more precipitously than its 1980 contingency schedule called for.

Still, the stand-by draft is barely more plausible a fall back. The last stand-by draft to be reactivated, in 1948, took over seven months to produce the first conscripts, a record that presumably can be improved upon, but not likely to the levels prescribed for the AVF. As with reliance on the reserves, there is simply no historical experience on which to base expectations; nor are the consequences of inadequate performance—in deterrence, cost, equity, military effectiveness—easily grasped. And to undertake both a reserve call-up and a draft reactivation at the same time would seem only to compound the confusions and uncertainties.

Furthermore, it is debatable whether an AVF, forced to expand quickly or steadily beyond its peacetime active-force strength, could do so without creating considerable inequities and attendant political furor. The equities involved in a reserve call-up (as between different units, between the regular reserves and the national guard, and between individual reservists who have already served on active duty and drilling reservists who have not) were matters of fierce dispute in the early days of Korea, as was the recall of reservists before the induction of citizens who had never served. The same concerns and considerations would probably apply to a contemporary call-up. And a stand-by draft, rushed to existence in the midst of emergency, with little machinery in place and with a mandate to produce as many as 100,000 conscripts in less than a month but from a pool of draft-eligibles that is much larger, is likely to be more frantic than fair, and create its own share of political distemper.

A volunteer active force of 2 million is nevertheless a formidably-sized piece of defense machinery. Standing alone, relying on neither the uncertain prospect of augmentation by additional volunteers nor the risky terms of a reserve fall back or stand-by draft, it is no doubt capable of responding to a host of contingencies of limited demand and duration. The difficulty lies beyond the limited contingency and in the face of emergency or sustained requirements for additional active-force manpower;

these are the circumstances for which we most depend on an armed force, and for which the AVF is structurally, hazardously, inflexible.

Gains, Losses, and Decades

The single most attractive feature of the all-volunteer force has been its avoidance of compulsion in peacetime. But this has seemed achievable only by losses in other respects:

1. in security, in the sense that a defense manpower procurement policy tied to the whims of the labor marketplace is a highly uncertain, cyclical adventure;
2. in military dependability, in that in time of emergency it offers no great confidence that additional manpower can be produced quickly enough to be militarily effective or even usable;
3. in pursuit of foreign policy goals, for much the same reasons as the foregoing;
4. in credibility, in that great leaps of faith are necessary in order to find comfort in the strategems that were devised in the seventies to shore up its logic;
5. in equity, in the sense that the profound inequities of previous peacetime drafts seem merely to be postponed and compounded in the AVF's stand-by, call-up measures.

Moreover, in the one decade that most favored the volunteer experiment, the AVF steadily lost strength across its active and reserve components. By the early eighties, these favorable circumstances had not only run their course; they had begun to reverse sternly.

The difficulties with the concept lay not so much in its management as in flaws in the underlying vision. It is certainly conceivable, as the AVF's architects contended, that an active force of adequate size could be maintained (at least while the manpower was abundant) if the nation would pay recruits truly competitive wages; but it was also somewhat pollyannaish to expect that America would. The predictable result was a wage scale high enough to lure many but not high enough to lure enough. It is also conceivable that a force recruited according to the norms of the civilian labor market would continue to draw secure levels of volunteer manpower in time of danger or armed conflict, but historical experience is not the parent of this particular faith. And it is also conceivable that the reserves could perform a role on a scale never previously assigned to them, but it was also risky to come quickly to rely on the expectation that they could. It is somewhat less conceivable that the stand-by draft could perform according to plan; it was hazardously ironic that national defense had come to rely on it doing so. The AVF had been deduced from a theoretical preference and molded by the axioms and corollaries of a book of mathematics. In this sense it has more to do with syllogisms than with experience, the necessities of the time, or common sense intuitions.

These considerations make further great efforts to preserve and repair the volunteer force a much more debatable proposition than is a search for credible alternatives. And the alternatives invariably entail some form of conscription.

Still, a precipitous lurch back to a draft would be terribly unwise. For while the case for peacetime conscription seems ever more relevant with the passage of time, it comes with its own imposing difficulties and provocative choices.

The Draft Alternatives: Versions and Purposes

The threshold difficulty with conscription as a policy alternative is that it is seldom expressed with particularity, admits of no single vision, implies no obvious set of terms, and alarms or reassures largely on the basis of which speck or gleam is in the beholder's eye. Apart from some general understandings of its character—it involves involuntary military service; selective service is, by definition, selective; the burdens of conscription fall with some natural persuasiveness heavier on the young than on the not-so-young—conscription is not a self-evident thought. The past—even the most recent past—offers no obviously preferable theory or design for a peacetime draft. Between 1940 and 1972, America had not one, but many, drafts; modern American conscription is a legacy of versions. Also, it is not evident that the best (or even the allowable) choices concerning peacetime conscription in the 1980s would bear much resemblance to those made by previous generations. Subsequent judicial rulings may well have put the past beyond recall in some key respects. Many past shifts in conscription policy were matters of immediate and incremental "reform," not of fresh conception. Few of these may be particularly enlightening or germane after a near decade's absence of the draft. In addition, there is much that has been proposed (universal military training, a draft for the reserves, endless versions of "national service") which has never been tried.

One difficulty with merely resuming the last draft is that America had very little experience with it. Changes in 1969 (reversal of the order of call to "youngest first," selection by lottery), in 1970 (court rulings substantially redefining conscientious objection and altering the ways the draft could be enforced), in 1970 and 1971 (pay increases for conscripts and volunteers, prospective elimination of several traditional deferments and of the so-called "doctor draft") were quickly followed by the termination of draft calls in late 1972. We really do not know how, or how well, the last draft would have worked over time.

Moreover, much depends on the principles and purposes a draft would be intended to advance in the 1980s. A primary objective, of course, would be to provide manpower for the armed forces. Yet there are several quite different ways to accomplish this, each advancing a set of secondary purposes at the expense of competing objectives. A demographically "representative" force, a high-caliber force, a young and vigorous or an older, better-skilled armed force—each can be pursued by manipulating the terms of a draft, although not without loss to other values (equity, cost, military effectiveness).

To speak generally of a resumption of conscription, then, begs many questions: a draft of whom, with what, if any, exemptions, satisfying which military needs, and advancing what political values, for what kind and duration of service, compensating on which theory and enforced by what means, at what cost? These questions reach much beyond the limited scope here, but they are the correct questions, and ultimately, the most pertinent questions. If the nation is to resume compulsory service, it is essential to focus the debate early on questions of how to, as well as on questions of whether to, walk such a path.

Still, it is possible to draw some broad threshold distinctions and derive some general statements about the purposes conscription would most properly serve in coming decades.

THE "UNIVERSAL" ALTERNATIVES

From the perspective of simple equity, it would seem that the most defensible manpower procurement policy would be to draft everyone. The option has been regularly, if never convincingly, proffered since the turn of the century, usually in one of two forms. First, all (or nearly all) youth would be required to undergo military *training;* but, in peacetime, actual military *service* would be expected only of volunteers. Accordingly, a reasonably-sized standing force could be maintained; a formidable reserve of trained manpower could be developed (and turned to in the event of a military emergency); and a near universal distribution of a common military obligation could be achieved. Alternatively, compulsory "national service" in civilian public work would be added to conscripted military service, thereby enlarging the "demand" for manpower to approximate the size of its supply without having to enlarge the armed forces to do so. Both come in near endless versions. Neither has ever been attempted in the United States.

Neither, also, presents a serious policy alternative for several reasons.

First, neither quite means what it implies. Proposals of this sort generally do not contemplate emptying hospitals and prisons to provide youths for training or service, or induction of the halt, the blind, and the otherwise lamentable. This, however, is more than a minor conceptual blemish. If universal conscription is not universal, it is selective, and, if it is selective, it amounts to little more than a large selective draft.

Second, with respect to their contributions to national defense, universal military training (UMT) and universal national service have never been quite persuasive. The military utility of rotating an entire generation of young males (and, in some schemes, of young women as well) through basic training and into some vaguely defined reserve status as a hedge against a future mobilization is not self-evident. Save for defending against a ground invasion of the United States, the circumstances in which the training investment might be repaid by militarily useful service are difficult to imagine. At the same time, UMT would necessarily require an enormous military training establishment, with its attendant dislocation of men and materiel from the "tooth" to the "tail" of the force structure, in order to create these reserve pools. This only begs the question of how manpower is to be procured to maintain the training base, however.

Less sure are the contributions of universal national service to military effectiveness, partly because the concept's formulations are endlessly varied. Still, since the overlay of compulsory national service on compulsory military conscription adds compulsions for civilian, not military, service, any effects on the military would be indirect at best. Some have argued that compulsory national service "legitimizes" compulsory military service, but this rests on the fragile assumption that conscription is politically dismaying, not because it limits the freedom of those subject to it, but because it does not do so equally for every person.

Third, there is reason to doubt that either measure produces much beyond a veneer of increased equity. UMT might provide the same training obligation for all, but unless all UMT graduates were to be called to active duty in a military emergency, actual service would be a selectively allocated burden. National service produces different, and yet more stubborn, equity concerns. While a duty to serve may be imposed on all, it is unlikely that compulsory civilian service can be tailored to be an equal alternative to the risk, regimentation, and restrictions on personal freedom of military service. Nor is it likely that within civilian service itself, burdensomeness could be fairly distributed across activities. Further, there is the matter of economy. If there is no obvious requirement to conscript everyone, is it equitable to compel more than are needed in order to maintain a universality of compulsion? The question would seem to require no great pause for wonderment. To need ten persons but to draft twenty would appear to foster its own inequities in the case of the additional ten.

Fourth, the social value of compulsory training or compulsory public service rests with questions for which answers have never satisfactorily been fashioned. What would be the costs? What, specifically, would be the benefits? Where, indeed, are the training facilities and personnel, jobs and service opportunities, on which such schemes would be predicated?

Lastly, both, but particularly compulsory national service, are constitutionally suspect. "Involuntary servitude" is proscribed by the Thirteenth Amendment (a prohibition from which the

Supreme Court long ago rescued the military draft). It is difficult to envision the courts exempting from the prohibition work compelled merely to promote the general welfare or to accomplish tasks associated with enumerated powers of Congress other than the military/war power. Indeed, if the conscription of an entire generation for involuntary public service does not run afoul of the amendment, it is not quite clear what would.

SELECTIVE SERVICE

This, however, returns the nation to where it has always been with respect to conscription: some, but not all, will be selected to serve. The fundamental benefit of selective service is security of defense manpower supply. The fundamental disadvantages are two: it involves compulsion, and its burdens fall only to some. Still, if—as the foregoing suggests—an AVF is unreliable in practice, and universal conscription is unmanageable in theory, the basic policy choice narrows sharply.

In past drafts, America has demonstrated both that it can manage conscription with reasonable fairness, economy, and military effectiveness, and that it can bungle badly as well. Depending on its terms, a selective draft can effect substantial changes in both military force make-up and civilian behavior. It can alter the racial composition of the ranks; it can spur the young to college, early parenthood, flight, and the feigning of ailments; it can make prisoners of conscientious objectors and exempted ministers of persons with little more than a viewpoint. And it can be both vagrant and venal in its attention to special interests. (House Armed Services Committee Chairman Carl Vinson once complained in the early fifties that "as it is written today, there are only a few lines in the draft about who is being inducted, but page after page as to who is being deferred. It is written almost like members of a State Assembly would write a sales tax just before the election.")

Still, there is no requirement that precedent be embalmed in future policy. It is possible to fashion a selective draft which:

1. imposes a liability to induction broadly and rationally across the youthful population;
2. selects from this draft-eligible population fairly and randomly, and with few exemptions, deferments and excusals;

3. balances equities between those who are selected and those who are not through a host of postservice benefits that are reserved for those who serve; and
4. pretends to no greater ambition than an economical, flexible, and secure provision of the numerical strength of the armed forces.

Such a draft would not strive to cure the many perceived social sins of the AVF (for many of these reputed ills are properly the attributes of military service and of the general population, not the consequences of a particular manpower procurement policy) nor seek, as did the draft of the sixties, to "channel" young souls into preferred, draft-deferrable, life styles or behavior (for the power to compel service is so awesome in potential that it begs for restriction to national defense in practice). Born of necessity by the inadequacy of the alternatives, it would do no more—equitably and economically—than necessity requires: provide a predictable and secure flow of manpower into the armed forces in time of peace and war. It is in these terms, and probably in no others, that the case for conscription is most relevant, credible, and cogent.

"The great thing in the world," said Oliver Wendell Holmes, "is not where we are, but in what direction we are heading." The great challenge of the eighties, it seems quite properly, is not to further rationalize or mummify the policy choices of the last decade, but to articulate and debate with fine particularity the prudent and attainable choices for the next.

Index

The American Assembly was established by Dwight D. Eisenhower at Columbia University in 1950. It holds nonpartisan meetings and publishes authoritative books to illuminate issues of United States policy.

An affiliate of Columbia, with offices in the Graduate School of Business, the Assembly is a national educational institution incorporated in the State of New York.

The Assembly seeks to provide information, stimulate discussion, and evoke independent conclusions in matters of vital public interest.

AMERICAN ASSEMBLY SESSIONS

At least two national programs are initiated each year. Authorities are retained to write background papers presenting essential data and defining the main issues in each subject.

A group of men and women representing a broad range of experience, competence, and American leadership meet for several days to discuss the Assembly topic and consider alternatives for national policy.

All Assemblies follow the same procedure. The background papers are sent to participants in advance of the Assembly. The Assembly meets in small groups for four or five lengthy periods. All groups use the same agenda. At the close of these informal sessions, participants adopt in plenary session a final report of findings and recommendations.

Regional, state, and local Assemblies are held following the national session at Arden House. Assemblies have also been held in Engand, Switzerland, Malaysia, Canada, the Caribbean, South America, Central America, the Philippines, and Japan. Over one hundred thirty institutions have co-sponsored one or more Assemblies.

ARDEN HOUSE

Home of the American Assembly and scene of the national sessions is Arden House which was given to Columbia University in 1950 by W. Averell Harriman. E. Roland Harriman joined his brother in contributing toward adaptation of the property for conference purposes. The buildings and surrounding land, known as the Harriman Campus of Columbia University, are 50 miles north of New York City.

Arden House is a distinguished conference center. It is self-supporting and operates throughout the year for use by organizations with educational objectives.

The background papers for each Assembly are published in cloth and paperbound editions for use by individuals, libraries, businesses, public agencies, nongovernmental organizations, educational institutions, discussion and service groups. In this way the deliberations of Assembly sessions are continued and extended. The subjects of Assembly programs to date are:

1951——United States-Western Europe Relationships
1952——Inflation
1953——Economic Security for Americans
1954——The United States' Stake in the United Nations
——The Federal Government Service
1955——United States Agriculture
——The Forty-Eight States
1956——The Representation of the United States Abroad
——The United States and the Far East
1957——International Stability and Progress
——Atoms for Power
1958——The United States and Africa
——United States Monetary Policy
1959——Wages, Prices, Profits, and Productivity
——The United States and Latin America
1960——The Federal Government and Higher Education
——The Secretary of State
——Goals for Americans
1961——Arms Control: Issues for the Public
——Outer Space: Prospects for Man and Society
1962——Automation and Technological Change
——Cultural Affairs and Foreign Relations
1963——The Population Dilemma
——The United States and the Middle East
1964——The United States and Canada
——The Congress and America's Future
1965——The Courts, the Public, and the Law Explosion
——The United States and Japan
1966——State Legislatures in American Politics
——A World of Nuclear Powers?
——The United States and the Philippines
——Challenges to Collective Bargaining
1967——The United States and Eastern Europe
——Ombudsmen for American Government?